Tetelestai

"It Is Finished"

The Renfro Family Faith Walk

Τετέλεσται

Koine Greek of Tetelestai

"Fear them not therefore: for there is nothing covered, that shall not be revealed; and hid, that shall not be known." Matthew 10:26 (KJV)

Dr. Donna Renfro, PhD

Tetelestai
"It Is Finished"

The Renfro Family Faith Walk

Written by
Dr. Donna Renfro, PhD

Founder and Minister of Pistis, Inc.

Cover illustration Photo: Jeff Miller
Photos: Dava Lee Russell, Kevin Renfro, Jeff Miller, Miranda Taylor, Sierra Nesseth, Glen Prince, and Dr. Donna Renfro
Editors: Glen Prince, Dr. Donna Renfro

Library of Congress Catalog Card Number

ISBN 978-1981895397

The Dedication of Tetelestai

I would like to dedicate this book to Brandy Russell.

Brandy Russell
Born: September 24, 1977
Died: April 17, 1984

Brandy Russell

Miranda Renfro

Brandy Russell was a cousin of mine. She was like an angel from the day she was born. I recall seeing her the first time at my Mamaw's house. She was in a beautiful dress and literally glowed. I was seven years old. Brandy captured a room when she entered it from day one. Brandy, like Miranda, was born with a genetic disorder. Unfortunately, during the time frame of her precious life, no cure was found. I remember pastors praying for Brandy to live, and not be sick.

And, I remember when Brandy died. Brandy was only six-and-a-half years old. Although her life was short, it was powerful. Her life and death inspired me greatly. Even as I write, tears fill my eyes, her life or death was not in vain. For, you see, the pain her death caused inspired me to fight, no matter what it cost me, to get the answers for my daughter. In the above pictures, you will see Brandy and Miranda. This particular picture of Miranda seared truth into my heart long before a doctor confirmed my worst dreams. When I saw Miranda in the photo, I had a flash back to my cousin Brandy. Instantly, I knew in my heart something was wrong. I just did not know what. Brandy was a gift from God, and an inspiration for me to refuse to quit. I did not want the pain of burying my child. I had witnessed it in the eyes of my Aunt and Uncle. I was determined to avoid Miranda's death at all costs. I knew how hard Brandy's parents fought to keep her here, but there simply was not enough knowledge. I also knew the prayers of the pastors and many others who believed were also not enough. Brandy's life taught me love, pain, and I needed more than just prayer and parental fight.

I needed knowledge!

"My people are destroyed for lack of knowledge." Hosea 4:6 (NRSV)

It would simply be up to God to provide the knowledge, but I was not going to quit until we received it. Regardless of the cost to me physically, mentally, emotionally, spiritually or financially, I wanted Miranda to live and be well. Time would prove our entire family would need miracles while truth unfolded.

CONTENTS

Preface

Tetelestai

The last word spoken by Jesus Christ was Tetelestai, which means "it is finished." When Jesus said, "Tetelestai" just before He died on the cross, He had accomplished His mission as mandated by God for all of humanity to have the ability to freely access God the Father to receive all the promises as a child of God through the price paid by Jesus.

Embarking on a journey through the valley of death, one must know Jesus has already paid the price. Victory is not in the end result. True victory in life is having the ability to walk by faith daily, enjoy the life you are given, and trust Jesus paid the price at Calvary regardless of the pain, disappointment, or suffering you may face this side of Heaven. Whatever circumstances, you face – this life is temporary. Knowing Jesus suffered the shame of the cross, took your sins upon Himself, finished His race, and rose again will enable you to do whatever this life requires of you. As time passed and our life unfolded, we needed far more than I could have imaged. However, no matter how painful, God's grace carried us through. Ultimately, we learned God was faithful to His will and promises at every turn or twist in our testimony.

As a reader, look at my life as a large puzzle with over 1,000 pieces. As you travel through this journey, you will see how God takes all the pieces to a very complex story and puts them together into a beautiful picture. Latch yourself in and be prepared. Although this is a testimony of God's miraculous power, it is not easy to realize the depth of pain and suffering my family endured. Due to the nature of this story, I have changed the names of people involved as not to expose who said what at different points. Just know, although the names are not listed, this true testimony is our walk of faith.

What I would like to do is take you on a journey of the heart. As you read the events in my life and my family, I pray you will see the hand of God and His faithfulness. Please remember I am flesh and bones, and in writing this book my desire is to be completely honest with the reality of serving Jesus through the good and the bad. Our family is not perfect, and we have faced trials, pain, and temptations. We did not always make the right choices, and we have sinned. But, due to God's grace we were able to choose faith, endurance, and forgiveness while we walked our path. Remember, God loves you just as much as He loves my family, and you have the same access to His love, mercy, grace, healing, and forgiveness. My goal is to testify of the faithfulness of God and fulfill my destiny.

In Christ,

Dr. Donna Renfro

CHAPTER 1

BIGGEST BATTLE

At the age of fifteen, I was desperate. I had struggled from birth. When I was born, my legs were turned backwards, and I had to wear leg braces as a baby. My skin would randomly break open and bleed. And, every day of my life I had a headache. The final straw was being diagnosed with Anorexia Nervosa. Doctors told me I would never be healed, but I could learn to live with it. Truly, I wanted to die. I cannot even explain the torment. I went with a church youth group to the beach. After walking up and down the beach, I decided it was time to put an end to my misery. The plan was perfect because no one could rescue me. I began to swim out into the ocean. I knew eventually I would get so far out I could not make it back. I would drown. As I was swimming, I began going to the bottom of the ocean and coming back up to the surface. At this point, I was past the pier and the water was deep. I was confident no one could stop me or rescue me out in the ocean. I pushed off the bottom of the ocean floor, and BAM! I was hit in the head by a boat! A young boy pulled me to the shore. As you can imagine, there was quite a bit of commotion. I could not believe it! The youth leaders had me call my Mom. She said, "Are you okay? I have been praying for your life. What is going on?"

> ➢ Suicide is never the answer to your pain or problems. If you are desperate ask someone for help. God has a good plan for your life.

Several months had passed, and I was still miserable. I was in counseling for the anorexia, but still extremely underweight. I cried out to God, "God, IF you are real, I want to know someone will love me. I want to know who my husband will be."

Two months later, my cousin and I were in a musical at our high school. After the performance, my cousin wanted to go to McDonalds. I asked my Mom who agreed to let me go. My cousin and I went expecting to get a soda and go back to my house. When we arrived at McDonalds, several young boys who had obviously been drinking alcohol were there. I was very fearful and introverted, but not my cousin. She went over and began talking to them immediately. I went to the counter and ordered a diet drink. One of the boys yelled "Hey Donna! Come on over here, and talk to us."

I slowly walked over and stood quietly. The boy who had attracted my attention appeared to be the life of the party. He talked a mile a minute to me. After about ten minutes, I told my cousin we needed to go. The boys walked out with us, because they were leaving at the same time. I almost accidentally hit the "life of the party" with my car. I was so embarrassed, but he did not seem to mind. He smiled, joked about women drivers, and left the parking lot. My cousin and I began talking about the experience. As she was talking, I heard a still, small voice, and I knew immediately it was God. Do not ask me how I knew it was God. I just knew. He said, "That is the man you will marry."

I was shocked. Who was that boy? Didn't God know he was drinking alcohol? My cousin was still talking about another guy. She did not seem to notice the God of the Universe had just communicated with me. I interrupted her and asked, "What was the name of the guy who kept talking to me?"

She said, "Kevin – he is a baseball player."

We laughed and talked all the way home. I never told her God had spoken to me, because it seemed a little odd.

Kevin was very cute. I began to watch him at school, and we talked a little. Kevin was different when not under the influence of alcohol, he seemed shy and quiet. I thought since God had told me he would be my husband, we would fall madly in love and live happily ever after. Well, as you can imagine, it did not happen the way I planned it. Kevin began dating another girl; so, he did not even seem interested in me when he was sober. I handled the situation with teenage grace. I cried like a baby in my bedroom – *patience*, not a word in my vocabulary. Where was God? And what did He mean?

God wanted to show me He means exactly what He says! On July 6, 1986, Kevin asked me on a date. It had only been about two months since we first met at McDonalds. Kevin and I went to a local ice cream parlor. I ate a single scoop of chocolate-chip ice cream on a sugar cone. I do not remember what he ate. I just recall the warm, safe, cuddly feeling he brought to my heart. Kevin and I grew in love as we dated. I use the word grew over fell, because our love continues to grow even today. Kevin is such a gift from God to me. He loves me exactly the way I am. He doesn't care if I am fat, thin, nice, mean, right, wrong, etc. Kevin loves me. What an awesome gift!

God used Kevin's unconditional love toward me to bring healing. Kevin knew I was diagnosed with anorexia, and according to the doctors, there was no cure. He did not mind. He just took me as I was. Do not get the wrong idea. Our relationship was not perfect . . . just pre-ordained. Kevin and I would argue. We were both opinionated and strong. Neither of us ever wanted to lose at anything, which could create interesting conflicts. But, I knew in my heart he would be there for me no matter what. I knew I was safe.

In 1987, Kevin graduated from high school. I made the decision to skip my senior year of high school and went to college as well. From the time I was a little girl, I had a dream of becoming an elementary school teacher. My dream motivated me to make up my mind to live and not die. Even if I had to live with anorexia, with Kevin by my side and a destiny ahead of me, I was going to survive.

Since God answered my cry of desperation, I became more interested in Him. I had heard about a new church nearby. So, my sister and I went to see what it was like. We had been members of another church since we were children. The new church was very different from our other church. When they began praise and worship, I felt the presence of God in the church. Once again, I cannot explain how I knew it was God or even what it felt like. I just knew, and I knew I wanted more. Kevin and I were in college. The church offered a small college ministry led by the youth pastor. Kevin and I became very involved. The youth pastor was Tim. He and his wife Sara impacted our lives greatly. They lived the Word of God before our very eyes. He showed amazing love for his wife, and she was a Godly woman who prayed continually. They did not judge, but always provided counsel. I wanted what they had, but I did not know how to get it.

I always performed at the best of my ability to please others. College was no different, and even brought out more of my drive for perfection. I had learned to handle the mental torment caused by anorexia, but I was not free from it. My weight would fluctuate with stress, headaches, fear, or any other situation I could not control. I pushed myself to carry extra classes and make excellent grades. In the fall of 1988, Sara met me at the campus. She listened quietly while I explained my stress and fears of failure. She shared with me how she could not live the way she lived without the Holy Spirit. I questioned her with a heart which wanted the truth. She patiently answered each question and described what transpires when an individual lay down their life to serve Jesus Christ and allows the Holy Spirit to lead them into all truth. I remember her using the example of an individual standing at the edge of a cliff. When they look down, they cannot see, but they jump with the knowledge God will catch them. Honestly, I was a control freak! The thought of asking the Holy Spirit to enter my life was more like jumping off the Grand Canyon. After much talking, we prayed. Even though it was a profound day, it was still not the full transformation I needed.

In the summer of 1989, Pastor Tim called me at home to see if I would consider going on the youth revival at Jekyll Island to baby-sit his children. Without even hesitating, I said yes, because I loved his children. As soon as I hung up, I knew something was happening. God was on the move! Again, I cannot explain it – just a knowing in my heart.

The youth raised money to go on the trip, so I decided to help. As always, Pastor Tim used this as an experience to teach us. We asked people to sponsor us to read out loud for an hour. I know it sounds odd, but it began a process which would change my life forever. Originally, Pastor Tim had said we would read the Bible, but He had just read a book he felt would interest us. So, we read *This Present Darkness* by Frank Peretti. I was not a person who enjoyed reading, but this book captured my attention. After one hour of reading, I was hooked. I went home and finished the book immediately. It was amazing the way the author clarified the spiritual and natural realms, not to mention the impact of just a couple of people praying. The book is fiction. But in my heart, I knew this author saw spiritual truths. God was preparing me to receive healing.

We left for the youth event in vans and had a wonderful time. I remember talking to Sara for hours. I do not even know what we discussed; but, I do recall how she was continually an example of Jesus Christ, which caused me to admire her greatly. When we arrived at Jekyll Island, Pastor Tim asked me if I would stay with the youth girls as their counselor. Of course, I agreed. During all of the sessions with the youth evangelist, I babysat their children while the youth group received ministry. The rest of the time I spent with the girls in our youth group. After a couple of days, the girls noticed I did not eat. Like I had said earlier, I had learned how to cope with anorexia, but I was not healed. Often, unfamiliar food would cause me to regress. For some reason, I felt better when I did not eat. As strange as it sounds, not eating some foods brought me peace and made me feel better physically. The girls were concerned; so, they went to Pastor Tim. As always, Pastor Tim was an example of Jesus Christ as he confronted me in love. I remember feeling angry and saying, "You do not understand! Nobody understands!"

He calmly corrected me with love and patience, telling me he wanted me to go to the next ministry session, and I would have to eat. Easier said than done,

I thought. The session was the easy part. Eating was not. I wanted to be normal, without torment. I just did not know how to arrive there.

The girls had told me about the evangelist, so I was okay about going to the session. The room was relatively large. There were probably over 1,000 teenagers in attendance. I was only 19 myself, so I fit right into the crowd. When the evangelist opened his mouth, I felt like God was talking directly to me, which was very interesting. It was as if this man had lived my life and had been in my brain. He taught on "Self-Pity." Boy! I was the master of self-pity. He said you would always feel like "Nobody understands." As he taught, I knew God was reaching out to me. I left the service and went out alone with my Bible.

I found a quiet place on the steps of an old church. I prayed the only way I knew how, which was honest open communication. I told God I wanted peace and freedom. Somehow, I knew to look up *peace* in my Bible. The concordance directed me to Numbers 6:26 which states *"the Lord turn his face toward you and gives you peace."* In the margin of my Bible, I wrote "God grant me peace – August 10, 1989." Although there was no lightning, thunder, or a direct blast from Heaven, I knew God had once again spoken clearly to me and directed my life. My heart was now prepared for the encounter yet to come.

Pastor Tim told me I would be returning to the night session with the young evangelist. He and Sara agreed that I needed ministry. So, she kept her children. I went with expectation in my heart. I was not looking for God to do anything for me, but I was looking for God.

The evangelist preached on forgiving others and letting go of hurts. At the end, he had an altar call. I believe every teenager in the place went forward, myself included. We stood huddled together at the altar as he instructed us. He led us through a prayer. Then, he instructed us to cup our hands and visualize the hurts we harbored in our hearts. I did as instructed. Finally, he told us to throw up the unforgiveness and hurt to God. I threw my arms up and a tingling sensation went all over my body. I had truly released my hurts and forgiven my offenders. Young people all around me had done the same. One girl who was born with a crippled leg was instantly healed. I was in awe. I had never experienced anything like it. The corporate anointing was tremendous. Corporate anointing is a term used when the power of the Holy Spirit comes among a group of true believers just like He did at Pentecost as described in Acts chapter 2. When Christians agree in prayer, Jesus Christ is present with His power through the presence of the Holy Spirit.

Standing somewhere in the middle of approximately 1,000 teenagers, the evangelist caught my eye. He asked me to step to the side of the altar. Even though I was not sure what to expect, I obeyed. I found myself talking with this minister. He asked me a simple question. "Do you want to be free?"

I said, "Yes."

He instructed an altar worker to get behind me. Let me just say my immediate thought was I was not going to fall. I had seen some people fall down on the ground when they were prayed for, and it appeared fake. I thought people who fell when they received prayer were weird, and I was not joining the crowd. The evangelist asked me again if I wanted to be free. Again, I said, "Yes."

Then, as if he could not hear me or did not believe me, he asked again. "Do you want to be free?"

With force and determination, I answered, "Yes!"

The evangelist began to pray for me with power, and I could feel the presence of God. He barely touched my forehead with one finger. I fell backwards into the arms of a man who gently placed me on the floor. The power which came over me was indescribable. I knew what was going on, but was surrendered to the Spirit of God. My body was not still, and I recall the evangelist walking around me and praying. I did not know what he was praying, but I knew I needed help. After more prayer, the evangelist reached down, and he lightly touched my forehead again. My body became completely still and the peace that passes understanding enveloped me, which is exactly what I had asked God to give me. The evangelist then prayed for the Holy Spirit to fill me with His living water, so it would flow from me freely. He instructed me to pray. When I opened my mouth, I prayed from the bottom of my heart. I do not recall how long I lay there or how much I prayed. But when I sat up, everything seemed brighter. Lights were brighter. People seemed more alive. I was different. The torment was gone. I could not even make myself think the things which bound me. I was truly transformed.

I called my Mom immediately to let her know what God had done for me. Later that evening, I explained to the girls in the youth group what Jesus did for me. I knew in my heart I would never be the same.

We went home the next day. Sara and I shared all the way home. She instructed me to write what God had done for me. Her instructions came from much wisdom. She explained to me how God encounters were incredible, but would quickly fade if not recorded. I thought my victory was unshakeable, but Sara's words would ring in my ears.

Sunday morning, August 12, 1989, Pastor Tim had the youth share their experience. He had me testify last. It was such sweet victory for my parents who had earnestly prayed for my healing. I opened my mouth, and God filled it (Psalms 81:10). My testimony was well received. I thought I had won the biggest battle I would ever face.

Christmas 1988

Kevin age 19

Donna age 18

CHAPTER 2

THE ABORTION

As I recall the events following the victory I received, my heart is grateful for a God of grace and mercy. If you had asked me in August of 1989 what the next year of my life would hold, I would have very confidently told you I was a disciple of Jesus Christ. I was never going to be the same. Because, I had experienced God in an awesome way – I knew He was real. However, my misconception was I thought I would never need God's supernatural rescue from sin, torment, or Satan again. I thought I had won. Pride goes before a fall.

While I was at the altar, one of the things I confessed as sin was being sexually involved with Kevin. We had dated for three years, and while we dated things happened. I was completely convicted by the Holy Spirit. Kevin and I discussed my experience at the altar, so we agreed we would not have sex again until we were married.

In the fall, I began my senior year in college. I was on my last semester of classes and was excited about the future. Kevin and I were in church all the time. We were growing daily in the knowledge of the Word of God – a good season for both of us. We had much to learn, but we were eager to learn it.

In January of 1990, I began my student teaching. Even though I thought I would love it, the schedule proved to be extremely stressful. I began to trust my abilities over God's. I had to spend a lot of time preparing for teaching, which left little time for Kevin, not to mention God. I simply was too busy. The Bible tells us in James 4:17, *"If anyone, then, knows the good they ought to do and doesn't do it. It is sin for them."* (NIV)

My sin began when I chose life over the Life Giver. I became busy. Ginger, my sister, often says, "If the enemy cannot get you beat, he will get you busy." Slowly, over a period of months, I became caught up in the demands of the day. Kevin and I continued our relationship, but God was on the back burner.

In May of 1990, Ginger and I graduated from college, which was a wonderful event for our parents. Ginger had completed a double major in four years, and I was graduating with honors at the age of twenty. I had completed my B.S degree and could teach elementary school. My parents had trained us in the Word of God and had given us every advantage to be successful in this world. The day was so wonderful, and I was on top of the world. I had achieved my goal of getting a college degree. Now, I could fulfill my dream of teaching.

In June 1990, I received a phone call from Pastor Tim. He told me he was taking a job as a music minister in a church up north. I had not attended church recently, because I had been too busy with my student teaching. Missing just one service had somehow turned into several months of absence. I could not believe they were leaving. I loved them. He assured me it was God's plan for them to go, and he knew God's hand was on my life. He also instructed me to look to the senior pastors. Throughout our journey many pastors from multiple churches would help guide us. God was faithful to send someone at every bend in the road.

My heart was saddened to see Pastor Tim and his family leave. I loved them so much, and I regretted missing the past few months of church. Because it broke my heart they were leaving, I did not go to their going away service. I am not saying it was not the will of God for them. I am simply saying I loved them and respected them greatly; therefore, I hated to see them leave. I wanted them to be a part of my life.

Around the same time, I became tired and nauseated. I thought I had the flu. After several days of feeling sick, I received a telephone call from a woman at church who faithfully prayed for me.

She said, "I know by the Spirit of God you are pregnant."

I was in shock. "I am not!" was my response.

She said, "I believe you are."

We hung up, and I immediately told Kevin. He and I were both sure the call was a mistake. The only time we had broken our commitment to abstain from sex was the night of graduation. I could not believe I was pregnant. The doctors had told me I might never conceive a baby, because of the abuse I put my body through with anorexia. Kevin and I had been so careful and used protection. Both of us felt miserable. We had broken our commitment to each other and God. We had confessed our sin to God and asked His forgiveness. How could I be pregnant?

We drove to town, bought a pregnancy test, and returned to my house. I took the test immediately, and it had a positive result. I could not believe it. So, we drove back to town and bought a different name brand test. We went back to my house. I took it. It was positive as well. I was in shock. How could this be? Kevin and I were both in shock. I wanted some time to think, so he went home.

When I went to bed, I cried out to God in prayer. For the second time in my life, I heard the still small voice of my Heavenly Father speak to me. He did not tell me what to do. Simply, He said, "It is a girl."

This night was one of the darkest moments of my life. After some consideration, I made the decision to abort the baby. No counsel. No friends. Not even Kevin. I could not bear the idea of bringing a baby girl into this world. Fear gripped me. I never wanted anyone to experience the physical issues which had tormented my life. In my limited thinking, I thought my daughter would suffer like I had. I simply could not handle the thought of watching her suffer.

The next day, Kevin and I talked. He loved me and wanted to do whatever would make me happy. We told Ginger about our plans, and she tried to change my mind, but I would not consider any other options. My mind was made up. She asked if she could go with Kevin and me. She did not want me alone. I agreed. Kevin, Ginger, and I went out of town. I had an abortion sometime during the month of June 1990. I do not know the actual date.

The reality of my actions did not sink in during the process. I spent the night at Ginger's house the day of the abortion and went home the next day. It was amazing. I had just aborted my baby and nobody knew. Life went on. Kevin and I even attended church the Sunday after the abortion. I mention this to point out you never know what the person sitting beside you in church is going through.

I said nobody knew. Well, do you remember the call I received from Stacy, the woman at the church who faithfully prayed for me? She called me in August 1990, and asked if I would come and see her. Of course, I went because I loved her. She was an awesome woman of God. When I arrived at her house, she and I sat on the front porch and talked. After a little while, she looked me directly in the eyes and said, "I know you were pregnant. What did you do?"

I looked her straight in the eyes and said, "I was not."

She again said, "I know you were pregnant. What did you do?"

Again, I denied it.

Without even flinching, she said, "Donna, I know you were pregnant! What did you do?"

The third time was the clincher for me. I cracked. I began to cry and told her everything. She was a Godsend to me. Do you know she did not say one judgmental thing to me? She had so much compassion it overwhelmed me. We went inside to her bedroom, and she held me in her arms while I cried. Hours passed, but she did not leave me until all the hurt was gone. We prayed together, and I repented before God. Abortion is a secret sin. God was gracious to reveal my sin. He did this not to attack me, but to bring healing to my wounds and forgive me. I claimed the same scripture Jonah prayed in Chapter 2 of his book in the Old Testament. Jonah asked God to forgive him for his disobedience and sin. I had the abortion in June, and on August 12, 1990, I repented. God did a quick work on my behalf! I am forever grateful.

Stacy promised me; it was our secret. I did tell Kevin and Ginger, and they were both thankful God had ministered to me through Stacy. Truly, I thought it would never come up again.

CHAPTER 3

DREAM JOBS

I applied for a teaching job all over the area. The superintendent in our county had told me I would have a job. During the second week of August 1990, my sister received a position in the county teaching special education. I felt confident they would call me soon. Time passed, and no call came. Finally, during the week teachers attended work before classes started, I went to see the superintendent. He looked me square in the eye and said, "I do not have a position for you."

I was stunned. He had told me I would have a job, and now he was saying I would not. I went home in shock and disbelief. All I had ever wanted to do was teach. Now, I had my degree and no job. My mother was sitting in the kitchen when I came home. She told me to not get too upset. Because, she had prayed and God would take care of it. I was not too thrilled with her words. Where was God? Did He not know school was starting?

My mother was a teacher also, so she and my sister went to in-service, while I stayed home. I had learned how to sew, so I worked diligently at the sewing machine to pass the time. There were three days of in-service before actual teaching began, and my mother came home each day totally expecting I would have a job. Thursday afternoon she came in and inquired whether I had heard anything. I was annoyed by her hope. I told her again what the superintendent had said. I reminded her school started Monday. I wanted her to "get in reality." I did not have a job, and I was not getting one according to the man who hires teachers. However, my mother continued to believe despite the circumstances and my attitude.

After everyone left Friday morning, I sewed. I worked hard and tried desperately not to think about the disappointment in my heart. About two o'clock in the afternoon the phone rang. I answered, and it was a company offering my Dad a job. In February 1990, the company Dad worked for shut down, and he had been unemployed for months. I was so excited for him. I was home alone and would have to wait to give him the news. As soon as I hung up the phone, it rang again. I was just sure it was the company calling back with more instructions, but to my surprise it was the school superintendent offering me a teaching position. I was shocked, amazed, thrilled, and without words. I hung up and could hardly wait for Mom to come through the door. She had been right. God was faithful!

I began teaching third grade. It was wonderful. I loved teaching. It was so easy for me. The children were a blast to work with daily. Kids are great. They say what they think and are innocent in their perceptions. The entire school year was much like a fairy tale for me. My dream of teaching was a reality. Kevin and I were in love with each other and growing closer to God every day. And finally, we set the date for our marriage. We picked March 9, 1991 as our wedding date.

This season of my life is precious in my heart. My Mom was great. She did all the work for the wedding. It was fun and exciting. Kevin and I knew we would marry. We had dated for 5 years, and we had God's word on it. So, great peace led the way for our wedding date.

In December of 1990, I moved into a small yellow house in the city, which was a big deal for me. I had never lived alone. My Dad was great. He would call to check on me, and as he put it, "see if you were still alive." I really had to face fears living by myself. During those three months, I learned how to pray and trust God to protect me.

Finally, our wedding day arrived. I was a nervous wreck, which quite honestly surprised me. Kevin did not want vows. He wanted us to just say, "I do." Well, not me. I wanted vows. So, of course, we had vows. Well, I could not say any of them. Kevin said his vows, and he did a great job. He sounded so confident. My turn came and out of nervousness I began to laugh. I laughed and laughed. I could not control myself. I laughed so hard my back was shaking. My pastor handled it well. He just kept the service going. Kevin was wonderful. He just looked at me with love in his eyes. When Pastor said, "You may kiss the bride." Kevin grabbed me and kissed me like there was no tomorrow. The congregation clapped. It was profound for me. I knew I was safe. I knew our marriage was from God. We went to Epcot at Disney World for our honeymoon, which was a lot of fun. I would have probably made it a point to enjoy it even more if I had known the future.

After we returned home, I was up praying one night and studying in the Word of God. I knew God was drawing me into His presence. The next morning, I was getting ready to go to teach, and while I was curling my hair, God spoke to me. This is the third time I had ever heard His voice. Clearly, God said: "You will have a son. Name him Micah James."

I was peaceful, but shocked. I had honestly thought I would never have any children. I knew God had forgiven me, but I did not think he would bless me with the very thing I had destroyed. I had a lot to learn about God's grace. Immediately, I went to Kevin. I had to wake him up, because it was so early. I told him God had spoken to me, and we would have a son. Not quite awake,

Kevin said, "That's nice, dear" and fell back asleep. I left for work. I could not shake my experience with God all day. I was amazed we would have a child. I was amazed once again the God of the Universe had spoken to me.

People have asked me how to know if it is God speaking. Let me just say – you know. That is all there is to it. When He speaks, there is no denying it. The Bible states in John 10:4, we know the voice of our shepherd. I promise you – if He wants to tell you something, you will know.

Even though God had spoken to me, I did not expect to get pregnant immediately. It was May 1991, and we had only been married two months. I did receive in my heart what God had spoken to me. I just thought it would be later down the road, at least a year or two. I had many career plans to accomplish: I wanted my master's degree and eventually a doctorate. Not to mention the fact Kevin was still in college. We were living on my salary, which was fine. He only lacked a few credit hours to graduate.

Well, the last week of school, I did not feel well. I was extremely tired and nauseated; therefore, I took a pregnancy test the morning of the last day of school. The test was positive. I was shocked. The timing seemed a bit off from my perception. However, God's timing is perfect.

Kevin and I were both excited, even though we had not planned for a baby immediately. I had already signed up to teach summer school, and Kevin did not even have a part-time job. It is interesting how the thought of a baby changes your whole way of thinking. Almost immediately, I wanted a house, and Kevin wanted a job. God set us on a path which would not be easy, but would be extremely rewarding.

Kevin began looking for a job. Meanwhile, I became very sick. Pregnancy was hard on me. I vomited all day and had migraine headaches. I will not get into details. Just image the worst flu for months on end. It was not fun. Kevin was not able to get a job, which worked out well for the summer. I was so sick he had to drive me to the school to teach. Often, I was on the couch in the teachers' lounge and vomited into the trash can. Misery was a new word for me.

While I was feeling sorry for myself one day, a teacher walked into the lounge. She inquired about me, so I told her I was pregnant. She told me how she would give anything to be lying on a couch and vomiting into the trash can. I was amazed. She went on to tell me she could never have children, which was really sad. My heart went out to her. Again, my perception was greatly adjusted. No matter what I had to endure, this pregnancy was a blessing. She shared with me how she was trusting God to give her the desires of her heart. During the next year, she adopted a precious baby. God fulfilled her request.

The summer ended, and the fall school year began. I had been teaching at my old elementary school, but due to financial cutbacks faculties were being shuffled. I was moved to a different elementary school, and I was not happy about it. I prayed and asked God to please not make me move, but every time I knew when I was praying it was God's best for me to go. The new school was approximately fifty minutes from my house, which added thirty-five more minutes of driving each way. I had a long drive every day. It gave me a lot of time to pray. Also, I had the opportunity to enjoy the view. I fell completely in love with a house, which I drove by on the way to the school. Every morning I would slow down when I passed by it. I loved it. The house was a two-story farmhouse with a wrap-around porch. It was the desire of my heart, but I did not think there was any possible way we could have my dream house.

Kevin was desperately trying to get employment. We agreed he would not complete his degree, but instead go to work full time. Kevin wanted to be a police officer. It was his dream – the desire of his heart. So, he applied for a position on the local police force. He was qualified and had great favor with the people hiring. The process to get a police job is long and drawn out. First, he had to take a written test, on which he scored 100%. Then, he had to take a physical test. Again, he had an excellent score. Finally, they narrowed the applicants down to twenty and were going to hire twelve. Kevin had only one remaining test. The applicants had to endure a psychological exam where they are put in a motel room and interrogated. Kevin did well, but came home upset. He never went into much detail about it, but the test emotionally drained him. Daily, I lifted Kevin in prayer concerning his job. I had much time to pray while I drove to work. We both felt confident he would get the job, after all it was the desire of his heart, and God gives you the desire of your heart – right?

It was almost December 1991, and Kevin had been interviewing and testing with the police force for six months. The new officers would be hired just before Christmas. I had been teaching and was on my way home from school when God spoke to me. He said, "Kevin will not get the police job."

I could not believe it. Kevin wanted to be a police officer more than anything. He was doing great in the testing and interviews. Why would he not get the job? The Bible clearly says God will give you the desires of your heart. I had been diligently praying, and I was now seven months pregnant. Kevin needed a job. I responded quickly to God with a simple prayer. If Kevin was not going to get the police job, please send another one and quick. I continued to pray by faith, believing Kevin would have a job before I had the baby.

In a couple of days, we received a letter from a new business which was getting ready to hire in the area. I encouraged Kevin to apply. He did not want to because of the police job, but I continued to encourage him, so he eventually applied. He was still confident he would be a police officer. I chose not to tell him what God had spoken to me. I was not trying to be deceptive with Kevin. I wanted to protect him and handle the knowledge I had with prayer. I was also hoping I was wrong.

The week before Christmas, Kevin was called in for his final interview. He was so excited, but I was reserved. When he walked through our door after the interview, his face said it all. He did not talk for a few days, but eventually he opened up. The chief of police told Kevin how he impressed them greatly. If he would go through the application process one more time, he would be hired. Because he was only twenty-one, they wanted him to show his commitment by repeating the six-month interview process. Also, it would give the needed time for him to be a little older. Kevin was devastated. I explained to him what God had told me, and he became angry. He wanted to know why God would not give him the desire of his heart.

This disappointment sent me into fervent prayer. I wanted to understand God. Were the promises in God's Word lies, or what? After seeking Him, it became clearer to me. God does give you the desires of your heart; however, your heart should be full of His desires. He grants the very best for our lives. Often, we make decisions based on our fleshly desires, in other words what we want. God makes decisions based on truth. He knew our future. We did not. He knew Kevin and his innermost parts. God knew what job would truly fulfill the desires of his heart. For now, we would have to wait and trust God.

My prayers were constant. I wanted Kevin to have a full-time job before Micah was born. I wanted a miracle. Kevin had been job searching for a while. We needed God to intervene in a big way.

Christmas break ended, so I had to go back to work. By now, work was difficult, to say the least. I was huge and not due to have Micah until February. I had already gained over seventy pounds and swelled daily. This was no normal pregnancy. I went to get my paycheck at the central office late Monday afternoon and due to my size, I fell down some steep stairs. I was not hurt, but my body was affected by the fall. I could not rest at all during the night after the fall. While I was awake, I prayed. I was desperate to end the pregnancy, because I was so uncomfortable. I was retaining so much fluid my arms would go numb; the vomiting had not stopped; my headaches continued; my ribs had turned out to make room for the baby; my weight gain was around one hundred pounds, and exhaustion was a new experience for me. I was ready for the baby to come, but Kevin did not have a job yet. I lay before God on the floor and cried out to

Him. I asked Him to please let me have the baby. I expressed my complete trust in Him. I even surrendered my request for Kevin's job. I no longer cared if he worked. I just wanted the pregnancy to end.

Early the next morning, I had signs of early labor. We went to the hospital, but they sent me home. I was not happy, but was too tired to get upset. My parents hung out with Kevin and me most of the day. I did not feel like eating and slept most of the afternoon. My parents went home when I woke up, and Kevin left as well. Around 4:00 p.m. in the afternoon, the phone rang. It was a wonderful woman from the church. She had called to arrange my baby shower. I stood up to move the phone while we were talking, and my water broke. I was so excited. I yelled into the phone and quickly ended our conversation. I called my parents and Kevin. We all headed to the hospital.

Upon arriving it became obvious the night ahead of us would be long. I had not dilated at all, but my body was in labor. After some time, the doctor hooked me up to I.V. medication to speed up the process. I requested my epidural and the anesthesiologist came. After inserting the epidural, they informed my mother they would be back when they did the C-section on me. My mother did not tell me this until after the delivery. She knew I had prayed, and believed by faith I would deliver Micah naturally. Several medical people had told me I would not deliver my baby naturally due to my size and shape, but I prayed and trusted God would somehow aid me in a natural delivery. I had to go back to work seventeen days after Micah was born.

Just before 4:00 a.m., the monitor, which showed the baby's heartbeat, became dead silent. The nurse moved a few things and then found the doctor. The doctor quickly came in and placed me flat on my back. He flipped the baby and told me to lie on my left side. All the fluid was now gone, and the baby had cut off his oxygen by lying on the umbilical cord. It was quick and scary, but as quickly as it happened it was over.

Finally, I was ready to deliver. I pushed for three hours. It was long and hard, which is not uncommon for most first babies. At the very end, I told the doctor, "I quit! Please, just take the baby." Calmly, he responded, "You cannot quit. You have gone too far now – push!"

Within minutes, Micah James was born. I had delivered him naturally, so once again God had faithfully answered my prayers. Micah weighed eight pounds and fifteen ounces. He was several weeks early, but perfectly healthy! I was excited and exhausted. Kevin went home to sleep, and I rested between visitors. Kevin came back late in the afternoon. He had a grin on his face. I inquired about his expression. Kevin replied: "I have a job!"

The new business where he had applied in December called and gave him a position over the phone. He would start work on Monday. I was amazed. I knew it was God. The timing was perfect! This job was obviously hand-picked for Kevin. My prayers were answered, and Kevin had a job not before the baby was born. But on the very day he was born. God is always on time.

My pregnancy taught me to trust God. He had been so faithful to every request. He caused my body to deliver Micah naturally despite all the people who did not think I could, and He gave Kevin a job at the exact moment in time we needed one. I had learned endurance and reward. I had also caught the concept concerning "desires of our hearts." Simply stated, as you seek God with all your heart, His desires become your desires. Therefore, the Bible is the truth. Due to your personal submission to a Holy God, you do get the ultimate desires of your heart by going the way God directs you. God did not give us what we asked for. He gave us what we needed. You see, He was the only One who knew our future! God was walking with me daily and training me for the future.

CHAPTER 4

DENIAL IS A POWERFUL FORCE

Life is not always what you think it will be…

Kevin had received his new job, and I thought all would be well. He went to work on third shift, which meant I was home alone every night with Micah and had to work as well. Micah was only seventeen days old when I went back to work. With Kevin just beginning his job and all our medical bills from Micah's birth, we could not financially afford for me to have days without pay. So, I had to go back to work. Anyhow, I found myself frustrated and angry. I had to do it all – teach all day, pick up Micah from his caregiver, pay the bills, buy the groceries, clean the house, cook, and take care of everything else. I felt very much like a single parent. It was not Kevin's fault; nonetheless, I was frustrated and headed quickly towards anger.

I had prayed diligently for Kevin to obtain a job. Kevin wanted the police job, which God had told me would not come through. So, I prayed as directed by God, expecting a great job for Kevin. Expectation is another thing which can greatly disappoint you. God always sends you the right way, but the right way is not always the easy way. I thought and prayed Kevin would love his job. He did not! As a matter of fact, he hated it. Kevin was working on a deck, making wheels for cars in extreme heat. He related it to working in a pit. Also, he had to wear steel-toed boots, and they were painful for his feet. He complained constantly, and it was the last thing I wanted to hear. When Kevin was hired, the plant was brand new and required him to work twelve-hour days, seven days a week. The little bit of time we had together Kevin was angry and miserable, which in no way helped my own frustrations.

We were living in a tiny rental house. I wanted a house of our own. We tried to buy a house when I was pregnant, but nothing was right or worked out. Three weeks out from the birth of my son, I was miserable. I strongly considered getting a divorce from Kevin. Not because I did not love him. I did. I wanted a divorce, because I wanted to divorce my life. Although God told me I would have a son, and I loved Micah, he was a lot of work. Even though God had given Kevin a job, it took him from me day and night. My life was not the way I had imagined it, and I was tired. I also justified divorce by the fact I did it all anyhow…why did I need Kevin?

Basically, I was feeling sorry for my situation and myself. But, as always, I prayed and had no peace about divorce. I would just have to adjust to my new life, not the life I had dreamed of, but the life God was leading us to live.

I began to pray about our house. The rental house was only 400 square feet and simply too small for two adults, a baby, and a poodle. We needed a house. I had a dream three separate times. In the dream, the house we were renting burned to the ground. First, the house up the street from us caught on fire, and then our house caught on fire. In the dream, I could hear my Dad saying, "Pack your bags and get out!"

Each time I had the dream, it bothered me. I told a lot of co-workers, who were teachers, about the dream. It definitely made me feel uneasy, but I had never had a dream from God before. Therefore, I did not even realize God was speaking to me through a dream.

My Dad continued to encourage me to get a house and after much thought and prayer, Kevin and I decided to build a house on some land my parents gave us. We could use the land as collateral, which helped us since we did not have any money for a down payment. The next step was selecting a house. I had fallen in love with a farmhouse I passed each day while driving to work. I loved the house with the big wrap-around porch. But, I did not think we could afford it. So, I put it out of my mind. Kevin and I chose a split-foyer type of house, which would have met our needs. But, it was not the desire of my heart. We hired a wonderful contractor who was going to do a turnkey job for us. As days went by, I continued to pass the farmhouse I wanted. I had no peace about our current house plans. Finally, I drove Kevin out to the house I loved and showed it to him. He liked it as well, but thought it would be way out of our price range.

I stopped the car right in the driveway of the house. Then, I walked right up to the front door and knocked. A sweet woman opened the front door; so, I told her I loved her house. She explained to me that it was a model home, which had been built in another state and brought in by a crane. It was a two-story house with a full basement. I had never heard of such a thing. She gave me her house prints for free and told me to call her any time. Kevin and I went out to eat and talk about the house. He simply suggested we ask our contractor how much it would cost to build the house. So, I did.

Amazingly enough, there was only a $5,000.00 difference in my dream house and the house I was going to settle for, because I did not think there was any possible way we could have the house I wanted. I had completely left God out of the situation. With God, all things are possible. We agreed with our contractor on my dream house. The only thing left was getting a loan, which I thought would be easy.

I had asked around and was directed to a specific bank by several people. We applied and paid the bank the application fee. I called them regularly and they kept putting me off. Kevin and I were young. We were both only twenty-two. Although we had perfect credit, we apparently did not have enough credit to get a construction loan. I was angry and frustrated. We had finally found the house. We had the land and the contractor. All we needed was a loan, but the bank would not budge. My Dad told me, "Donna, where there is a will, there is a way."

We contacted a local farm lending company and had our loan within days. It was great, because the interest on the money we borrowed was much less with this company than with the bank. Also, this company took great interest in the actual building of our house and watched our contractor like a hawk. Our contractor was wonderful to us, but I think God, in all His wisdom, denied our first request for the bank loan to save us money and to give us an overseer with wisdom and knowledge, so the contractor could not take advantage of our youth. The contractor was required by this institution to provide all receipts before he made financial draws on the money. Because he did exactly what they required, the construction worked out great for all of us.

We moved into our new home in October 1992. I was so excited to have the house, which was about 2,000 finished square feet. It seemed like a mansion to us. I had fun decorating the house and fixing up Micah's room. I had adjusted to being a new mommy and wife. Kevin had adjusted to his new job, although he still did not seem too happy about the type of work. Life seemed to be settling out and getting better. I simply had no idea what was just around the corner for us.

Interestingly enough, weeks before we moved out of our rent house, the house up the street caught on fire and burned just like in my dream. We were in shock and took pictures while we watched the fireman try to stop the house from burning down. I became a little concerned. I had never had a dream which predicted the future before. The house-burning dream was my first. Anyhow, we moved out and within six weeks of moving, the house we had rented caught on fire and burned. It was on the local television news. Of course, all the family and friends I had told about my dream were amazed. Let me just say, I was more amazed than anyone. I realized God was speaking to me in dreams and my Dad's voice had been the key. If we had not packed our bags and moved out, we would have been there when the house burned. But, we did pack and move. By the way, the owner rebuilt the house.

When Micah was nine months old, Kevin went to the pediatrician with me, which was odd. Kevin had never gone to an appointment before because of his job, but for whatever reason he went with me to this specific appointment. We waited in the waiting room for a long time, and finally we were called back to a treatment room. Micah was there for a well-baby check. The doctor walked into the room and looked Micah over from one end to the other. He then pointed out to Kevin and me, Micah had a large discolored spot on his stomach, which went around to his back – no big surprise to us. Micah had been born with the brown skin in that particular location. The doctor then looked Kevin and me in the eye. He asked us some questions. He asked if anyone else in the family had a marking like the one on Micah or if any relative had any problems, and we told him no. The doctor then said, "That marking is an indicator your son, Micah, will grow tumors and have cancer."

I was speechless. I was in shock. Micah was completely normal. He had no indicators of tumors or any other sickness. My shock quickly turned to anger. Kevin and I took Micah home and talked very little about the doctor's comments. Promptly, I decided the doctor was wrong, so I changed Micah to a different group of pediatricians. I was not going to let some crazy doctor tell me my son would grow tumors or be sick. Anyway, I believed God had made the way at Calvary for sickness to be taken away from us. Therefore, I justified my denial with scripture and decided simply Micah was fine, and the doctor was wrong. Truly, I gave it no place in my mind or heart. I was not going to receive the report of the doctor. My son was healthy and that was that!

Denial is basically saying something is not correct or true even if all evidence is present. Let me point out, denial of truth is not faith. God never intended for us to use scripture and deny our circumstances or any truth. God intended for us to use our faith and the Word of God to change our circumstances. The Bible never promised a life without pain. It does promise tests, trials and even tribulation, but it also promises as believers we will overcome. I took the scriptures out of context and used them to bring me a false sense of peace. I took the Word of God to deny my situation and Micah's disease. I did that –

not God. I had been taught about God's miraculous healing power; therefore, I simply made up my mind how God would make the entire thing go away. All I had to do was give it no place and ignore it – not confess it. God would make Micah grow whole, because the Word of God promised sickness was taken away at Calvary, but I was wrong.

I was wrong on so many levels. Please listen to me. Denial of your circumstances will not make them go away. Denial will keep you in the middle of your circumstances forever. You can bury your head in the sand, but basically you will just end up eating sand.

Hearing the words my son, whom, by the way, God had prophesied to me, had a disease which would cause him to grow tumors or have cancer was more than I could handle. So, I simply chose to not handle it at all.

I would also like to point out God is the Healer, and there are times where the right action is NO action. But, I believe the only time a person can choose no action is if God, Himself, divinely directs you to be still.

"Be still and know that He is God." Psalm 46:10 (NKJV)

Walking in a close relationship with God will allow you to know what to do or not to do. I did not make my decision based on prayer or guidance from God. I made my decision of denial, because the pain was too great to acknowledge. If I acknowledged what the doctor said about my son, I would have felt as if God had failed me. I would have been angry with God for even allowing my child to be born with a sickness. I would have had to face my faith and beliefs. Therefore, without consciously realizing all this, I simply chose denial, which was the easy way out.

My choices to ignore the doctor would catch me years later.

CHAPTER 5

MILLION DOLLAR FAMILY

Kevin and I loved Micah. He was such a blessing – truly a gift from God. One I did not deserve. Although God had forgiven me and I had forgiven myself, somewhere deep in my heart, I thought I had to pay a price for having an abortion. I thought I did not deserve children at all, much less a child as wonderful as Micah. He was the easiest child in the world to love and very easy to care for. He had a wonderful personality and brought much love, light, and fun into our lives.

Kevin wanted another child. In my heart, I did too, but I still had the memories of how very sick I was pregnant. I feared getting pregnant and being sick again. During Micah's first year, I went through a lot of adjustments and knew another child would bring more adjustments, but Kevin desired more children. We were talking about trying to plan a pregnancy – now there is a novel idea. Planning a pregnancy had not been a luxury Kevin and I had ever experienced. Anyhow, we thought I should become pregnant at the beginning of the school year and have the baby at the end. Then, I would have the entire summer off with the new baby and time to adjust before going back to work.

Well, as usual, God had another plan. I found myself pregnant in June 1993. Micah was eighteen months old and a lot of fun. Kevin and I were both thrilled! The excitement in me was so great – even I was amazed. I loved Micah so much and knew another child would be such a blessing. Immediately, I began searching for scriptures in the Bible about healing and not being sick. I wrote them down and posted them all over the house. I was older and had learned more about healing. I was determined I would not become sick during this pregnancy. I single-mindedly decided to believe God would make a way for me to enjoy this pregnancy without sickness, pain, and suffering.

After knowing I was pregnant just a few days, my body began to have problems. I was bleeding and cramping. I recall sitting up all night long. It appeared as if I was going to have a miscarriage. I prayed and asked God to save the baby, and He did. It would be the first of many times, I would pray for God to save the life of this baby.

Determination is not enough, although it can be a huge key. Belief is not enough, although it is necessary. Sometimes you simply need a miracle from God. It is not in our ability to modify the laws of nature or change the circumstances. It is only in our ability to believe God will. I did believe from the bottom of my heart, yet I was sick anyhow – desperately sick again. I had horrid headaches, pain, vomiting, and sugar level problems throughout the entire pregnancy just like with my previous pregnancy. Even though I believed I would not be sick, I was. Although I prayed and trusted the scriptures, I still suffered. I was not too concerned because I knew when the baby came, the sickness would go away. So, I simply endured the pregnancy knowing the fruit of my labor would be worth the pain.

Within weeks of knowing I was pregnant, God spoke to me, "Donna, quit your job and stay at home."

I thought resigning my job was a bad idea! I could not quit my job. I loved my job. I loved teaching. After all, I had always wanted to be a teacher. I made more money than Kevin at that time, and it was illogical for me to quit. Not to mention there would be no way we could pay our bills, if I stayed at home. It was impossible in my mind, and not even something I wanted to consider. I was not going to quit my job.

Even in writing the truth of my story, I am amazed God never gave up on me. I was stubborn, prideful, and a pain in the neck. Just ask Kevin. But, God never gave up on me. He never stopped loving me or pouring grace on me. He is an amazing God. He made a way through Jesus Christ, and the price He paid at Calvary to cover us in His mercy and grace without our perfection being required. I am simply saved by grace, and nothing can change my salvation. I am sure God would look down on me and get a good laugh. He knew I would make the right decisions. I was the one who did not know.

As the summer went on, I became more and more convinced God wanted me to quit my job. Kevin agreed. I thought it was a bad idea. I did not want to quit. I wanted to teach. Do not get me wrong. I loved Micah and missed him while I worked, but I had a great job which allowed me to be home with him 180 days a year and take any sick day I needed with pay. I had great hours – by 2:30 p.m. I had picked Micah up every day. He basically only spent his mornings and an afternoon nap away from me. Not to mention the fact God had given him a great caregiver. God had moved on the heart of one of my mother's friends, who had retired from teaching, to keep Micah for me. Micah was the only child in her care, so he received all her attention. She and her husband were retired, and they loved Micah. She would come out to my car in the mornings and get him out of his seat. She loved him, and he was very safe. God had created a wonderful situation for us. Why would He want me to quit my job?

Kevin and I also began conversations about what to name the baby. I was just sure I was having a boy. God had not told me. I was just sure because I had aborted my baby girl – I would never have another girl. I loved Micah and was thrilled at the thought of having another boy. So, we came up with the name John David. Notice how I said, we came up with the name. As always, God had another plan.

I went for the ultrasound, which would tell us the sex of our child. Kevin and I went together. I remember the day well. The technician was great. She talked us through the entire ultrasound showing us every detail of the baby. She asked us if we had any other children, and we told her about Micah.

Then she said, "You are a million-dollar family! This one is a girl."

I was stunned beyond belief. Kevin was thrilled. He would have been thrilled with a boy, too. Kevin loves babies and was thrilled we were having another one. I was shocked for a different reason. I began to cry. I could not get over God's grace. I never thought I would ever have a girl, because I had aborted my baby girl. Although, I knew I had forgiveness, I simply did not understand the amount of grace God had given me. I was overwhelmed with joy. Our lives would be complete. We would have a boy and a girl. A million-dollar family – the dream of most was the reality for us.

Well, obviously, the name we had chosen would not work. So, for the next few months Kevin and I argued over what to name this precious little girl. I had a name of a little girl I had taught and loved, but Kevin refused the name. Because, he thought I would continually compare our child with her. Then, we both wanted to name her after our grandmothers, but neither of us would bend on which name came first or in the middle. By the way, did I ever mention Kevin is just as stubborn as I am? We are well matched. We argued until the name *Miranda* came. We were sitting on the bleachers at a basketball game when I suggested the name. Immediately, he jumped on it! Our daughter would be named Miranda Audrey-Ruth Renfro. The middle name was a compromise of both grandmothers being honored by our child.

When I was about seven months pregnant, I was praying over Miranda in my living room one evening. I prayed diligently over both my children, even while I was pregnant. Anyway, the oddest prayer came out of my mouth. I prayed, "Miranda will never be overweight, not one day of her life."

I want to add here that Miranda's obesity was going to be a symptom of her health problems. At the time of the prayer, I had no idea she would not be healthy. God was giving me a piece of the puzzle, and I did not realize it. I would also like to add I do not judge or think less of overweight people. I love people exactly how they are created – short, fat, tall, skinny, black, white, male, or female. It matters not to me. But the clue in the prayer was, for Miranda obesity was a sign of her disease. In the natural, Miranda was overweight for several years, but ultimately the prayer would rule over her body, and God knew that when it came out of my mouth.

The words caught my attention, because I had never feared I would have a daughter with a weight problem. My fear was having a daughter who would deal with my physical problems. The prayer would prove to be a place I would hold in my heart for many years as we battled for her life. A prayer, when prayed had no meaning to my mind, but I knew it had come from the heart of God.

I sought God diligently for a word over Miranda. God had prophesied Micah to me, but, with Miranda, He had been silent. Just after Christmas, God spoke to me, "Miranda will be born on February 7, 1994."

Miranda was not due until the first of March, but Micah had come early so it was not a big surprise to me to think Miranda would. I simply wrote down God's word and went on living.

Kevin and I decided instead of quitting my job; I would take a year off. I had tenure and could take a year without pay and still walk back into my job. It was not what God had told me to do, but I was going to quit for a season. Financially, I did not think it was possible for me to stay at home permanently.

So, I applied for the year off and my request was granted. A wonderful young woman who had been the school's secretary was going to get my position, temporarily. She had just finished her degree, and she was excited. I gave her all my teaching equipment. I felt led of God to do it. Oddly enough, on my last day, when I walked out of the school, deep in my heart, I knew I would never teach elementary school again. The season of teaching in an elementary school, for me, was over. Truly, I did not give it too much thought. It was just a knowing.

Just as God prophesied, Miranda was born on February 7, 1994. She was beautiful. Kevin and I were elated – having a wonderful son and a beautiful daughter. What more could we possibly want?

However, the million-dollar family was quickly tossed into a nightmare of medical problems. Before we left the hospital, Miranda was diagnosed with jaundice. Every day for two weeks we had to take her to the hospital to be tested, her liver levels went higher each time. I kept praying and finally the jaundice went away. It was scary, as any mother with a newborn would know. Then, by the time she was three weeks old; she had her first infection and was placed on antibiotics. Also, Miranda cried relentlessly – day and night without a break. When I would tell the pediatricians, they said it was probably colic. I thought colic sounded reasonable, but Miranda cried so much. She cried persistently and without ceasing.

During her three-month check-up, the bomb was dropped. I was told Miranda had a metabolism problem. I guess you could call me the "queen of denial." I refused to believe the words of the medical professional. In shock and disbelief, I refused to accept my daughter would have a metabolism problem. Miranda was a beautiful baby. She had recently gained several pounds, but don't all babies? God would not let anything bad happen to my baby…especially a weight issue! I left the "well baby" checkup on June 15, 1994, hurt and angry. Wednesday night at church I saw my sister in the hallway outside of the infant nursery. She could see the anxiety in my face. I explained to her what I had been told, and she too said, "No way!"

Together we prayed over Miranda. We claimed the blood of Jesus and cursed sickness and disease. I never gave it another thought. Again, I chose to deny the truth. Again, I chose denial. I refused to believe anything was wrong with either of my children. I was not willing to accept it. Regardless of who said it or why they said it, I believed my children were completely healthy. I was not willing to accept any other option.

Again, years later, this decision would catch me and almost kill my daughter.

By the fall, God would not get off my back about quitting my teaching job. I was distraught about the decision – torn apart in my heart. My heart knew exactly what to do, but my brain thought the idea was completely illogical. I prayed and prayed, but God would not change His mind. I had been Miranda's mother for six months and saw how difficult she was to care for daily. I knew it would be hard for anyone else to handle her. I cannot say enough how very much I loved her. However, the truth was she had daily issues with her sickness and crying. I never knew what a day would hold. Finally, I became desperate. I prayed and asked God to confirm His word to me through someone else. That very night, I went to a prayer meeting. At the end of the meeting a woman was led to pray for everyone. She prayed for me last. When she reached me, she said, "There are things you want to go and do, but God has called you to stay at home and be a mother."

Of course, I cried. But, the very next day I turned in my resignation, which was very difficult for me. I was not quitting a job – I was giving up my dream. However, I decided God knew more than I did, so I chose to obey Him. Financially, things were tight, but we had managed. If God wanted me at home, I assumed He had a good reason for it. You know it is so simple to quote scripture or read the Bible, but to live the life is different. Truly quitting my dream was a crucifixion of my flesh. I knew the scripture in Galatians 2:20, *"I have been crucified with Christ and I no longer live, but Christ lives in me. The life I now live in the body, I live by faith in the Son of God, who loved me and gave himself for me."* (NIV) This was one of the first times I had to live the scripture and truly submit my will to His without knowing why.

Miranda was a completely different child than Micah. I am sure all children are unique, but mine were night and day. Micah had been so simple and easy going. Miranda was demanding and constant from the moment she was born. I loved her equally, but she required so much more of me. Miranda was constantly sick. The first life threatening illness was at age nine months. I went to meet with a friend who had two children the ages of mine at a local place for the boys to play. Miranda was quiet. She always cried, without exception, especially in her car seat. On this particular day, Miranda did not cry. She did not cry in the car or when we were with the other family. She did not cry at all. I knew something was not right. I went home and put her in her bed thinking maybe she was simply tired. I had never in the entire nine months of her life known her to not cry. I went to do other things in the house. Suddenly, I was prompted by God to go and check on Miranda. When I checked on her – she was burning up with fever and lethargic. Her fever was over 105. I called the pediatrician, and they said to come immediately. Kevin drove me there while I held her lifeless body in my arms.

My heart knew something was seriously wrong, but my mind would not receive it.

We arrived at the office, and they ran several tests on her to get to the root of the problem. Finally, it was decided Miranda had a severe urinary tract infection. This would be the first of about thirty urinary tract infections she would have over the next four years or so. We were sent to the hospital, and they ran more tests to see why she had the infections. Apparently, reflux can occur in little girls and they wanted it ruled out. Well, Miranda did not have reflux. I recall coming home from the hospital and lying on my bed. Deep in my heart, I knew. I knew something was wrong, but what?

Miranda continued down a path of sickness and disease. She was always sick or in a trauma. Her first hospitalization overnight happened at about thirteen months of age. She became ill, and I knew in my heart she needed help. The odd thing was she appeared okay. But, my heart told me differently. I watched her closely all day and by the evening, I decided to take her to the hospital. Miranda was dehydrated and at a very serious point. The doctors immediately admitted her and ran fluids through her veins. It would be the first of many hospitalizations.

What I would like to do at this point is simply list the major-medical visits and hospitalizations. We were always at the doctors with Miranda. I have only listed the extreme visits. It is overwhelming, and I believe a list is the best way to show you what we endured.

February 7, 1994	Miranda was born
February 8, 1994	Diagnosed with jaundice
February 21, 1994	First infection treated with antibiotics
March 16, 1994	Colic diagnosis
June 7, 1994	Sick with fever and cough/chest cold
June 15, 1994	Diagnosed with a metabolism problem
July 20, 1994	First Ear Infection treated with antibiotics
November 2, 1994	First Urinary Tract Infection
November 1994	First Hospitalization with testing
November 16, 1994	Urinary Tract Infection/Flu
January 1995	Brother accidently cut her finger with scissors
February 13, 1995	Fell out of baby bed on her head
April 13, 1995	Hospitalization for dehydration
August 1995	Chicken pox
September 4, 1995	Emergency room visit: Miranda was sick and kept at the hospital

April 4, 1997	Strep throat/tonsils swollen
April 23, 1997	Sinus Infection/ fever 103 and up
September 23, 1997	Sick treated with antibiotics
January 29, 1998	Hospitalization for sickness/fever over 105/told again by a doctor metabolism problem
May 4, 1998	Urinary tract infection
May 26, 1998	Strep throat
June 2, 1998	Large tonsils/ still sick/pharyngitis

Miranda had strep throat without a negative test for about a year, before we had her tonsils surgically removed.

We were constantly taking Miranda to the doctor for one reason or another.

During her third year of life, it appeared as if she was getting better. It was one of the healthiest years she had. I really did not know why, nor did I question it. I was simply thankful for the break. I thought maybe she would just outgrow her problems. It was one thing after another with her. Simply there were too many traumas!

Miranda was driven to drink poison. She drank whiteout at the church, which caused great panic. She ate hair gel and shampoo. She drank an entire bottle of fever reducing medication. She drank bleach and many other strange things. I was constantly trying to keep her out of chemicals and keep her from drinking them. Honestly, I was afraid I would eventually be accused of child abuse, because it happened so often. Many times, I did not even report it, or I would call the poison hotline and handle it from the house. Believe me, I did everything humanly possible to keep her safe, but she was determined to ingest these items. It happened when she was in my care, and when she was with others. Family and friends also witnessed this odd behavior.

I am going to complete this chapter with a list of Miranda's symptoms from birth.

Miranda's Symptoms:

Constant Crying/Emotions out of Control
Strep Throat Multiple Times
Multiple Urinary Tract Infections
Drank Poisons/Ate hair gel and shampoo
Fell Often – Balance was off
Difficulty healing from scratches and scrapes
Headaches
Double/Blurred Vision
Even Went Blind on Occasion
Acne
Red Face
Weight Gain
Bruised Easily
Difficulty Sleeping
Backache
Right-side Pain
Fatigue
Urinary problems/ Loss of Urinary control
Central Obesity
Buffalo Hump
High Blood Pressure
Heart Arrhythmia
Heart Murmur
Chest Pain
Extreme Thirst
Nausea/Vomiting
Loss of leg control/ unable to walk
Ate salt/ she would pour it in her mouth

CHAPTER 6

THE CALL

In the fall of 1995, we went to the beach with our family as we did every year. While at the beach, God told me I would break the spirit of infirmity off my family – it was a generational curse. Generational curses are passed from parents to children. I did not think much of it, because I thought I could simply pray "it" away! When we were leaving the beach, I had my first vision from the Lord. It was odd. In the vision, I was standing on a large stage and giving my testimony. Then God spoke to me that I would testify and begin a ministry called, "The Word Works!"

I was a bit stunned. I did not want to be in the ministry. I wanted to teach elementary school. I wanted a career. I had plans for my life and being in the ministry was not one of them. I simply wrote down the vision and shelved it in my heart. Over the next twelve months, God was going to change my life forever. He was going to require me to get honest and truthful about my hidden sins.

After quitting my teaching job in obedience to God and staying home to be a mother, I began serving at the church more. I quickly became the nursery coordinator by the fall after Miranda's birth when she was about nine months old. The nursery was a hard and demanding job, but I loved a challenge. Not being paid was irritating, because honestly, I did more work as the nursery coordinator than I ever did as an elementary school teacher. Although the nursery position allowed me to stay at home most of the time, I still put in many hours a week working in the nursery organization. Before I became head of the nursery, one person had overseen it and did all the work by herself. I tried her way for one year and at the end of the year I chose to resign. I went to the pastors and told them I loved them very much, but I simply could not continue as the nursery coordinator any longer. I gave them a thirty-day notice, which I thought was a generous offer and plenty of time for them to find another person to take the volunteer job.

I truly had no idea of God's plan for my life. I had my own plans, and although I had obeyed God in quitting my teaching position, I still thought in my mind it would be a temporary situation at best. Although my heart had said I would never teach in the schools again, my mind insisted I would. At that season, I made choices based on *my will* not necessarily *God's will*. I was in the process of learning how to let God be in control of my destiny instead of me.

God was setting me up for my future, and I did not even know it, nor did I want to know.

A couple of weeks after meeting with the pastor, I was in praise and worship when God moved on my heart to go "back to the nursery." Honestly, I thought it was Satan tormenting me. I thought absolutely no way was I going back to the nursery. I had worked myself to death for nothing. People lied to me, accused me, yelled at me, basically treated me with no respect, and I was not even paid to do the job. I had a job of respect in the school system and truly did not like serving the Body of Christ.

Some of the worst people to deal with are Christians. I hate to say it, but it is true. Just because they are saved does not mean they have character. Character causes a person to do the right thing, because it is the right thing to do, and I found little to no character in most of the people working as volunteers in the nursery. For instance, a person would commit to serve and not even show up, not to mention call and let me know. So, I was stuck trying to fill positions to care for children in the nursery as the church service was beginning. I was shocked by the lack of character I found. Our nursery was large and required many volunteers. I was exhausted by the entire situation, and there was no way I was going back.

I always loved prayer and went faithfully to the prayer meetings. I remember a person praying for the new nursery coordinator, and I agreed with her in the prayer. I thought whoever takes the position needs prayer, and I am glad I am finished with that job!

I decided to leave town for a couple of days to visit my sister who lived about five hours away. God would not get off my back about the nursery. I studied diligently in the Word of God during the visit and was convicted in my heart about Jonah. God had asked Jonah to give a message to a community, and he refused. Jonah ended up in the belly of a whale until he agreed to obey God. I could see where God was going with this, but honestly, I did not want to take the nursery back. I wanted to run as far away from it as possible. God did promise me I would begin to be financially compensated for my work, but He was very clear to me, I could not ask for any money, only pray. God wanted me to see He could change things simply through prayer. He did not need me to physically go to the pastors to ask for pay. I simply had to pray.

When, I returned home, I notified the pastors of my church I would stay on as the coordinator. However, I was not too happy about the entire situation. We, as a church body, were in the middle of building another building because our congregation was large. So, we had to meet at a local hotel for three months. My children were ages three and one when this transition took place, and Kevin was working nights. I recall one Wednesday afternoon I was getting ready to go on to the hotel because I had to set up every nursery room with all the equipment prior to time for the church service, so I had to go early and, of course, take my children with me. Well, I had put Miranda, who was not yet two years old, in her room with a gate at the doorway. I had gated her because we had stairs, and her room was safe. As I came down the hallway to get her I could smell something horrible. When I entered her room, she had taken her diaper off and rubbed it all over her walls. She had done number two, if you know what I mean. I was pressed for time and simply left the mess to clean up when I arrived home.

The trials of running the nursery were constant, but proved to be good training ground for me. I had multiple opportunities to get upset, angry, and even ugly at times. God was faithful to show me how to fix the problems. He taught me how to use a team effort instead of a one-man show. The nursery was simply too big for one person to run it well, so I built a team which would help me. We had clerks, teachers, helpers, and I had my own special sidekick who would train me in seeing situations from others peoples' perspective. I was not good at observing other people, and God knew it. So, He put people in my life to help me grow and change.

After I recommitted to the nursery, the pastors called me into the office and offered to pay me just like God had said they would. The monetary pay was little, but the benefit I received from it was God's promise and delivery of His word without my asking people. Simply, I had prayed as God instructed, and the door opened just like God said it would. I learned a great deal from that lesson, and it would help me in the journey ahead.

I began serving as the nursery coordinator, in the fall of 1994. It was the fall of 1995 when God gave me the vision of testifying. The years 1995-1996 would prove to test my character and obedience to God at a much greater level. God revealed to me in a church meeting where my sister lived that He wanted me to testify about the abortion. I immediately clammed up and thought "absolutely not!" After all, only a couple of people knew. I was the nursery coordinator at my church. I was not willing to tell anyone about the abortion. All I could do was think about how people would judge me and accuse me. I was extremely fearful of what people would think, and at that moment I told God, "No."

God was going to teach me His thoughts about me were all that mattered, and He loved me regardless of my sins or flaws. He loved me exactly how He created me, and I was saved by grace. I knew in my heart, God was okay with me, but I also knew people were not like God.

Months passed and God would not let up on me. I literally shook with panic at the thought of telling people. To tell people, I would have to tell my parents and pastors. They did not know. As I had stated before, abortion is a secret sin and not one person wants to talk about. I had put it in my past. I had asked for forgiveness and had forgiven myself. I did not want to bring it up again and get it out there for the judgment of the world. God continued to press me. I called my sister. She said she believed it was God, and I simply needed to tell Mom and Dad. I was scared to death.

I waited until she came into town, so I would not be alone when I told them. When I had the abortion, I had never had a baby and now I had two. I did not realize the life I was sacrificing at the time. I did not realize I was killing my parents' and Kevin's parents' grandchild. The thought never entered my mind. I truly did not understand the effects of my decision and how far reaching they were. I thought it had only hurt me, and I saw no reason to expose it now. I knew it would cause pain, and I did not want to hurt anyone. I wanted to hide from it, but God refused to let it go.

Finally, I met with my parents to tell them. Ginger was with me. Kevin did not want to be present. I was so scared. I cannot even put into words the fear I faced with telling my parents. It was horrible. My parents came over to my house, and I just spit it out. My Dad was amazing, he simply said, "Donna, I love you no matter what you have or have not done."

The victory was sweet, but bitter. I had taken a precious gift from them, and they loved me enough to forgive me and not judge me. How blessed was I?

The next step was telling my pastors, which was just as scary. I had attended their church since I was sixteen. I was attending their church when I chose to have the abortion. At the point of telling them, I was on their paid staff as the nursery coordinator, of all things. In my natural mind, I would have thought God would have chosen a different person to head up the nursery; for instance, someone who had not killed a baby through abortion. Grace is much larger than our brains can wrap around.

I do not recall the date I met with them, but I do recall their response. I told them what I had done and my pastor came over to me. He bent down in front of me and said, "Donna that must have been so hard for you. I am so sorry you went through that. We love you and support you. We will pray for God to open the right door for your testimony."

You could have blown me over with a feather. I totally expected judgment and for them to beat me up with their words. Not to mention the fact, I figured they would want me off their ministerial staff and certainly not serving in their nursery. But, instead I received love and understanding. To say the least, I was shocked.

In July 1996, I received a call from a local woman's group and they asked me to testify. They did not know my testimony at all. I agreed, and the date was set for August 12, 1996. I knew it was God. The first testimony I had ever given was on August 12, 1989. God had spoken to me that I was called to testify and build "The Word Works!" ministry on August 12, 1995. Now, God had opened a door for me to testify on August 12, 1996, but this time it would be much harder. None of my closest friends knew about the abortion, and I refused to tell them.

> ➢ Note that it was exactly seven years from August 12, 1989 to August 12, 1996. The number seven is completion in the Word of God. The steps of the righteous are definitely ordered by God!

All my friends came to the meeting. They were all there the first time I testified about the abortion. I was scared to death. I wanted to run out of the building. My flesh was weak, but in my heart, I knew God wanted my testimony out there. So, I obeyed. When I stood up, I prayed and claimed Psalms 81:10 over my mouth. That scripture states when you open your mouth, God will fill it. I was graced by God to testify, and it was amazing what He did in that group of women. At the end of my testimony, I gave an altar call and over thirty women came forward for prayer. It was something I had feared so much, yet the truth was my testimony gave freedom to others! I learned a lot from the lesson of listening and trusting God. Even if circumstances speak against you and even if your own mind is against you – trust God. God is bigger and knows better.

I did not tell Kevin's parents about the abortion until the year 2004 when God told me to start "The Word Works!" ministry. It was heart wrenching. My reason for waiting was truly timing. I wanted to tell them in God's time, and I waited until God moved in my heart to let them know. They were also very supportive. Of course, they grieved the loss of their grandchild, but never attacked Kevin or me. They simply loved us and supported us. I was truly amazed. Love is a powerful tool if used in the right way. It can break a heart, but it can also heal one. Choose to use love to heal.

A sense of relief filled my heart as the truth was finally out there. I healed further in my journey and in the end, was thankful God had pushed me. I learned lessons, which would give me the strength for the journey ahead. I learned to trust God. I learned to trust my parents. I learned to trust my pastors. I learned to trust my friends, who also never judged me. I learned to trust the leading of God, regardless of the cost to my flesh or the fears in my mind. Ultimately, I learned more about my own inner strength, myself, and truly with God all things are possible!

Still, even with working on the church staff and testifying, in the back of my head, I thought I might still fulfill my original dreams. I kept what I like to call plan "B" in my mind for many years. God had required Kevin to give up his dream of becoming a police officer and was requiring me to give up my dream of teaching in public education. Dying to your dreams and living God's plan is no easy task. Literally, it took me years to truly die to my agenda and choose God's. But, God had time and apparently was not concerned with how long it would take or what it would take.

God had called me to stay at home and be a mother. That was my first calling. During the early years of my children's lives, I prayed diligently and studied in the Bible daily. I poured the Word of God into their little hearts and played praise and worship music all the time. The children either listened to praise or the Bible on tape every night as they slept. I had no idea of our future. I had no idea of the journey ahead. I simply did what God instructed me to do daily. This particular season of preparation would prove to be the power in our walk as we would face sickness and death.

Without the preparation, I truly do not know if I would have made it through the fire, but all I know is this: if you obey God one day at a time, He will lead you. He will show each one of us as individuals what we need. What is God for one person may not be God for another. He created each one of us uniquely, and we all have separate destinies. I just knew in my heart what God expected of me, and I obeyed Him by doing what He said.

THE ACCUSED

Mark 15:3 (NIV)
"The chief priests accused him of many things."

This information is added after the journey was complete. It was simply too difficult to write about all the accusations while we were in the process. So, as you read our story you already know the odds were greatly stacked against us, not just for lack of knowledge, but pride and ignorance were weapons of the enemy.

The thing you fear the most is usually what the enemy will use against you. Our seven-year journey to get to the root of Miranda's problem began in 1998. During this journey, we were accused of horrible things. One night Miranda had bleeding in her private area, years later we would realize the bleeding was due to her hormonal imbalance, and it terrified me. So, I immediately called her pediatrician, and we took her to the hospital. We were accused and questioned about sexually abusing our daughter. It was awful. And this was the first of many accusations, which would follow us during our journey to find the truth. I have chosen to list the accusations here to avoid stating personal names, but just know we, Kevin and I, or just me by myself were accused over and over. The enemy wanted me to quit and at times honestly, as you will read I wanted to quit, but my heart and love for my daughter would not allow me to give up.

During the journey, I was accused at one point of being one of those sick mothers who needed a sick child. I was accused of physical abuse, due to her bruising. I was accused of feeding Miranda poison to make her sick. Due to the diagnosis of Anorexia Nervosa in my past, I was accused of wanting a perfect sized child. I was accused the entire ordeal was in my head, and I was making it up. I was accused of being a mother who wanted a perfect daughter, and due to my perfectionism, I had created a sick child. I was accused of pushing Miranda too hard and making her sick by expecting too much of her. I was accused of lack of faith by the fellow believers in the church. I was accused of "micro-managing" my daughter to make her sick. Doctors, friends, family, and Christians accused Kevin and me!

The enemy used anyone he could find. The accusations always came at pivotal points in the journey. Points where I could either give up because of fear, or continue in faith. Each accusation hurt Kevin and me greatly, but I chose to take the position of proving each person wrong. I knew in my heart, I had never harmed my child in any way. I loved her and the only accusation that would have been the truth was: I was desperately trying to get her help!

I found ignorance, which is not stupidity, in every place I was accused. Stupidity is knowing what to do and not doing it. Ignorance does not know what the problem is or how to fix it. Every person who accused us was ignorant and prideful. It was their flaw, not mine. But, I had plenty of time to figure that out and forgive each accuser along the journey. It would become part of my challenge.

As the journey would continue for years, my fear changed from accusations, to the sheer fact that maybe no one would ever find out the truth. My Dad taught me growing up, "Donna, all you have to fear is fear itself!" Due to the length of the trials we faced, many people abandoned us in our time of crisis. I am loyal to my bones, and when people we loved walked away I had to learn to let them go.

My Dad was right! My Dad had also taught me growing up where there is a will there is a way and to never quit. He never allowed me to quit at anything I began. He insisted I complete whatever I started. The training from my childhood would be a key to my determination as an adult. Trying to find answers which did not exist was going to prove my character and training. It was going to change me forever, but to be the best I could be – not destroy me. It ultimately was going to save my life, Miranda, Micah, and prolong Kevin's life. We were also told more than once to simply give up, because there was no hope! I refused that as well. I did not need the world's hope. I had faith in God's ability to be the impossible problem solving God! I had God on my side, and He was enough!

CHAPTER 7

LET THE JOURNEY BEGIN

In June 1998 at a regular prayer meeting at the church, the Holy Spirit moved in my heart to tell the people they were not released. We were to commit and pray every night for ten straight nights. As God was moving in my heart, my flesh wanted to rebel, but I knew in my heart God had extraordinary things to accomplish and obedience was imperative. So, I instructed the people praying with me what God had placed in my heart. We committed to pray from June 4, until June 13, 1998.

Prayer was awesome. I simply cannot put into words what we experienced. The heartbeat of the prayer was repentance, and the focus was Jesus Christ, crucified. We prayed for unity and for the church to be consumed with seeing people saved, spirit-filled, healed, and walking in victory. The last night of intercession was profound. Directed by the Holy Spirit, seven of us marched around the grounds of the church seven times in complete silence. At the end of the march we shouted in victory and declared the walls that separated us would fall. We prayed for unity in the Body of Christ.

One night during these intense prayer meetings, I shared with a fellow prayer warrior that in my heart, I knew something was wrong with my daughter. It was the first time I had ever told anyone. This person promised me they would pray until Miranda was well.

After such intense prayer, we as prayer warriors were not prepared for the attack each one of us would face. We had gained tremendous victory in prayer, but also had alerted the enemy to our individual lives. The enemy attacked each prayer warrior with the ultimate goal of divide and conquer. We all faced different attacks, but each attack was deadly. The person I had shared my concerns about Miranda came under life threatening attack. He had surgery for a broken neck within weeks of the prayer effort and over the following two years had multiple heart problems, which eventually led to a heart by-pass surgery.

As for us, our family, the company where my husband worked laid off all employees for the most of July and part of August. It was frustrating, but the real blow came about the second week of August 1998, when Kevin's father became blind for no reason at all. Kevin was devastated, and I personally began to wonder where God was. Many people prayed for my father-in-law, and he did receive partial sight back. However, he was declared legally blind and was unable to continue working. Kevin became angry. All I could do was pray.

I was personally gripped, in August 1998, by a pediatrician's words. This particular doctor was not going to let me ignore the fact something was wrong with my daughter. Basically, he was going to say whatever was necessary to get me to listen. At a recheck visit for Miranda, at the age of four, I was told if I did not do something for her, she would weigh 300 pounds by the time she was eighteen at her current weight gain. And, if she went to kindergarten other children would label her as "fat" which would be next to impossible to overcome. I was devastated by these words. I knew Miranda was overweight, but I had done everything humanly possible to help her. Until this point, I was unable to admit my daughter had a "metabolism" problem, but the reality was "growing" larger every day before my very eyes. I asked the doctor what to do, and he suggested we test her for possible problems. For the first time, I agreed and the medical tests began.

I recall the sick feeling I had in my gut. I remember the feeling of shock and buckle up for the long haul. I knew deep in my heart, I had just agreed to open a can of worms. Let me add here how very faithful God was to me. If I had known what the future held, I would not have been able to go forward. In God's grace and infinite wisdom, He protected me and only allowed me to have enough information to continue to go forward.

The first tests for Miranda in the doctor's office was for blood sugar abnormalities and thyroid problems, because those were the most common. All tests came back normal, so the doctor sent me to a dietician. I was mortified and angry. I did not want to go to a dietician. I was so tired of people thinking I over fed my daughter. I knew it had nothing to do with her food intake. I was angry, frustrated, embarrassed, and tired of the bony finger of accusation coming my way due to Miranda's size. The doctor's office made the appointment and notified me of the date. After some consideration, I canceled the appointment. I rationalized God surely did not expect me to go to a dietician. After all, I had been freed from watching every bite of food go into my mouth. I was not about to watch every bite of food go into my daughter's mouth. I buried my head back in the "sand" and assumed it was God's will.

About a week later, I was at home alone reading the Word of God at my kitchen table when the phone rang. I answered it and to my surprise it was the dietician. She was very kind and simply said if I would come and see her, she believed she could help me. Very reluctantly, I agreed. However, I told her I would not bring Miranda. She said that was fine.

On October 9, 1998, I went to the hospital to meet this dietician. I did not want to be there, but I decided I would get it behind me, and then I could say I had done everything possible to help Miranda. I brought with me a chart I had to keep before going to the dietician. I had to write down on paper everything Miranda ate for one week.

I was sitting in a waiting room, when a very nice woman called my name. I stood and walked over to her. She looked a little surprised, but greeted me warmly. She introduced herself and asked me to walk with her to a room where we could talk. I immediately felt safe with this woman. She was extremely kind and very interested in what I had to say about Miranda. I could tell she too knew there was more to Miranda's weight gain than food. After some conversation and her observation of Miranda's food intake for a week, she looked me in the eye and said she wanted to be honest with me.

The dietician proceeded to explain to me a mother who is not overweight would not produce such obesity in her children due to genetics. She observed my size and structure. I was 5'1" and wore a size 4, so I was considered small. As she spoke it was as if for the first time I had ears to hear Miranda may genuinely have a problem. The dietician told me she knew a man who could help us. She spoke very highly of him and said he was an excellent endocrinologist. I had never heard the term before, but she felt confident Dr. Endo #1 could help Miranda. She added endocrine disorders were extremely rare, but she believed Miranda may have one.

I left the visit in a bit of shock and dismay, but feeling the possibility of a problem might be true. I went home and told Kevin. He and I looked up endocrinology on the computer and read about different diseases associated with the endocrine system. One disease, in particular stuck out to me because it described Miranda to a tee. The disorder, Cushing Syndrome, stated the individual had easy bruising, weight gain, infections, skin healed poorly, and retarded growth. It was the easy bruising which caught my eye. Miranda had always bruised easily, and I had never understood why. But, when I saw retarded growth I dismissed the disorder. Because, I mistook retarded growth for mind retardation. Miranda was extremely gifted in her intellect, so I totally dismissed Cushing Syndrome as a possibility.

Miranda had struggled with strep throat since January 1998. In December 1998, I took her to an ear, nose, and throat specialist, because her tonsils were so large she had difficulty swallowing. I knew she needed them removed. The doctor took one look and set the date for surgery.

On December 26, 1998, Miranda had her tonsils removed. It was not fun. The doctor had made it clear to me the procedure would be painful, but I had my tonsils removed as a small child with little discomfort. So, I expected Miranda would not suffer. I was wrong. She came back from surgery in a lot of pain. Kevin had left the hospital to go get lunch, and I was alone with her. She was pitiful and it broke my heart. Miranda began vomiting blood, so the nurse gave her a shot which did settle her down. At one point, I took Miranda to the bathroom. She was hooked up to an I.V., and I carried it. I laid the IV on the floor to help her get undressed. She began to scream. I looked down and blood was going up the tube into the I.V. bag. I went and found the nurse. She was wonderful. She explained to us how the IV bag must be held up. When she lifted the bag, the blood went back into Miranda. I was learning things I never wanted to know.

Miranda was discharged, and we went home. For days, she would not eat. She often even spit out saliva, so she would not have to swallow. I weighed her with the hopes she would be losing weight and to my surprise Miranda gained. I was gripped with devastation. What was wrong with my baby? How can a person gain weight when they have not even eaten? Again, I just put my emotions and questions on a shelf, buried deep in my heart.

CHAPTER 8

STORM BREWING

My pastor had an awesome message concerning "breakthrough" on the first Sunday in January 1999. It was a message which would change my life forever. He often challenged the congregation to act on the message we would receive, and this challenge was to write down on paper anything that had ever disappointed you with God. He specifically mentioned desires of your heart. Immediately, I knew what would go on my list.

There were only two areas in my life where I felt God had failed me. Miranda was the most important one to me. I had never understood the prayer God had me pray while pregnant with her, and why she had been obese her entire life. I loved her, but I felt devastated by the prayer as well as the evidence in her life which was contrary. Also, I had sought God for years about being debt free. Kevin and I had obeyed God and stood on the debt free scriptures, but nothing seemed to change our situation. Being debt free was a desire I had, but in comparison to Miranda it did not even hold a candle. I wrote down these two items in the back of my Bible and prayed a simple prayer. I had no idea at that time what my future would hold.

The Holy Spirit moved in my heart to study the four gospels, which are Matthew, Mark, Luke and John in January 1999. Daily, I read through them. I would only read the words Jesus spoke. It was definitely a time of increasing my faith. Also, I began to confess I would apprehend what I was apprehended for – no matter what.

One night in February 1999, at the age of five Miranda became extremely upset and emotional. Over and over she would say, "Why am I like this? What is wrong with me?"

Emotional outbursts were normal for Miranda. She had screamed and cried from birth. But this one broke my heart. Kevin and I watched her emotional crisis with pain in our hearts. Miranda was different and it was not her fault, but we did not know how to help her. I held her for what seemed like hours and prayed over her. Eventually, she fell asleep, and I went downstairs. Kevin told me to do "whatever it takes" to get her help. I felt hopeless and without direction. All alone in our living room, I began to pray. The words of the dietician resounded in me concerning knowing a man who could help. I could not recall his name, so I called a man in our church who was a nurse. I explained our situation, and he said it sounded like an endocrinology problem. As soon as he said the word, I knew that was what the dietician had called the doctor who could help. Before we hung up the phone, he prayed with me. I asked him to please not say anything. I explained this situation was extremely painful for us, and we did not want others knowing.

As soon as I hung up, I went to the yellow pages of the phone book. I found the pediatric section and located his name: Dr. Endo #1. The next day I called his office, and the receptionist informed me we needed a referral to see him. I was irritated, but knew I had to go through their protocol. I called and made an appointment for Miranda to see her regular pediatrician. The appointment was set for the first part of March 1999. We waited. Little did I know that it would be the first of many opportunities to wait.

March came quickly and Kevin decided to go with me to the appointment. I had prayed daily about the entire situation and was prepared to ask the doctor for a referral. The doctor was wonderful. He checked Miranda from head to toe. I recall him sitting on a stool and flipping through her chart. He looked up at Kevin and me with compassion and said he felt we should go see an endocrinologist. I was stunned. I had not even had the opportunity to ask yet. He then proceeded to say his office would make us an appointment with Dr. Endo #1 – the exact doctor I was going to request. I had confidence God was ordering our steps, and this doctor was a key to Miranda's health.

Miranda continued to deal with multiple problems. She was beautiful, but because of her size and shape often other children said unkind things to her. It was devastating to her when children would ridicule her and call her "fat." Also, she dealt with severe fatigue, headaches, infections, loss of bladder control, emotional outbursts, frustration, bruises, sweating, and a variety of other things. Her symptoms varied daily, and kept our lives constantly disrupted.

The pediatrician's office made the appointment for May 3, 1999. I was annoyed. Why was it going to take so long to get in and see this man? I asked the office if we could get in any earlier, and they said no. Waiting was not something I enjoyed. I wanted answers. I wanted Miranda to get help. Why in the world should we have to wait?

As the days passed, I became discouraged. I prayed often, but still felt frustrated. I did not understand why Miranda should have to go through this, or why we even needed doctors. I wanted God to heal her without the medical profession. I knew He had the power and ability. As I prayed and sought God, He spoke to me, "Your faith has made her whole."

By the end of April 1999, I was ready to cancel the appointment. I began to rationalize if my faith made her whole, then she did not need the doctors to help her. I went before God in prayer. As I sought Him, it was clear to me He wanted us to see Dr. Endo #1. Also, I felt I needed to write down Miranda's symptoms and go to the doctor prepared.

At this point, very few people in my life knew of the trial we faced. The day of the appointment, Miranda and I went alone. My family and my two closest friends knew and were praying. As I sat in the waiting room of the office, I knew deep in my heart, I would be coming there for years. It was odd and not at all what I wanted to think, but a reassuring peace came with the knowledge. I had no idea what to expect. I knew absolutely nothing about the endocrine part of medicine. I was anxious about the entire situation.

They called us back to see the doctor. Miranda and I were led to a small room where they took her weight, height, and blood pressure. Then we were placed in a small treatment room to wait for the doctor. Shortly, a very nice young man came into the room. He introduced himself and said Dr. Endo #1 would be in later. He checked Miranda and began asking me a lot of questions.

God had instructed me to go prepared, and I regretted I had not. I had to answer everything off the top of my head while under pressure and stress. The doctor took an extensive family history and began to go through a list of questions concerning Miranda. He was extremely interested in the fact she fell down a lot and had headaches. I was surprised. I did not know how her other symptoms could relate to obesity. The young doctor left the room and said he would return with Dr. Endo #1.

Within minutes, Dr. Endo #1 entered the room and shook my hand. He seemed very kind and compassionate. Both men began looking at Miranda. Dr. Endo #1 commented on the pigment in her hands, which I thought was odd. He then began to talk back and forth with the other doctor. I just sat and listened while they discussed the probability of a tumor on Miranda's pituitary gland. Dr. Endo #1 began to address me. He told me endocrine disorders were extremely rare. He said he would check her out for every possible problem, but there was only a chance of about 1/100 that they would find anything. Also, he was extremely clear that 99% of the time obesity is caused by overeating. I ignored the comment about her weight, because I was numb to the accusations as well as comments. I had already learned to ignore them. I knew the world blamed me for Miranda's situation, so I had accepted it as part of life. He listed probable disorders and diseases, one of which was Cushing's Disease. I began to feel dizzy.

The words were starting to go over my head. I wanted to run out of the room, but instead I sat there trying to receive the information I was being given.

Dr. Endo #1 began ordering tests. He ordered lab work, a 24-hour urine, and an MRI of her brain. By this point, I was in shock. These men had just discussed the possibility of my child having a tumor as if it was a hot dog. It was all I could do to stay focused enough to follow directions. The lab came in and drew blood, which greatly upset Miranda. I was handed an orange jug and a "hat" to place on a toilet to catch Miranda's urine. I was handed a piece of paper with specific instructions on how to "catch" her urine for 24 hours. And as we were leaving, Vicki, the doctor's nurse, handed me another paper with a date for Miranda's MRI and explained to me where to go to the hospital to pre-register her for the procedure. Because Miranda was only 5 years old, she would have to be put to sleep during the MRI; therefore, she would have to go through pre-admittance.

As Miranda and I walked out of that office, I had the overwhelming feeling this was much bigger than I had imagined. I was unnerved to say the least. When I arrived home, I called my closest friend. I told her everything the doctor had said. I was upset. Very calmly, she reassured me God would take care of it. Specifically, I was greatly upset at the thought of a tumor. She simply stated it was not the end of the world, and if it was a tumor, they could just remove it and Miranda would be fine. My sister, also shared the same attitude. She encouraged me to stay focused on Jesus, and do whatever the doctors said.

I cried out to God. I wanted answers. My prayers were continual. My pain was great.

I decided I would take Miranda's urine over the weekend. She was in pre-school, and I thought it would be easier if we did the test on a day when she was at home. Every time I would try to test her it did not work out. As I mentioned earlier, Miranda did not have bladder control. She often wet herself several times throughout the day. Her lack of bladder control had been evident for about 6 months and grew worse daily. We had to collect ALL the urine without an "accident." Finally, I started the test on Monday, May 17, 1999. I had to take the jug to her pre-school and have her teacher help. It worked out fine. I turned in the test and did not give it another thought. My thoughts were consumed with the idea that she could have a tumor. I did not think I could handle this medical crisis at all.

After I turned in the urine, I made an appointment with the hospital to come and pre-admit Miranda for her MRI. I really struggled with the entire idea. The thought of putting her to sleep did not bother me, because she had done well with anesthesia during her tonsillectomy. It was the thought of a tumor. I could not even go there in my mind. I tried to rationalize why I should cancel the appointment and not go through with this. I prayed. I cried. I talked to my friend. She encouraged me to go through with it, constantly reminding me God was in control. The day I had to go to the hospital for the pre-admittance, I stopped for gas on the way to Miranda's preschool. When I went in to pay for the gas, Dr. Endo #1 was there. I did not recognize him at first, but then it dawned on me who he was. I said "Hi," and he replied. Although it does not seem like a big deal, I know the steps of the righteous are ordered by the Lord. Seeing the doctor was a confirmation for me to go through with the MRI.

I dropped Miranda off at preschool, and I went to the hospital to pre-register her for the MRI. I signed my name and sat down. A few minutes later a man in a wheelchair was placed behind me. He had a trachea in his throat to help him breathe, which totally unnerved me. My grandfather had died from throat cancer and had a trachea the last few months of his life. The noise an individual makes breathing through their neck is difficult to hear. It brought back horrible memories and made me want to run out of the hospital. I sat there and quietly prayed for God to get me through. Finally, Miranda's name was called, and I could go back.

I was placed in another waiting room with about three people. One woman kept talking to me. She shared her entire medical history with me. I simply sat and listened. After she was finished, I offered to pray with her, and she was delighted. Then, she began to question me about why I was there. I hesitated, but she persisted. I revealed to her there might be a possibility of a tumor located on my daughter's pituitary gland. So, I was there to sign her up for a MRI. She was a very loving person and promised she would pray for Miranda as well as me.

A nurse came and called Miranda's name. I followed her to another room where I filled out papers and signed consent. She explained the procedure to me and asked if I had any questions. I had none. Then, she asked me if I would mind telling her why my 5-year-old daughter needed an MRI. The emotions of the day were too great for me at this point, and I began to cry. I told her Miranda was severely overweight and there might be a tumor on her pituitary gland. She teared up and asked if she could pray with me. I was amazed. She also promised to keep us in her prayers.

When I went to my van, I fell completely apart. I recall hitting my steering wheel with my fists and crying out to God. Where are you God?

Why does my daughter have to go through this? Is this really necessary?

Then, I began to feel like it was not even real, or maybe I had done something to make the doctors think Miranda had a tumor. I wanted out of this situation, but did not know how to get out. I cried until I could not cry anymore. I spent time trying to pull myself together before picking Miranda up from preschool.

Miranda's MRI was set for June 10, 1999, which was a Thursday. On Tuesday, at the prayer meeting, the power of God was evident. My prayer for Miranda was simple. I simply asked God for answers. My constant friend and prayer warrior, turned to me and said she had a word from God for me. She laid her hands on me and said, "Fear not. Fear not. Fear not."

The weekly staff meeting followed the Tuesday morning prayer. I walked over to the Education Building to attend the meeting, and thought about what God had just said to me. It seemed simple enough, yet sobering to me. At the end of the staff meeting, I asked them to pray for me. I explained a little about Miranda, which was the first time I had told them. The staff gathered around me and prayed. The presence of God was strong. I was peaceful, but I strongly sensed a storm brewing.

CHAPTER 9

YOU WILL WALK AND NOT FAINT

Wednesday night, June 9, 1999, I was at church during praise and worship when the voice of God spoke to me: "You are about to set sail on an exciting adventure. My hand is heavy upon your daughter. I love her more than you do. I heard your prayer and Miranda will not be overweight. You are going to the other side. Miranda will live to be very old. I will carry you for the next six weeks. You will run and not be weary. You will walk and not faint."

I fell to my knees. My heart trembled at the thought of our future. I was not a person who liked adventure. I enjoyed safety. Roller coasters were not one of my favorite rides. I like flat ground without bumps. Also, my mind immediately went to the word tumor. Surely, God would not let my daughter have a tumor. This cannot be real. The doctors are just being extremely careful. Why did God say Miranda would live to be very old? I had never thought she would not. What was going to happen? The praise music continued, and my mind settled down. I wrote down what God had spoken, and decided I would hide it in my heart.

Bright and early Thursday morning we reported to the hospital for the MRI. Miranda had to be prepared as if she was going to have surgery, because of the anesthesia. She was dressed in a gown and placed on a gurney. We did not have a room. Instead, she was in an area where patients wait to be taken to surgery. There were eight separate stations for patients. Miranda was in the one closest to the door. The nurses and doctors were great. They entertained her the entire time we waited. The gloves became balloons which quickly took the shape of a chicken when the nurse drew eyes and a mouth on it. Kevin and I nervously watched as our daughter interacted with the medical team. Again, we had to answer questions and sign more forms. Miranda had a way of capturing their hearts. She looked so small on the hospital bed. As one nurse was taking more information, another nurse began to cry. The thought a child had a tumor is overwhelming even to strangers.

God carefully ordered every step. As we were waiting for Miranda to go to the MRI, Katie, our church pianist, walked by the room. She saw us and stopped. We explained to her about Miranda's situation, and she told me she would be Miranda's recovery nurse. I had great peace. I was amazed at how God had perfectly met our needs. As they rolled my baby away, Katie put her arms around me and began walking me to the parent waiting area. She reassured me God would take care of her. I literally trembled when we had to walk away from Miranda.

Kevin and I passed the MRI station on our way to the waiting room. As unbelievable as it may seem, we saw another woman from our church who was also a nurse. She had been assigned to Miranda's MRI. She would be there while Miranda was being tested. Great peace was my comfort. We had no idea what to expect. As we waited, God spoke to me, "They will find it."

I was irritated. Didn't God know I did not want them to find anything? Didn't God know I wanted them to come back and tell me she was normal?

God's voice grew louder, "They will find it."

Over and over He said this to me as I waited. I tried to ignore Him, but I could not. When God speaks to me, it overrides my own thoughts. I could not get away from the fact He wanted me to know . . . "they will find it."

Time passes slowly as you wait for your child to be tested. Katie called us on a phone in the room where we waited to let us know she was out of the MRI. We waited for the call to come back and see her. To my surprise, Dr. Endo #1 walked into the waiting room. He had been with her during the MRI. He introduced himself to Kevin and shook our hands. He went on to say the MRI was completely normal. I was shocked. I felt a burning sensation from the top of my head all the way to my toes – this is a strong feeling I get when something is not right. I had difficulty thinking. The doctor went on speaking, but I do not even know what he said. I did manage to ask him about the other tests, and he said they were all normal. He asked me if we had seen a dietitian. I reminded him the dietitian sent us to him. He told me to call him, so we could discuss her test results. He said he wanted time to "scratch his head and think."

I was in shock. Katie called us back to see Miranda. She was awake, but not alert. We were given instructions for her and discharged. I had no peace. As bad as I did not want them to find a tumor, I knew what God had said. Something was wrong . . . bad wrong, but I did not know what.

When we arrived home, I painted. I had begun painting Micah's room the night before. Work is often how I handle things which are out of my control. I work on a project, something I can change. I was painting murals on his walls. Kevin helped me, which was a good way to sort through the day. As I painted, I went over the day in my mind. God had appeared to order every step. He had told me, "They will find it." I questioned whether I heard His voice. I wondered if I might be losing my mind. My heart knew Miranda needed help, but even the doctor said he could not find anything. I rationalized I needed to put the entire thing behind me. Just let it go. After all, I had done everything humanly possible to help her and had found no help.

One of the most hurtful things was the way some people responded to me. By now our family and part of the church knew about our situation. I had tried so hard to keep it private, because it just hurt too bad for others to know. My pain was deep, and I wanted it left alone. When I shared with some close people in my life how the MRI found nothing, I received the response maybe now "I" could put this behind "me" and just accept Miranda the way God had created her. I felt like burning flames of arrows were piercing my heart. Surely, God did not make my child obese just to teach me to accept her. What about all her other symptoms that did not involve weight? Was I just expected to accept them as well? I loved Miranda more than my own life. Why was this always my problem and my hang up? I was devastated. I decided not to even call Dr. Endo #1 back. Why should I? He had already said the tests were normal, and he did not know what the problem was. I really was not up to being sent back to another dietitian.

The next few days proved to be painful. Even the Bible speaks of a heart without hope. Hopelessness is dark and bitter. I refused to answer the phone. I tried to keep busy and put my mind on other things.

Friday, June 18, 1999, I was working around the house and the Holy Spirit softly spoke to me, "Call him."

I ignored the nudging. I rationalized there was no point in it. Why should I? I will only get the same advice. I knew Miranda did not overeat, and I was tired of the insinuations.

Again, the voice of God spoke, "Call him."

Surprising even myself, I picked up the phone and called. The receptionist took my name, number, and a brief message. She said she would have Dr. Endo #1 return my call. I immediately thought it would be days, maybe even weeks before he called me. I set the phone down and walked off.

Within ten minutes the phone rang. I answered and it was the endocrinologist. He began to go over the test results. I walked upstairs to my bedroom. I found a piece of paper and a pen. Slowly he read several results, which were all normal. He commented on her good cholesterol. He said it was extremely low, but quickly stated more exercise would raise it. I did not respond. I knew Miranda was active unless she had a day of severe fatigue, and I

53

was tired of trying to justify myself and my daughter. I could hear the doctor flipping papers. There was silence for a minute, and I instinctively knew he had found something. He began to explain to me her cortisol level was extremely high at 175 which was an indicator Miranda had Cushing's Disease. From my heart, I responded, "Can you help her?"

Quickly and with much reassurance he responded, "Oh, yes! We can help her."

He went on to explain to me we would do one, maybe two more urine tests and then more tests would follow. We hung up.

I fell to the floor. I just sat there in a heap. Out loud, I said, "It's not my fault. It's not my hang-up. I did not cause her problems. She has a disease."

I cried, trembled, and tried to let it sink into my brain. After I calmed down, I called my friend. She was so supportive. She promised me she would be there for me. While I was on the phone with her, my sister called. When I answered, she said she had tried to get a hold of me all week. She went on to tell me that a prophet of God was in her house and had seen a picture of Miranda. When she saw the picture, she told Ginger to tell the mother of that child, "If must go all over the world, get her help. She has a pituitary problem."

I told Ginger Dr. Endo #1 had found it. Miranda has high cortisol. I told her apparently high cortisol is an indicator of Cushing's Disease, and they can help her. I was amazed at how God had sent a prophet to confirm Miranda needed help.

I knew nothing about Cushing's Disease. Kevin and I had read less than a paragraph about it last October after I had seen the dietitian, but I remembered thinking it sounded like Miranda except for the fact she was not mentally retarded. I went on a hunt for knowledge. The Bible is clear about the fact people perish for a lack of knowledge. I wanted to know everything about Cushing's. I wanted answers. I was glad they had found the problem, and I was thankful it was not a tumor.

We hooked up the internet to our computer. Cushing's is extremely rare; therefore, I was not having any luck finding any information. The internet proved to be an incredible source. I simply typed in Cushing's and found lots of articles. I spent hours researching. As I studied, I quickly learned I had made a mistake last fall. Growth retardation is not mental retardation. Growth retardation means the child slows down on their height. Also, I found a 24-hour urinary free cortisol test was extremely diagnostic of Cushing's. There is no other reason for high cortisol. Basically, if your cortisol is abnormal, you have this disorder.

I learned there were two basic types of Cushing's. A person could have Cushing's Syndrome, which is caused by tumors in the adrenal glands. Or Cushing's Disease, which is caused by a tumor in the pituitary gland. Again, I was faced with tumors. However, in reading and studying, I realized the tumors could be removed, and the person becomes completely normal. I saw hope. As horrible as a tumor might seem, the thought of Miranda being well was worth it. The more I studied it became clear the difficult part of Cushing's was diagnosing the cause of the high cortisol. There were several tests the individual would have to go through to find the tumor. Also, 50% of the time a pituitary tumor cannot be seen on an MRI. Therefore, Miranda may very well have a tumor on her pituitary gland even though the doctors did not see it on the MRI.

My hunt for knowledge kept me busy. It took hours to find information and understand it. I had never been interested in the medical field, but this brought a hunger for truth that could not be quenched. I wanted to know every facet of this disease. I also found – if this disease went untreated, it led to death.

Sunday morning after the church service, I sat down beside a fellow staff member and told her what the doctor had said about Miranda. She asked me if there was treatment for Cushing's Disease. I explained to her Miranda could be completely healed if they could find the cause of her abnormal cortisol level. I told her from what I had studied, it appeared to be caused by a tumor. She began to pray for me. I knew God was there. At the end of the prayer, she looked at me and said, "Donna, it is strong in my spirit the ax head will float."

I knew of the passage in the Word of God located in II Kings 6: 5-6. It was an impossible situation. An ax head had fallen in the water and had to be found. Elisha, a prophet of God, threw a stick into the water, and the ax head rose to the surface and floated. God made the impossible, possible. I received the encouragement and felt confident God was going to reveal the root of Miranda's problem.

At the very next prayer meeting, I was seeking God on behalf of the church when He spoke to me, "Yea, though you walk through the valley of the shadow of death, fear no evil."

I was blown away. I was not going to walk through any valley. Why had God spoken Psalms 23 to me? My family had covenant with Him. We were safe from valleys, or so I thought. I had trained my children in the promises and victories the Bible had to offer. I was not about to receive the possibility of a valley. I chose to dismiss the word. Once again, I was the queen of denial.

The endocrine doctor ordered another 24 hour UFC test for Miranda. I went by his office and picked up the orange container to start the test. It was frustrating. Miranda was wetting herself an average of five times a day. It took several days of trying before I was successful in catching all her urine for 24 hours. I turned in the test on Monday, June 21, 1999. The results would not be back until Thursday. Waiting was hard. I felt as if her entire life depended on these results. Knowing Cushing's Disease untreated led to death put tremendous pressure on me.

I decided to paint my porch, because it helped me to work on something I could do something about. A friend came over and helped me paint. We began painting early Thursday morning. I called the doctor's office when it opened, and expected they would call right back. I did not receive an immediate call, so I started painting again. I constantly watched the clock and jumped every time the phone rang. The morning passed slowly. I wanted the results. I began to worry. Why weren't they calling? What was taking so long? I began to wonder if these results were normal and then dismissed the thought. How could they be normal? After all, they had found the problem. It was time to move on and get her help.

Finally, the nurse called me around 2:00 p.m. She said the results were within the normal range, and the endocrinologist wanted me to do as we had previously discussed. I was shocked. I quickly began questioning her about the results. How could they be normal? What does that mean? She was very kind and told me she would have the doctor call me.

Within minutes Dr. Endo #1 called and explained to me that Cushing's can cycle. I inquired further, so he explained that it can come and go. In other words, the hormone can surge for days, weeks, or months, and then disappear for a period of time. He went on to tell me to take her urine again in four weeks. I explained to the doctor the difficulty I experienced taking her urine due to her lack of bladder control, and he suggested Miranda may have a urinary tract infection. So, he ordered a test to check.

I was devastated. Last week they had found something, and this week it is gone. I cannot even put into words the emotions I felt. Not one part of me wanted Miranda to have a problem. But, I knew in my heart she needed help. I thought they were going to help her, but now I had to wait four more weeks and take her urine again. Little did I know in the summer of 1999, I would wait for years.

That night I did not sleep at all. I went to the computer to find any information on cycling Cushing's. I was not successful. As I researched, I sensed God drawing me into His presence. After a while, I prayed. While seeking God, I was reminded Miranda's weight gain was not consistent. That was one reason it was easy for me to think maybe she would outgrow her "problem," or maybe it was going away. I went to our photo albums and was amazed. It was obvious in pictures Miranda's weight gain was not constant. Also, I noted in the pictures how her tummy and upper back held most of her weight gain. Miranda was beautiful. Her little fingers reminded me of a toddler that never lost their baby fat. As I looked through the pictures, I became more peaceful and felt in my heart Dr. Endo #1 was right. Miranda very well may have cyclic Cushing's.

Miranda's test for a urinary tract infection came back positive. So, she was started on antibiotics. I was hopeful she would regain her bladder control. After the first round of antibiotics, Miranda was retested. Again, it was positive. Miranda went on a different type of antibiotics. The medicine did not seem to help her bladder control at all. Miranda's loss of control was getting worse by the day, and her urine had a horrible odor to it. The smell was like a cheap perfume. Nothing seemed to help her.

The time came to test Miranda again for cortisol. I tried to take her urine, but her problem was much worse. It was frustrating for both Miranda and me. She tried so hard, but still wet herself. The lab was insistent we had to have all the urine. To catch her urine, Miranda and I had to stay right beside the bathroom all day. I set the timer for ten minutes, and she would go every time. Finally, we were successful, so I turned in the collection. Again, I waited. I hoped this time it would reveal something, so we could get her help.

The endocrinologist called with the results. I was not doing well when he called. From the stress of waiting, I had developed a migraine headache accompanied with vomiting. I had been in the bed all day and felt hopeless. He was pleasant as always and reported to me her results were normal. He began flipping through her previous test results and talking at the same time. I was listening, but not really believing what I was hearing. He went on to say maybe the first test was a lab error. He made an appointment for Miranda to come back to see him in August 1999.

The darkness I felt was without words. I was beyond being devastated. I could not believe now it was a lab error. What kind of cruel joke was this? After studying Cushing's, I knew Miranda had it. She had almost every symptom, and her body shape was exactly how the articles described people with the syndrome. How in the world could this be a lab error? I was angry, hurt, and terribly disappointed yet again. I recall sitting on my couch and crying for hours. My anger towards God was unmerited, but still very real. How could He say to me "they will find it" and not keep His promise?

Within hours of Dr. Endo #1 call, I received a call from the teacher Miranda was going to have for kindergarten. She was excited about the new school year and having Miranda in her class. As we were on the phone, she mentioned to me the county had openings for teachers. I hung up and decided to get a teaching job. From my heart, I had served God without exception. I had been a bond-servant of Jesus Christ. I could not believe God was failing me with my daughter. I was not willing to be a hypocrite. I live what I believe.

If God was real, then His word was the truth and my daughter should be whole. I had suffered heartbreak over Miranda since her birth. I had prayed and walked by faith for what appeared to be no avail. I was not willing to continue to serve a God that did not heal my daughter.

The very next morning I went to the central office and spoke with the superintendent. He offered me a job on the spot at a local school in the county. I accepted the offer, but I was miserable. I knew in my heart, God did not want me to go back to the classroom. I loved working at the church and the people I served. Boy, I had changed. But, I was just so hurt. I wanted out of this nightmare. I felt as if God failed me, and my life dedicated to Jesus Christ profited nothing. If God would not heal my child, how could I declare He was faithful? Kevin and I were tired of the financial strain, so once again I rationalized God right out of the situation. I could not see a way in the natural for our finances to increase without me going back to the classroom.

I had walked so closely with God. I spent my days in prayer and praise. I served Him from my heart, not wanting anything in return. I simply wanted to be an obedient vessel. Suddenly, I found myself in a situation where I wanted Him to move and He did not, as far as I could tell. There were other situations in our finances, family, and at the church where I had been frustrated by His timing. However, He was always faithful. This particular time was different for me. This was my baby. I wanted her whole, and I wanted her whole right now! My very life and breath depended on Him. He was my source. When I took the teaching job, my Source was cut off. I could not find Him. Devastation was not the only emotion I felt. For the first time since I had given myself to Jesus, I felt truly alone.

I could not stand being without Him. If you have ever walked closely with Him, you know what I mean. As much as my heart broke for Miranda, I could not stand the separation from my Savior. Within 48 hours, I broke. I went before God and repented for my disobedience. I submitted to Him. I promised Him I would serve Him all the days of my life and honor His word – no matter what. I even released Miranda with my words. I declared whether she lived or died, well or sick, I would serve Him.

I notified the superintendent, I would not be taking the position, and I let my pastors know I could continue working at the church.

Peace was restored to me even though I did not know my future. I rested in the fact God had me.

CHAPTER 10

YOU ARE NOT ALONE

I was reminded of the word God had spoken to me in June 1999. He had told me I would run and not be weary and walk and not faint. I knew these words from a scripture, so I looked it up to see if I could get any more direction.

Isaiah 40:31

"But they that wait upon the Lord shall renew their strength. They shall mount up with wings as eagles. They will run and not be weary. They will walk and not faint." (KJV)

I was not exactly excited over the discovery waiting was the prerequisite for the promise. Patience is a difficult skill. People may think they have it, but testing proves the quality.

Also, I thought back to our annual family beach trip. In June 1999, I went to the beach with my children, parents, sister, and her children. We had a wonderful time. It was actually the week before Miranda's MRI. During the week, I had sought God concerning Miranda. He had ministered to me about breaking the spirit of infirmity, which is a curse of sickness and death brought on by sin entering the world, over my family. God showed me how it had been a generational curse and it was time to have victory over it. The thought of breaking a curse excited me. However, I was beginning to see it would not be easy. God had spoken the same thing to me in the summer 1995 – I was called to break a generational curse of sickness and disease.

On a Wednesday night in July 1999, God spoke to me again. He said, "The process you are in will seal you to Me. You will know My voice beyond any doubt. Miranda will be safe. My hand is on her. It is not about her - the process was predestined to train and equip you for the call. Every step is ordered. You are not alone. I am with you. She will be completely healed! Fear not!"

Again, I was not excited about this word of the Lord. I wanted Miranda to be whole without any process. I wanted victory, but not through pain. I really had to work through my emotions. God had allowed this process. Why? Did He want to destroy me? How could He possibly think this process would be beneficial? I knew God was the Healer, and Satan was the destroyer. I knew Satan caused the disease, but God was choosing the way to make her whole. I wanted God to choose the easy way. I wanted to lay hands on her and have the entire "thing" disappear. People received miracles all the time in the Bible. However, God would not direct me to those passages for Miranda. I struggled with Him. In my heart, I knew we were going to the other side, but my flesh screamed for escape from the journey. In Mark 4: 35-40, Jesus declared to the disciples, they were going to the other side. As they went a furious, demonic, storm came up, and the disciples were afraid. Jesus was so confident he was asleep during the storm. The disciples woke Him up, and Jesus spoke to the storm, which calmed down completely. Jesus then turned and rebuked the disciples for their fear. The disciples had greater respect for Jesus after the journey. They knew Him better and trusted His authority at deeper levels. I felt confident Jesus wanted to instill the same in me, but I really did not want to surrender to the journey.

Let me say, it may seem as if God spoke to me often, but He did not. I had many days, weeks, and even months without hearing anything. I am sure as you read it seems close, but the words came weeks, even months, apart and without any light in between. The journey was dark and time passed slowly.

Miranda was not well. August 1999, had come, but she still had a urinary tract infection. Also, she had started having a horrible pain in her right side. The pain was not consistent, but very intense. She would grab her side and scream, "Mommy, Mommy, help me!"

This was a difficult time, to say the least. I had no power to help her or make the pain go away. I became very concerned. She was grabbing her side where her kidneys are located – always in the same place. I knew she was not making it up. It was obvious she was in pain. I questioned the doctors, but no one had any answers.

On a Wednesday night during praise, just before our appointment with Dr. Endo #1, God spoke to me, "Your daughter has Cushing's. You will have to fight for her."

I fell to my knees in disbelief. We had taken two more tests after the first one came back abnormal, both of which were normal. Did God not know her recent tests were normal, and Dr. Endo #1 felt the first one to be a lab error? What was I supposed to do? Who was I fighting against? I prayed. I did not know what else to do.

Miranda and I went to see Dr. Endo #1 on August 20, 1999, which was not a pleasant experience. I had the knowledge of what God had said to me, yet I was faced with the natural realm and test results.

Miranda was called back to the little room where they weighed her, took her blood pressure, and measured her height. Then, we were sent to an examination room to wait for the doctor. A young man, who was a doctor in training, came in before the endocrinologist. I did not recognize him. He checked Miranda and asked her how her summer was. He then went on to say everything was completely fine. He commented on the fact, Miranda had not gained weight over the summer and swimming/exercise was helping her overcome her obesity. He wanted to test her again for a urinary tract infection, which came back positive, and again this man commented on the fact she probably had scar tissue on her kidneys. By now, I am angry. Where was Dr. Endo #1? Who is this guy, and what does he know?

Finally, he went out and returned with Dr. Endo #1. They entered the room and discussed Miranda. I sat quietly, but I am sure it was obvious I was angry. I do not hide my feelings well. Dr. Endo #1 told me he was sending Miranda back to her regular pediatrician for the urinary tract infections. He felt she needed to be referred to a specialist in the urological field. Then, he told me he felt Miranda was fine. I questioned him about the first test result, and again he said he felt it was probably a lab error. He believed if Miranda had cyclic Cushing's we would have another high test by now. I was persistent, so he ordered two more 24 hour UFC's to be done six weeks apart, but made it clear to me that he thought she did not have the disease. A return appointment was set for December. Dr. Endo #1 told me he would release her at that time, if nothing else showed up.

I left the office furious. Where was God? Did he not know the doctors believed my daughter was fine? My mind was spinning. The first guy who came in the room had infuriated me with his comments about her "obesity." He had no idea what my child had endured. Who did he think he was to walk in the room and judge her? Also, how could he tell me she had kidney damage? What did he know? Why did Dr. Endo #1 let him even come in our room? It took me awhile to calm down. I wanted answers, and no one gave them to me.

I handled the visit as I always did. I prayed and worked on a project in our house. A friend helped me lay hardwood floors in Micah's and Miranda's rooms. Kevin was involved in the renovation. I somehow felt better when I could put my hand to something and change it for the better.

An appointment was set for Miranda to go see her regular pediatrician, who was a very kind man. On the way to the appointment, Miranda began to question me about being closer to God. I answered her questions, but wanted her to drop it. She was persistent and told me she wanted the Holy Spirit to lead her. I told her I was driving and this was not a good time. Miranda persisted.

She wanted it right then and would not take "no" for an answer. So, in the parking lot of the pediatrician's office, Miranda and I prayed together. She received the Holy Spirit. I was amazed. God was obviously not too concerned about the appointment we faced.

Her pediatrician reviewed her recent record of urinary tract infections. He told me we would try a different antibiotic, but if this did not work he would send us to a urologist.

At the end of August 1999, my pastors told me they wanted me to come on board as a full-time employee. I would be considered full-time at the beginning of September, which worked out perfectly with both of my children in school. It was such a blessing and helped to relieve the financial strain Kevin and I had faced for years. I was excited about working, because I loved what I did at the church. It was amazing to me how I almost missed this opportunity by taking a teaching job, and how God gave me the desires of my heart when I surrendered my future to Him. I did let my pastor know I had absolutely no idea what would happen concerning Miranda. He told me not to be concerned. They were in it with me and supported me 100%.

Miranda began kindergarten. She loved it, and her teacher was awesome. Miranda's bladder control was gone, so she wore diapers, which we called "special panties." Also, her other symptoms caused her difficulty at school. Fatigue was hard for her to battle. A normal child can go day in and day out, but not Miranda. She would get too exhausted. One morning, I recall getting her up for school and she began crying, "Mommy, I can't. I can't even walk."

I did not know what to do, so I went into my bedroom and prayed for her. I knew immediately to keep her out of school. I called her papaw, and he kept her while I went to work. I had to carry her to the van and into their house. She did not have the strength to walk. I left her and cried all the way to the church. I felt such desperation, but no hope was given.

Her urinary infection persisted. Her pediatrician sent us to a urologist. His office worked us in quickly. He was a wonderful man. He looked at her record and ordered tests. I was beginning to get numb to this routine. The doctor ordered a renal ultrasound and a scope. I was relieved he ordered a renal ultrasound. I hoped they could figure out why Miranda had pain in her side. He explained to me the scope would need to be done in the hospital, due to her age. Miranda would be put to sleep, and he would examine her. The urologist added more medication to Miranda he hoped would help her bladder control as well as the infection. The dates for the procedures were set, and we left the office.

A couple of days later, I was at the church in a prayer meeting with a friend. This friend of mine was new to the church and had a heart for prayer. After we had prayed for some time, she told me she believed she had a word from God for me. I looked at her with tearful eyes, and she began to speak, "God has seen you in the night. He has seen your pain as you have cried out to Him on behalf of your daughter. You have been placed in a dark tunnel, but there is light at the end. He has heard your cry."

I was amazed. This new friend knew nothing about our situation. I cried while she hugged me. I knew God was watching. I knew He was in charge – I just didn't know how everything was going to happen.

Miranda and Micah were on a soccer team, which began the first part of September 1999. Micah was having a great time, but Miranda was frustrated. She had difficulty keeping up with the other children as well as falling often. During the first game, the coach pulled her out because her face became the color of deep maroon while she played. It was bothersome to realize she did not have the ability to physically function without health issues.

Miranda's teacher would often call me from school to come and pick her up. She had difficulty getting through the day. Miranda could be extremely emotional, which was hard to handle. She would have horrible headaches and pain in her side. It was hard for me to know what to do. I had just taken a full-time position, which I felt God had given me, and now Miranda's health placed constant demands on my time. I was hoping the up-coming tests would shed light and help her.

My sister called me the first part of October 1999, and asked me if I had taken Miranda's urine again. I told her not yet. It was too frustrating and Miranda's bladder control was worse. She encouraged me to take the urine. She said she felt God had laid it on her heart. I told her I would after the scope if nothing showed up. Also, Miranda's kindergarten teacher spoke with me. She felt whatever Miranda's problem was it was happening right now. She expressed concern. I listened, but felt helpless.

I had to pre-admit Miranda to the hospital for the scope. This time Miranda had to go with me. They weighed her and to my shock, she had gained five pounds. I was without words. Was this nightmare ever going to end? How in the world could she be gaining weight? The child was in school, and we were on the go constantly. I just put it on a shelf in my heart - another unanswered problem in her life.

It is amazing how fast a person can forget or displace what God says. God had told me Miranda had Cushing's, but because the endocrinologist did not believe she did, I was ready to dismiss the entire thing. Also, after studying the disease, I did not want her to have it. Cushing's was extremely difficult to diagnose, and not all cases ended well. I would rather not deal with it.

Miranda had her renal ultrasound on October 7, 1999. The technicians would not tell me anything during the procedure. I am sure they are not allowed, but I wanted to know right then. We had to wait for the results. I hoped the urologist would find her problem. However, he came back from the surgery he performed with absolutely no answers. He told Kevin and me that possibly her endocrine problem was the root. I was shocked. How could she have so many problems with no answers? I questioned him about the renal ultrasound, and he instructed me to call his office.

When Miranda was discharged, we went home with no answers yet again. I was quiet, but not on the inside. Where was God?

Why did He not reveal her problem? Where was I to turn? What was I to do? I remembered Ginger suggesting I take her urine. I decided I would. Miranda was already scheduled to miss school the next day, due to the procedure. So, I took her urine for 24 hours beginning on October 8 and ending on October 9, 1999. I really did not expect anything. I did it out of desperation more than faith. I turned the urine in on Monday, October 11, 1999.

I often spent time in prayer while at the church. I had gone over to the nursery at the church to pray, and God moved strongly on my heart. He led me to a passage in Matthew that became my main prayer for Miranda.

Matthew 10:26

"Fear them not therefore: for there is nothing covered, that shall not be revealed; and hid, that shall not be known." (KJV)

I contacted the urologist's office, and they told me the renal ultrasound was completely normal. I hung up and became angry. I could not believe no one could find any problems with this child. She needed help and the darkness grew. I cried until I was over the disappointment. Then I pulled myself together and went on with our life. What other choice did I have?

Tuesday morning, October 12, 1999, we had our regular prayer meeting. Cara was a powerful prayer warrior who came. She had been one of the crew who had prayed for ten straight nights back in June of 1998. I had not seen her for months and had missed her as well as the strength she brings to the prayer meetings. At the end of the prayer, she asked me if she could pray for me. I agreed and went over and sat in a chair beside her. She laid her hands on me and began to pray. Suddenly, she stopped. She questioned me, "Donna, what is wrong with your daughter?"

I responded, "She has multiple problems, and no diagnosis."

Cara began to pray again. After a short period of time, she prophesied to me, "God is sending you a Godly man, doctor, with a diagnosis. Tumor capsulized - will be removed. Donna, you are called to stand between Heaven and Hell on behalf of the church and pastors – do not be distracted or diluted."

She then went on to say she saw Kevin standing with Miranda in his heart. She knew he had much pain associated with this, and God was going to heal him and restore our daughter.

Cara then said to me to consider the power of offerings. She felt strongly that offerings; specifically, financial offerings brought breakthrough and was tied to the covenant. God made covenant promises in the Bible for all believers, which can be found in Deuteronomy 28.

Several of my friends were at the prayer meeting along with others who heard the word of God. My closest friend would prove to be a strength and remind me of the word throughout the journey ahead. God continued, pointing us on this path with medical help, but the natural realm proved to bring no answers. It was truly a faith walk through much darkness.

The urine results for Miranda were back by Friday, but I chose not to call and get them. I decided I would wait until Monday, October 18, 1999. I really did not want to know. Before I turned in the urine, I had prayed and asked God to please shed light. I wanted to end the hunt for Cushing's if it was going to be a dead-end road. All day Saturday, God ministered to me. I spent time in prayer and praise. I was lying on my bed reading the Bible when in my spirit, I heard, "Her steps are ordered – go look."

Right then Miranda needed me. She was stuck on the swing set and could not get down. I went outside and helped her. On my way back in the house, God repeated Himself. I knew He was trying to tell me something, so I asked Him "Look for what?" I was instantly reminded the dietitian was a key person in setting us on our current path. I went back to the previous year's calendar and realized I had seen her on October 9, 1999. Exactly one year to the date from the recent UFC test. I immediately knew this test would tell the truth. I knew it would be abnormal. I just knew it.

Later it would come to my attention Miranda was dedicated to God on October 9, 1994. The steps of the righteous are truly ordered by God!

During the night, I went through Miranda's clothes. She had gained several pounds recently, and her clothes were too small. Always in the past, I cleaned out her closet and gave the clothes away. This time I felt led by God to save the clothes by faith, believing one day she would return to those very sizes. I stored the clothes in Micah's closet. Although it may not seem like a big step, but for me it was profound, because I had nothing in the natural telling me things would ever change.

I tried to tell Kevin. He was not happy about what I had to say. He became very angry and upset. I called a friend. She and her husband came over to help Kevin calm down. Kevin was out in the woods, and her husband went to find him. My friend encouraged me and listened as I unloaded the frustrations of being alone in this walk. I wanted Kevin to face this with me, but he would not. Her husband returned with Kevin, and we all prayed in the living room. My friend told Kevin while in prayer she saw Kevin standing over a person in a hospital bed and "making a deal" with God so the individual would live. Time would prove that person was me.

I was not exactly thrilled to hear those words, but knew it had come from God. At the time, of course, we thought the vision was about Miranda. I sat in front of Kevin and told him I knew with my entire heart this test was coming back abnormal, and we needed to be ready. We would have to walk through this together, getting our strength from God. Kevin listened, but did not respond.

The next day, I put in the call for the result. Waiting to hear was not my favorite part. I waited for about four hours. Finally, I called the nurse, and she told me Dr. Endo #1 would have to give me the results. I knew something was up. When the results were normal, the nurse always told me. The day passed slowly, and no one called. After Kevin arrived home from work, I called again. The nurse told me the endocrinologist was going to "dictate me a letter." I was to continue as we had previously discussed. I was not satisfied with the response. I wanted to know the results. I pressed the nurse, and she told me they were abnormal. I wanted the exact number, so she read the results to me over the phone. Miranda's cortisol level was 286. Anything over 91 on the scale for an adult was not normal – much less a child. I was raging with emotions by this time. I questioned her about the endocrinologist. What was he waiting for? She said she would have him call me.

Five minutes later, the endocrinologist called me. He was very nice. I was extremely upset. He explained to me that Cushing's was a "spoofy" disease and very difficult to diagnose. I told him I wanted to get her help. He set up another appointment for us to come and see him on October 29, 1999. I hung up the phone and told Kevin. He was very calm and strong. I fell completely apart. My body trembled, and I cried. I called one of my pastors, and she prayed for me. She told me I was not alone in this walk. Even though God had clearly shown me what was coming, great pain traveled with the truth.

Shock was something I was beginning to experience on a regular basis. I had great difficulty sleeping and my stomach often hurt. I was claiming the scriptures from the Bible and spending time with God on a regular basis, but my flesh did not handle the constant roller coaster this path was dishing out. I began to seek God on how to handle the stress of the process. I was without direction, so I survived as best I could.

On Thursday night, October 23, 1999, we had our regular intercessory prayer meeting. Cara was there again. I had not seen her since she last prayed for me. At the beginning of the meeting, she stood up and came over to me. She brought oil with her. She anointed my feet with oil and prayed for me to have strength for the journey. I knew it was profound, but I had no idea what the journey would entail.

The last abnormal test caused me to get organized. I put a notebook together with all of Miranda's doctor records, symptoms, and pictures I had found in June 1999, when the endocrinologist first suggested cyclic Cushing's. While compiling the notebook, I went back to her baby book to get information about her first year. I was shocked to read that Miranda had been dedicated to the Lord on October 9, 1994. I was amazed at how God had truly ordered her steps.

October 9, 1994   Miranda was dedicated to God
October 9, 1998   I met with the dietician who sent us to the endocrinologist
October 9, 1999   I collected Miranda's 24-hour urine, which came back abnormal confirming Cushing's Disease

At that time, I pulled Miranda out of school. She was sick and having difficulty almost daily. After much prayer, I decided to home-school her. A friend immediately offered to keep her while I worked at the church. God met every need. I struggled with leaving her, but I knew this particular friend, loved her almost as much as I did.

Kevin shared our situation with some friends at his work place. Together, they collected money for us to help pay our medical bills. We were amazed. No one had ever helped us pay our medical bills before. They gave us about $900.00, which totally caught up our current medical bills. God was meeting every need we had in amazing ways.

I went to our appointment on October 29, 1999, ready to find help for her. The endocrinologist was wonderful. He talked straight with me and seemed pleased with the information I gave him. I asked him what the next step was, and he suggested the Dex test. I questioned him concerning the fact she does not always have high cortisol. How would that affect the test? He did not know. Then, he told me he had never treated anyone with Cushing's before – it was just so rare. He told me I could do the Dex test from home. I would have to take her urine for 3 days while giving her medication during specific time intervals. On the last day, we would come to the office, and they would draw her blood. I was not certain about the whole thing. I did not like the reliability of the test dependent on my ability to catch her urine.

I wanted the pressure off me. However, I agreed to try. The endocrinologist told me to wait to test her. He wanted to check with the lab to see if the medications she was on for urinary tract infections would affect the test. Also, it was noted medically Miranda's blood pressure was high.

I left the office with several orange jugs and many questions. I was not aware Dr. Endo # 1 had never treated Cushing's. He seemed wonderful, but I was bothered. If this disease was so difficult to diagnose, I wanted people who had dealt with it. I did not have any direction or even know who could help her. It was just a concern – not really something I thought I would do anything about. After all, I rationalized, God had sent us to this endocrinologist, and he was relatively local.

However, I did want to know if the Dex test would be a waste of time if Miranda was not in cycle. As soon as I went home, I posted a note on the Cushing's bulletin board on the internet. Somebody responded to me and told me to check with the NIH. They could give me the information I needed. I had never heard of the NIH before and was not sure what it was. I simply typed NIH and "go" into the internet. It took me to the National Institute of Health. Although I was not familiar with anything, I retrieved a phone number after some digging.

Dr. Endo #1 called me Sunday with a new prescription for Miranda. He had not been able to talk to the lab yet and would let me know something by Tuesday. I did not sleep at all Monday night. I was up praying and seeking God. I wanted to move on with Miranda, but I had no peace about the Dex test. I felt confident I was not capable of catching her urine for three straight days. It was hard enough just to do 24 hours. As I sought God, I felt I needed to be honest with the endocrinologist and not attempt the Dex test at home. Also, I felt very strong about contacting the NIH and getting an answer about the reliability of the Dex test if she were not in cycle. Somebody had to know the answer, and I wanted it before I put Miranda through the test.

Tuesday morning, I called Dr. Endo#1's office and left him a message to call me. Then, I called the NIH and left a message with Miranda's test results from her UFC, urinary free cortisol, and my concerns about the Dex test. God moved in my heart to stay at home, but I rationalized the NIH would probably not even call me back. Besides my stress level was much lower if I did not sit by the phone waiting for it to ring, so I left and went to the church to work.

We were getting ready for a staff meeting when I was told Dr. Endo #1 was on the phone for me. I went to my office and took the call. He told me Miranda could take the Dex test while on the antibiotics, but he still did not know if the Dex test would be reliable if her cortisol was low. I told him there was no way I could catch her urine for three straight days. He suggested we do the test in the hospital, and I agreed. He said he would put in the order, and Miranda would go into the hospital that night. That night, I could not believe this was happening. We hung up, and I was in shock.

Almost immediately, the nurse called me with insurance questions. I answered them, and she told me she would contact me as soon as the order for the test cleared. We hung up the phone.

I walked back into the staff meeting, but my mind was not in my body. My pastor asked me what the doctor had said. I told the staff what was about to happen. The entire staff prayed for me, but I continued to feel shock. I knew Miranda needed help, and I wanted to get her help. I just was having great difficulty accepting this route.

After the staff meeting, I sat at my desk and tried to think straight. I called a friend to let her know. She said she would help us out. She encouraged me, but I had no peace. Finally, I left to pick up Micah from school. On the way, I prayed. I was trying to find peace. Out of my mouth, I kept confessing, "Miranda's steps are ordered by God." I picked up Micah and went home. As soon as I walked through the door, I checked our answering machine to see if the nurse had called. It was blinking, so I pushed the button to retrieve the message.

The voice simply stated, "This is Dr. Endo #2. Please call me."
He left a phone number on the machine. I wrote it down. I listened to the

message over and over. I was in awe. Dr. Endo #2 was the man who had written most of the articles I had studied about Cushing's. I could not believe his voice was on my machine. For the very first time, I felt like there was light.

Our current situation still stood. It was too late to call Dr. Endo #2. I would have to wait until in the morning. I was immediately reminded how God had told me to stay home, and how I thought I knew better and left. Quickly, I repented and asked God to please help me. I did not know what to do. I wanted to get an answer to my question before we tested Miranda, and I did not have an answer. I asked God to do something – stop this somehow.

The nurse called me around 5:00 p.m. and told me the insurance had not given her the authorization number yet. She felt it would be best to wait until tomorrow night. I agreed and instantly knew God had answered my prayers.

I was excited about the thought of talking to Dr. Endo #2. I knew he could answer my questions. He was an expert on the topic of Cushing's. I was in awe of his voice on my answering machine. When I called the NIH, I had no idea he worked at the NIH. Even if I had known; I would have never dreamed he would call me. God was definitely moving on Miranda's behalf. I was going to get answers.

The next day I took Micah to school and all the way home, I kept saying, "Thank you for the cross."

I said it over and over. I was so grateful Jesus had made a way for her at Calvary. I was excited and did not even know why. A friend came over and sat with me on my bed while I called Dr. Endo #2. It was incredible! The man personally answered the phone. I was shocked. I asked him if he was the man who had written the articles I had read, and he said, "Yes." I told him I had called to find out if the Dex test would be reliable if Miranda was not in cycle. He did not answer. Instead, he asked me to tell him about Miranda. I did and he told me, "Your daughter has Cushing's. Fax me the stuff."

I said, "What stuff?"

He said her doctor will know. Just fax him her information. I questioned him about insurance, and he said, "That is not a problem – everything is free." I was amazed. We had never had any free medical treatment. Then he told me, "We bring her up here. We test her. We send her home for a few weeks. Then bring her back for the surgery."

I hung up and began shouting, "There is light! He wants my baby!"

My friend and I were both ecstatic. I was so excited it was difficult to think. Within 24 hours her entire destiny had taken a turn. In my opinion, we now had the very best doctor involved. I was truly amazed at how God had moved on her behalf. Finally, someone was going to help my baby.

We cancelled the Dex test. When I asked the nurse to get Dr. Endo #1 to send Dr. Endo #2 Miranda's information, she was wonderful and seemed happy for us.

Waiting began again. I had never dealt with anything like this. So, I thought I would receive a call within days from the NIH. I was wrong. Two weeks passed and I was frustrated by the lack of communication. I called Dr. Endo #2 back. He answered and told me it was "not a problem." He had seen her records and an associate of his would be calling me. He did tell me it looked like she had a pituitary problem, but they were not confident it was Cushing's. Tests would tell.

I went to the NIH web page to find out more information. I soon realized the NIH was located in Bethesda, Maryland. I knew God had picked this doctor. Bethesda in the word of God is the healing pool of water. An angel of the Lord stirs the water and people rush to go in to receive their healing. Even on the web page, the NIH talked about being a place of hope for the hopeless. I had confidence that God had ordered Miranda's steps.

Waiting was hard. On November 15, 1999, at a meeting at our church, God spoke to me, "She will live. Fear not! Her steps are ordered."

I believed what God was saying, but I wanted them to call me with a date. I wanted to know when we were going. I wanted to see results. I was tired of waiting. Days turned into weeks – December quickly came. I was almost daily disappointed. I wanted them to call me. What could possibly be taking so long? God kept nudging me to fast and pray for three days, but I would not. I did not want to fast. I wanted them to call.

On December 12, 1999, the voice of God came to me, "You are about to walk into the pit of Hell. Fear not. She will live. She will live. She will live. I have ordered every step. Prepare yourself. Go full of the faith, power, and the word. It is very dark, but My light will shine. Fear not! I have redeemed her. I love you, Donna. I am with you. It is a journey of faith. Go! Be blessed as you go. Go! You have my release. You will know me as Healer! I have you, Donna. You are not alone. I am with you. No matter how dark. She will live."

Also, God gave me a dear friend to travel with me through this horrific journey. God told me, "She was a solid oak."

I wrote the word down, but still was extremely annoyed the NIH had not called me. Quickly the miracle of Dr. Endo #2 calling me was fading, and the waiting was producing discouragement. I sought God with my whole heart to please have them contact me by Christmas. After all, I had declared that 1999 would be a year of breakthrough for Miranda back in January when a pastor preached on it. I felt God should move for me. God was not moved by my prayers. He continued to nudge me to fast and pray.

Christmas came and I was devastated by not hearing yet. Finally, I surrendered to the fast God had been moving on my heart to do. I knew it would be impossible to hear from the NIH in 1999. The only week left was between Christmas and New Year's Day. I figured they did not even work during that week. I began the fast on December 27, 1999.

God spoke to me, "She will live. She will go to Bethesda. You will go. They will find it. They will remove it. It will end. You are on the "heels" of it – one more step and you will go."

The fast ended on December 29, 1999. A friend came over the next morning, because we were going to help my Mom take down wallpaper. We were standing in my kitchen talking around 9:00 a.m. when my phone rang. I answered it, and the woman on the other side identified herself as an "associate" of Dr. Endo #2. I was amazed. She told me she needed to set up the dates for Miranda to come. She asked me several questions and told me she would get back with me. I asked her if it would be soon or would I be waiting for weeks. She said I would know within the day, because the NIH would be closed the next day for New Year's Eve.

The morning moved quickly, because I had several phone calls. The date for Miranda's admission was set for January 30, 2000. She would be in the hospital for about 10 days or so. No one could be exactly sure, because it depended on the results they would retrieve while we were there. Within hours, it was set. We were going to Bethesda. We were going to get answers.

Once again, I was in awe of God's faithfulness. As soon as I obeyed Him with the fast, He opened the door. The timing was amazing. It was the very last working day of 1999. This was a tremendous breakthrough. I knew it was by the hand of God!

CHAPTER 11

SHOCK AND DISBELIEF

January proved to be a long month. I was glad to finally have the dates from the NIH, but we still had to wait. Waiting was hard. We had now been actively trying to find answers for eighteen months. I wanted to get to the bottom of the entire thing and end it.

We had an incredible church service the first week of January 2000. There was an altar call, and almost the entire church went forward for prayer. I was working at the altar by passing out tissue or information packets. It was a blessing to see so many people receiving from God. After my pastor had prayed for the others, she turned to me and placed her hands on my head. She was silent, and then began to prophesy. She said, "Satan has asked to sift you as wheat, but I pray that your faith will fail you not."

My pastor went on to pray for me fervently. I received the word and the prayer. I knew I was in a difficult season. I just did not know how difficult.

During the next Sunday morning service, God moved in my heart. It was odd. He told me to "go to Disney World" with my dear friend. He told me "to have fun and make memories." I was not a person who would just "go to Disney World" on a whim. I was a little taken aback by God instructing me to go have fun. After the service, I told my friend what God had said and immediately she said, "Let's go."

My precious friend said we could camp, and it would not be expensive at all. I had never camped and the thought of it was not too appealing. I liked safety. I was not too sure camping would be much "fun" either, but she encouraged me to give it a try. So, we decided to go the weekend before we would leave for the NIH. I asked Kevin, and he said for us to go and have a great time. Since I worked at the church, I had to ask for time off. My pastor told me to have a great time, so the plans were set. The kids were thrilled. I had peace.

My friend and her children, together with Micah, Miranda, and me set out for Disney World on Wednesday, January 19, 2000. We left a day earlier than we had planned, because a huge snow storm was expected in Tennessee. Of course, we wanted to get over the mountains before it hit. We rode in her van and pulled their pop up camper behind us. We camped on Disney property and arrived at the site just a little after midnight. My friend and her son set up the camper, and we all went to bed. Miranda and I slept together on a full-size mattress, which was really comfortable and surprised me greatly.

My dear friend loved Disney World. She really knows her stuff . She had planned an agenda for every minute of every day. The first day we went to Animal Kingdom, which was a blast. While at the parks, I rented a stroller for Miranda. She was too easily fatigued to walk and in pain. Everyone was great to be patient with her difficulties. The next day we rode a boat to another Disney resort and looked around. The kids swam in a pool and later that night we went to a "Chip and Dale" marshmallow roast, which was a great deal of fun. The third day, we went to Magic Kingdom, which was wonderful. God really graced Miranda throughout the entire day. Our last day, we went to Downtown Disney. There was a Lego play station, which the kids enjoyed. And shopping in Disney stores, which I enjoyed. It was a peaceful and magical trip. I was so thankful we went. I even enjoyed camping.

We headed home on Monday, January 24, 2000. There was a warning a snowstorm was moving across the nation, but we felt we would miss it. We were only on the road about one hour when the rain began to beat down on the van. We kept right on moving. The further up the road we went, the colder it became. I was not concerned, and my friend seemed to be handling the drive just fine. We stopped about forty-five miles outside of Columbia, South Carolina, to get gas for the van and food. While I was in the store a woman told me a snow storm was expected to hit Columbia. Still, I thought we would get through before the storm hit – it was still daylight. How bad could it possibly get?

We left the store, and God began speaking to me. He said, "The storm you are in will grow worse and worse, but you will get through. It is a type and a shadow of what you will experience with Miranda. Remember, I am the Shelter in the storm."

I told my friend, and she was as amazed as I that God had just spoken to me. We continued to head home. As we entered Columbia, the rain turned to snow. It was incredible how fast the snow was sticking on the interstate. We kept right on going. I became a little apprehensive, but my friend remained calm. We decided to pull off the interstate and gas up again. After she put the gas in the van, we decided to get back on the interstate, and try to make it home. By this time there were several inches of snow on the interstate and traffic was barely moving. We merged back into the traffic and noticed people were stuck. We were moving very slowly. Vehicles were sliding all around us in the three lanes of traffic. By now, I was stressed. I liked safety, and this did not appear safe. After almost an hour had passed, we had barely moved 100 yards up the interstate. Then it happened, we began to slide. The van was sliding, because we were moving so slowly when the interstate began to go uphill. We had no speed and no traction. My friend and her son went out in the snow to put chains on the van's tires. They were wearing flip-flops on their feet and had no coats. I sat in the van and prayed. People just kept passing us. No one stopped to help. After several unsuccessful tries, we called my friend's husband on my cell phone. He talked them through the process, and they were able to put the chains on the tires. I was extremely unnerved. I wanted off the interstate. I wanted to be somewhere safe.

We took the next exit and rented a hotel room. I called Kevin and asked him to come get us. Kevin, my friend's husband, and another friend headed our direction, while we waited in the hotel. The snow was beautiful. It was amazing how fast it had fallen. The news labeled it a blizzard. Apparently, it was the only one in the history of Columbia, and we were stranded in it! We were blessed though. Most of the city was without power, but the place we stayed had power and heat. Kevin arrived at the hotel around midnight and took our family home. My friend's husband stayed with her, and they traveled home the next day. It was definitely an adventure, but it ended well.

I thought about what God had spoken to me and how the storm did grow worse before my very eyes. I wrote down what He said and decided to "put it on a shelf" as usual.

Wednesday night at church, Pastor had everyone gather around us and pray. It was a blessing. After the prayer, several people gave us cards and money. We were blessed abundantly. All of our financial needs for the trip were completely taken care of by the gifts we received. I felt confident God was providing for us. One gift particularly surprised me. God had moved on my heart about sowing an offering on behalf of Miranda in the amount of $1,000.00. We did not have the money, but I still had sensed it was something God wanted us to do. One family gave us a card with this exact amount of money in cash. You might think I would have immediately given it, but I felt I should wait. I put the card and the money in a safe place to wait for the right time. I felt I needed to pray and seek God concerning the timing of the offering.

Kevin and I headed to Bethesda, Maryland with absolutely no idea what we would face. Miranda was admitted on Sunday, January 30, 2000. The NIH was gigantic compared to anything we had ever seen. Building 10 was where she was admitted. We were sent to 9 West, which was on the ninth floor. Miranda was placed in a room with another girl who was there as a volunteer in a research study. I was allowed to stay with Miranda in her room. The room was somewhat like a regular hospital room. I had a fold-out cot to sleep on at night. Kevin stayed at the Children's Inn, which was located on the NIH campus. It was like a Ronald McDonald house for families of sick children and proved to be a great blessing.

Almost immediately, a sweet nurse came into Miranda's room. She told me she did not want to overwhelm me with the test schedule. First, she would put in Miranda's heparin lock and go over the schedule with me. I did not even know what a heparin lock was, much less what to expect from a "test schedule." The nurse checked out Miranda's arms for good veins and applied a cream on areas she felt were the best. The cream apparently numbed the skin so the needle would not hurt as bad. After about an hour, we were led down the hall to another room where she inserted the heparin lock. It was similar to an I.V., but had extra tubes hanging from it. Miranda handled it well.

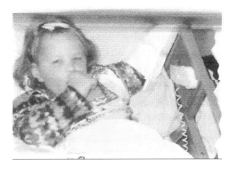

The nurse then brought in a piece of paper with tests listed under different days. She carefully went over Monday with me and told me the tests could change without any notice. We had been given a large amount of information that day. At the Children's Inn, they had gone over policies and procedures. At admittance, we were given a packet of information to digest. And now, I had to comprehend this test schedule. I was grateful I had studied about Cushing's. I recognized most of the tests on the schedule. I decided just to take it one day at a time.

Later in the afternoon, Miranda was in the playroom when a very pleasant woman came to see us. She introduced herself as a doctor. She said she was there to check out Miranda and make sure all was well for the night. I was apprehensive to say the least. Concern was written all over my face. With much compassion, she said, "Honey, you can take that worried look off your face. You are in the right place now. These doctors treat Cushing's all the time. They are the brains who will get you help. Just relax."

I really appreciated her encouragement, but still felt extremely apprehensive. She checked Miranda and immediately noted her body odor. She questioned me, and I explained how Miranda's urine had smelled strange for over a year. She took a lot of notes and told us to expect a doctor in the morning.

A doctor from the NIH, whom I will call Dr. Endo #3, came in sometime Monday and met with us. He checked Miranda from head to toe and asked me lots of questions. I was prepared with my notebook. I had learned from the past and was glad to give him the information he needed.

Tests began. I was instructed to catch all her urine. I explained Miranda's difficulties, but they wanted me to catch her urine anyhow. The nurses quickly saw for themselves catching Miranda's urine was no easy task. Miranda had an MRI which was difficult for her. The last one she had they put her to sleep, but at the NIH she was awake. I was allowed in the room with her. I literally had to crawl part way up in the tube with her to keep her still. She was pitiful. Being in the machine was scary for her. The tube makes a loud sound which resembles trash can lids crashing together. Miranda was in the tube for about one hour while I held her hands and encouraged her to hold completely still. There was a mirror, she could look in and see me. I could see tears running down her cheeks as she lay there. It was so hard for me to make her lay there. I wanted to rescue her, but I knew she needed the test. When we returned to the room, a nurse informed me Miranda would have a Diurnal Cortisol Blood test during the night and first thing in the morning. I was not familiar with it. She said it was simple. They would just pull blood from Miranda's heparin lock.

Tuesday came and the Diurnal test was over. Miranda was not allowed to eat or drink, because she was scheduled to have the CRH test. The Human or ovine CRH is given to test the pituitary for the ACTH deficiency to differentiate whether the pituitary gland was the problem or if the source was ectopic. Due to her bladder problems, a renal ultrasound was scheduled. The CRH test was put off until after the ultrasound. The ultrasound was interesting and not painful at all. However, Miranda was beginning to get upset about not eating. We finished the test and went back to her room for the CRH test. The nurses were not successful in pulling blood from her heparin lock. They informed us they would have to put in another one. Miranda became upset, after all she was only five years old. They put cream on her arm again, and we waited for the cream to numb her. Finding a vein proved difficult. They would dig in her arms while she screamed, which was emotionally taxing on me. I wanted to quit, but I knew she needed these tests to get answers. After trying for several hours, they finally put the test off until the next day and allowed Miranda to eat. She was exhausted and kept saying she felt like a pin cushion.

Dr. Endo # 3 came to me with test results. He said they did not see anything on the MRI. I was not surprised, because it was the same result we had received at home. However, again I felt a burning sensation and knew something was not right. Then, he informed me Miranda's cortisol level in the Diurnal test was low and showed variance. He went on to say that people with Cushing's have the same cortisol level at night and in the morning. This test pointed to the fact, Miranda did not have Cushing's. I could not believe what I was hearing. The tests for the day ended, and I was left with a child who had been through a horrible and difficult ordeal for results, which showed nothing. Miranda finally fell asleep around 11:00 p.m.

I went down to the playroom and called a friend on the watt's line. I was angry and again devastated. I was ready to pack her up and leave. Where was God? Why were we there? If she did not have Cushing's, why in the world had all the doors opened for us to come? What kind of cruel joke was this? I was so angry and hurt. My friend listened as I blamed God for sending us and questioned everything I believed. I hung up the phone still brewing with anger and went back to my room. My friend later told me she stayed up all night praying for me.

The next morning, I spoke with a nurse about our situation. She strongly encouraged me to stay. She told me it was obvious Miranda had a problem, and I should let them do all their tests before giving up. We took Miranda down to the room to get a new heparin lock. Just before the nurse was going to insert the needle, another nurse brought Miranda a piece of mail. It was a letter from Nana, my mother, which simply stated in big letters "Jesus loved Miranda." Miranda was excited about the letter and seemed more willing to let them insert the needle. The nurse walked over to the sink and washed her hands. When she returned, she inserted the needle finding the vein the very first time with no difficulties. I was amazed after everything we had gone through the day before. She told me while she was at the sink, she prayed and could tell Jesus had guided her hand as she inserted the needle. Her comment softened my anger towards God a little, but I was still hurting on the inside.

The day went quickly, and the CRH test was completed. During the night, I knelt by the bed in the hospital room and prayed. I repented for my anger and asked for forgiveness. Also, I asked God to please reveal the truth and not make us go through this again. He spoke to me, "It will get much darker before the light."

Although, the words were not what I wanted to hear, I had peace. Because, God was in charge. I slept well.

The next day proved to be a little more encouraging. Dr. Endo #2, who had called me and spoken with me before we went to the NIH, came by to see us. As soon as he walked in the room, I sensed hope. He examined Miranda and commented on her buffalo hump. He was very kind. I questioned him about cyclic Cushing's. He said, "Not a problem, about 15% of all his patients had Intermittent Cushing's." He was always peaceful and confident, which helped me greatly.

Dr. Endo #3 also reported the results of the CRH test to us. It had come back positive, which was an indicator Miranda's pituitary gland was her problem. When I questioned him, he said the CRH test was not diagnostic. Frustration does not even come close to what I felt. What did it take to get a diagnosis with Cushing's? He and a nurse explained to me the doctors would chart everything like putting pieces of a puzzle together to diagnose it. Miranda would have to meet the criteria in a lot of different areas. The whole concept was foreign to me. All other diseases seemed so simple. Why was this one so hard?

One afternoon it was snowing when Dr. Endo #3 came in our room. While he was looking out the window watching it snow, he began talking about his little boy. It was nice to see the human side of such an intelligent man. As he was talking, he made a comment to me, I hid in my heart. He said, "Sometimes we bring kids back in six months, and we can see the tumor on the MRI."

He continued talking, while I made a mental note. Sometimes was a whole lot better than never. Hope was hard to come by, and I took any glimmer I could find.

The night before we left the NIH, I was standing in the hall talking to a couple of nurses. My heart was broken, because I knew the doctors did not get the test results they needed. The nurses were wonderful and very supportive. As we talked, an older man with a foreign accent who was there with his child walked by us. He stopped, turned to me, pointed his finger at me and said, "You pray to your God – He will heal her."

I recall looking at him in disbelief. Tears were running down my face. I did not understand why I received continual encouragement from a variety of sources without breakthrough. When would God heal her? How long would I have to wait?

We completed a scan of her adrenal glands, a bone test, and a Dex test by Saturday morning, and we were dismissed. Dr. Endo #3 told me they would call me with the results. I was glad to go home, but was not really hopeful about getting the results. The week was unbelievable, and I knew in my heart the results were still not conclusive. Dr. Endo #3's final instructions to me consisted of going home and collecting urine if Miranda had a weight gain, or if I thought she was in cycle. I could not believe it. We were back at square one. Dr. Endo #3 told me if they were not able to get to the bottom of her problem, I needed to find another doctor, because it was obvious Miranda needed help. "It was obvious she would die."

Shock and disbelief consumed me for several days. I could not believe we had gone to the healing pool of water for nothing. God had told me, "They would find it." I was beginning to question my abilities to hear God and wondering who is "they?" God had said we would go to Bethesda, and God said "they would find it." We went to Bethesda, but they did NOT find it. I felt like I was living in a cruel joke!

CHAPTER 12

THE UNTHINKABLE – MICAH DIAGNOSED

We had been home about two weeks when I received the call from Dr. Endo #3. He said, "Miranda looks like Cushing's, probably intermittent. Take her urine when she gains weight, or if you think she is cycling."

Please keep in mind Cushing's Disease untreated leads to death, because it never left my mind while we traveled through to the other side.

I met with my pastor soon after my return to update her on our situation. I told her I had no idea how long this would take. She encouraged me greatly and told me to do whatever it took to take care of Miranda. I told her I did not know how much I could be in the office, but she was not concerned. She said I could work from home. I was amazed by her compassion and love.

They wanted Miranda at the NIH while she was in cycle. Well, that was going to take a miracle. Even if we were able to get another high UFC test, by the time we received the results, her cycle could be over. I was not happy to say the least. I knew we were in an impossible situation.

All of the test results would be sent to Dr. Endo #1's office. I contacted them to set up an appointment and let him know what our instructions had been. I really was not sure how he would respond, because I had not spoken to him since the end of October 1999. Dr. Endo #1 called me, and we spoke. He was kind as always. I told him about our experience at the NIH, and he said, "Yeah, they will do a million dollar work up and they will find it."

I was amazed by his comment. God continually told me, "They will find it." I was shocked to hear the words come out of Dr. Endo #1's mouth. We talked a little longer, and he told me his nurse would call me with an appointment date. I asked him if I could take her urine. He said it was fine.

The nurse called with the date, and I went to pick up the orange jug to take her urine. I was just sure Miranda was in cycle. I was positive God would not prolong this journey. I took her urine and waited for the results.

Dr. Endo #1 gave us the results when we went in for our visit. I was shocked. Miranda's cortisol level was 10. That was extremely low. Dr. Endo #1 checked her out and said he had not yet talked to Dr. Endo #2 from the NIH, but he would. Then he gave me the same orders I had already heard. Take her urine. He said to take it once a month, or if I thought she was cycling. I left the office discouraged. If the doctors did not know when a cycle was, how was I supposed to know when she was cycling?

I went home and made out a chart. I kept up with every symptom and her weight. I marked it daily. Miranda's symptoms varied, but were always present. Something was always going on in her little body. As I kept the chart, I became even more aware of her difficulties.

I sought God continually in prayer. Others, as well as myself, prayed and fasted for three days. It appeared as if our prayers were unheard or unanswered. It was extremely difficult to "press on."

By the middle of March, I was extremely discouraged. So, I called Dr. Endo #2 myself. He answered, and I questioned him. He said he had spoken with Dr. Endo #1 and told him, "Miranda looks like Cushing's, probably intermittent. Take her urine once a month, or if I think she is cycling."

I questioned him about the length of a cycle. He said nobody knew how long it might last. It could be days, weeks, or months, because it was different with each person. He did let me know Miranda was not in any danger when not cycling. I guess he thought his words would comfort me. Nothing really comforted me.

Well, all I could do was take her urine. One thing was certain. All the doctors were in unity. I was the only one not agreeing. They should try to take her urine. It was nearly impossible to catch it all without strapping her to the toilet all day, which would be cruel.

I took her urine again on March 15, 2000, with the hope she was cycling. I had really felt in my heart that spring was our season. Spring always brought new life. Disappointment struck again when her test results were 10.

I cried out to God. Where was He? I felt hopeless.

A woman from my church came by to pray with me. She said it was strong in her spirit the enemy wanted to torment my mind. I agreed with her. The entire situation was insanity as far as I could tell. She prayed for me, which proved to be a turning point in my heart.

March 18, 2000, I began writing this book by faith believing God would heal her. God reminded me of a scripture I had once claimed for my life. It is located in Isaiah 40:4 and states, *"Every valley shall be raised up, every mountain and hill made low; the rough ground shall become level, the rugged places plain."* (NIV) I began to claim the verse over my life. Even if this situation was a roller coaster, I was not riding it. I was going to walk as if the valleys were high and the mountains were low. I wanted to walk as if I had victory.

God began moving on my heart about offerings. In Malachi, a book in the Old Testament, the author talks about Jesus Christ rebuking the devourer on our behalf in relation to tithes and offerings. I was reminded of Cara encouraging me to seek God concerning covenant promises and money. As I prayed, I knew I needed to sow the $1,000.00 we were given, just before we went to the NIH, as an offering to God on behalf of Miranda. I called Kevin at work, and he agreed. I immediately drove to the church on Friday, March 24, 2000, at 11:30 a.m. and gave the money to the woman over the finances. She and I prayed together, and it was as if I could see Jesus standing between Miranda and Satan. Jesus was saying, "Stop It! That's enough!"

My pastor came into the office just as I was leaving. She and I prayed together. In my heart, I knew a spiritual breakthrough had been accomplished. I just did not know how long it would take to manifest in the natural realm.

Miranda was having multiple difficulties. She was extremely nauseated every morning and very tired. I became concerned, because her cortisol level was so low on her last UFC tests. Hormones need to be in balance. High or low can be dangerous. Miranda appeared to have signs of Addison's, which is the exact opposite of Cushing's. I called and talked to Dr. Endo #2 at the NIH. He told me they were not looking for low cortisol in Miranda, only high. I was still concerned, but was left with no choice except to trust their judgment.

Wednesday night, March 29, 2000, God spoke to me during praise and worship. He said, "You will have a diagnosis by Easter."

I was a little unnerved. God encouraged me to lean on Him. He was to be my strength and Shelter. He would sustain me.

April came and I was still hopeful for a high UFC test, especially since we were going to get a diagnosis by Easter. I took her urine with confidence the cortisol would be high.

I was on my way to the church to work when I decided I would call Dr. Endo #3 to see if he could get the results from the clinic faster than our local doctor. As I was driving, I prayed in the spirit. I could tell my prayers were strong and effective. Just before I arrived at the church, God showed me I had been praying for me. I had no idea what I was about to face.

When I arrived at the church, I called Dr. Endo #3. He said he would try to get the test results. Then he went on to tell me he was amazed I had called, because just yesterday he and Dr. Endo #2 had discussed Miranda. I immediately thought: Good! Boy, was I wrong. They were saying they did not believe Miranda had Cushing's, because her low tests are so low. Well, I was in shock. The last time I talked to Dr. Endo #2, he said it looked like Intermittent Cushing's. Unbelievable! Yesterday she had it – today she does not. I asked Dr. Endo #3 if this UFC was high would they rule out Cushing's, and he said no, but if it is low they would. He did tell me Miranda definitely had a metabolism problem and desperately needed help, but he had no suggestions of where to go or whom to ask for help. He only knew she was sick unto death.

I hung up and again faced shock and disbelief. How could they have possibly decided she did not have Cushing's based on low tests? Miranda had high tests. This nightmare seemed to have no end. I did not want Miranda to have Cushing's, but I did want someone to get to the bottom of this and end it.

I left the church immediately. I had to go home. I had to pray and get direction. I needed help; God was the only One who could help. On my way home, I felt in my heart I needed to call my pastor and let her know what we were facing. When I arrived home, I called her. She listened and encouraged me. Also, she decided to get the entire church to pray and fast. She asked me what to have them pray and I answered, "That Jesus Christ would make Miranda whole."

After our conversation, I quickly pulled myself together and reminded myself of what God had spoken to me. We would have a diagnosis by Easter;

therefore, this UFC would be high. It had to be for them to get the necessary results to help her.

Dr. Endo #3 was not able to get the results. We had to wait several days. The days were so long when we waited to hear. I spent time in prayer and praise. I was just sure this was it. Finally, they would find it. I was confident since the doctors were ready to quit God would reveal the root of her problem.

The nurse called me with the results. They were normal. I was shocked. Where was God?

Obviously, I did not hear His voice. I must be crazy or something. What was I going to do? The doctors at the NIH were going to give up on Miranda. Where would I turn? Who would help us?

I calmed down and called Dr. Endo #3 with the results. We talked for a while. He was very kind and compassionate. While we were talking, I asked him a lot of questions. I wanted to know what else could possibly cause her problem or where else to turn. During the conversation, it came up Miranda had not gained weight since we were at the NIH. He asked me why I had taken her urine if her weight had not increased. I told him I had based it on her symptoms, not weight. He told me to wait until she gained weight and take her urine. Also, he suggested we test her for Diabetes Type 2. He then said, "We will not drop the ball on Miranda."

I clung to those words more than once. I was frustrated by the lack of a diagnosis by Easter. Although, Easter was still two weeks away, I knew we would not get a diagnosis – or so I thought.

The Sunday morning before Easter, April 16, 2000, my pastor explained to the congregation our family needed a miracle. She asked them to pray all week and fast on Wednesday. She told them we were believing God to make Miranda whole.

Monday, Dr. Endo #1 ordered the diabetes test. I took Miranda to his office where they drew blood. Miranda was amazing. She held out her arm and was not the least bit bothered. The nurse drew the blood and off we went. I could not believe how strong she was. To see your six-year-old daughter just hold her arm out and let people put needles in without even flinching is odd. She and I were both getting numb to the entire experience.

Micah was struggling with a sore throat. I kept giving him acetaminophen and hoping it would go away. After several days, I felt like he needed a strep test. I took him to his pediatrician on Monday afternoon. His regular doctor did not have space for him, so we saw the nurse practitioner who was very kind. The strep test came back normal. She felt like it was probably a virus. As we were getting ready to leave, I asked her to check a dark spot on Micah's shoulder. I had been a little concerned, because it was so dark. I told her Micah had several spots, but not as dark as that particular spot. She checked it and began to question me about his other spots. I showed them to her and she said, "Mam, your son may have Neurofibromatosis."

Quickly and without any thought, I began to argue with this woman. I told her my son was fine. He was normal and had no difficulties. I knew what sick children were like, and he was fine. She left the room and came back with a medical book. She looked up the syndrome and showed me the criteria for the disorder. It explained people with NF Type 1 had multiple cafe-au-lait spots on their body from birth and other criteria would develop as the person grew. The next noted criteria would be freckling either in the groin or under the arms. Also, she was quick to point out, most children do not have difficulties in their first decade of life. Micah was eight. My thoughts immediately began to spin. Was this woman telling me my son's life would end at age ten?

Let me interject here, I had been told when Micah was nine months old, he had a problem, but I had chosen to deny it. Denial of truth is not faith!

Micah had several spots, but no freckling under the arms. We did not check the groin. I was just sure she has dead wrong. I wrote down the name of the syndrome and left. Again, shock was the only thing I could feel.

Once I was in my car, I called a close friend and told her. I asked her to call her husband and have him look up the word, Neurofibromatosis. I wanted to know what it would mean for Micah. I do not even know what she said. I just recall feeling numb all over. I was sure this was a mistake. It was unbelievable as far as I was concerned. How could someone have two children with medical problems? My mind was blank.

When I arrived home, I immediately went to the internet to get factual information. I studied just enough to learn that Micah's spots were a strong indicator he had NF Type 1, but he only had one criteria and to be diagnosed a person had to have two. I decided to check his groin for freckles. I was mortified to see small cafe-au-lait spots, freckles, in Micah's groin. I felt dizzy and light headed. I thought I might pass out. My life was a nightmare. I could not take the reality my son also had a horrible medical diagnosis.

I quickly learned NF is a syndrome caused by the lack of chromosome number 17. It is genetic and without a cure. NF causes the individual to grow tumors at random – it can be severe or mild, varying with every person. I was without words. I was living a nightmare.

Tuesday afternoon I received a call from the nurse practitioner who had seen Micah. She had met with Micah's regular doctor, and they felt they needed to check this out immediately. So, she set him up with a medical eye doctor. Tumors growing in the eye are apparently some of the first problems, so they wanted to see if he had any. Also, she set him up with his regular doctor for a physical. I could not believe it. I had done nothing, and these doctors were moving like crazy on his behalf. Yesterday, Micah had a sore throat, but was basically fine. Today, he has Neurofibromatosis type 1. When God had told me we would have a diagnosis by Easter, I thought he meant Miranda.

I had no idea Micah was even a possibility! I did not know what to do or how to respond. My immediate reaction was to tell no one. My pastor had just requested prayer for Miranda and the very week the church prayed, my son was diagnosed. Unbelievable, over and over in my mind, I would think: this is unbelievable!

Wednesday night we went to church. The pastors had asked us to bring Miranda to the service, so they could lay hands on her and pray. It was a communion service, and the church was packed. I literally felt the love from the people as they prayed for my child. The pastors prayed fervently for Miranda and our family. I recall my pastor saying, "As they walk through this fire, do not even let them smell like smoke." I knew the power of God was strong in the service, and I felt confident we would see results from the prayers for Miranda as well as our entire family.

Thursday, I received the results from Miranda's diabetes test and everything was normal. Again, my child with so many problems tested completely fine. I was thankful she did not have diabetes, but continued with great frustration nothing ever showed her problem.

Within days of the prayer, it was noted Miranda had not wet herself. She had not had bladder control for about 18 months. We were amazed to see her use the bathroom as a normal child. Time would prove she had received a definite miracle the night the church prayed. Miranda never wet herself again!

In my mind, I thought the bladder control was essential for the tests we needed to receive a diagnosis, and God was making the way. I had no idea what the problems were in her body at that time, but I knew God had done something to help her.

Doctor appointments were lined up quickly for Micah. I decided I needed to let the pastors know. I went into my pastor's office and told him. He was wonderful. He encouraged me to not be moved and trust God's Word over circumstances. I had peace when I left. My pastors proved to be a constant voice of peace and direction throughout the entire ordeal.

We went to the eye doctor within two weeks, which was interesting. They dilated Micah's eyes to see if he had any tumors growing. I felt sick at my stomach. I was still basically in shock at the thought of him even having a problem, much less tumors. We were in the office for about two hours. They did a variety of things to check him out. At the end of the appointment, the doctor told me he did not see any tumors now, but wanted to see him back in a year. I was relieved, but not okay.

The eye report was sent to Micah's regular pediatrician, and we went to see him a couple of days later. He checked Micah from head to toe. He counted Micah's spots and noted the freckling in the groin. After some time, he had another pediatrician come in and count Micah's spots. It really was amazing. They measured the spots to see if they were the "right" size. I was stunned by the entire process. His pediatrician recommended we go see a genetic doctor who specialized in Neurofibromatosis. So, an appointment was made with a genetic doctor at a Medical Center in Nashville, TN, for Friday, May 26, 2000. I now began to feel as if I were caught up in a whirl-wind.

CHAPTER 13

WILLING TO WAIT

Even as I look back to recount May and June 2000, I am amazed at God's grace. Darkness can be overwhelming. Sometimes we walk only by sheer necessity to get to the next step. I had no fire or fight left in me. I was weak and without desire to seek God's face. I wanted my life to go away. I had come to a place I never thought was possible after knowing Him. I had arrived at, a destination in my life which caused me to literally hate living. I hated my life. I loved my husband, children, family, church, and job, but I hated my life. I wanted out of this nightmare and no exit doors existed. Time was now my enemy. Waiting was my prison.

I knew exactly where we stood with Micah. We would have to wait until the end of May to get direction, and I was getting better at putting things on a "shelf" until it was time to deal with them. I knew I could do nothing for Micah or about the situation so I simply did just that – nothing.

Miranda appeared to be much better as we entered the month of May 2000. She seemed full of energy and life. I was hoping she had received a complete healing when the church prayed. However, in my heart, I knew we were going to have to "go through" to get to the other side. As always, Miranda's appearance of health was a deception.

Miranda had a small cut on the back of her leg. Really, it was not a big deal. A couple of days passed and the cut grew larger. It became apparent it was not healing. I treated it constantly with the hope it would heal. About four days after the cut, it began to have bubbles on the skin and appeared to be infected. By the next day, other areas on the back of her legs were looking like the first, so I made her an appointment. I had a fleeting thought she had strep on her skin. I had never seen strep on the skin, but my heart knew that was her problem.

I took her to the doctor on Friday afternoon. The pediatrician was concerned. He said she had impetigo. I had not heard of impetigo before. He went on to tell me what to watch for and put her on several medications. I told him Miranda had a runny nose and cough. He said the medication he had her on would take care of any infection in her body. I left and thought we had solved our problem. I was relieved to have it in her medical record that she still weighed 86 pounds.

Miranda began the medication on Friday afternoon. I felt confident she would feel better within days. Sunday night she woke up with a rash on her legs. She was miserable. When she was miserable, we were miserable. We were up all night with her. Nothing helped her discomfort. Monday, I took her back to the pediatrician. While waiting to see the doctor, I noticed a poster which talked about impetigo. The poster explained impetigo is a strand of strep on the skin. I was amazed. I knew in my heart Miranda's problem had been strep and again, my heart proved correct. When she was weighed, Miranda had gained 2 pounds. I was just sure she was beginning a cycle. Miranda had not eaten much at all over the weekend, because she felt so bad. Weight gain was an indicator of high cortisol; therefore, I thought she may be cycling. The pediatrician checked out her rash. He did not know exactly what to make of it. He decided to change her medication and see if it had been an allergic reaction. I told him Miranda had been on the antibiotics before and never had a rash, but he said a person can develop a reaction. I questioned him about what to do if the rash became worse. He said he did not know.

I left with great concern in my heart. Things with Miranda are usually not easy and never what they appear to be. All I could do was follow this doctor's instructions, and trust God was in control.

Miranda was up all night. Her rash spread all over her body. Kevin and I could not comfort her with anything, which made for a long night. I cried out to God the next day. What was I to do for her? I felt led to call Dr. Endo #3 at the NIH. He asked me some questions and told me to take her back to the doctor. Kevin came home from work and took her. I was simply unable to go back again. It may sound like not a big deal, but I was constantly running to the doctors with my kids. I needed a break.

When Kevin came home, he told me Miranda had scarlatina, which is also caused from strep. They tested her for strep throat and the result was positive. Miranda had impetigo, scarlatina, and strep throat all at the same time. Unbelievable! They changed her medications again. I questioned Kevin about her weight, and he said she was up another pound. I felt confident she was cycling, but decided I would wait till she felt a little better to take her urine.

Just a few days later, Micah woke up around 11:00 p.m. with vomiting. He was very sick. He vomited about every twenty minutes all night. I was exhausted and had very little patience. When was this going to end? We were constantly being bombarded by sickness. I contacted the school, and they said the virus was going around. Miranda was still on medication for all her infections. I tried to keep them separated.

Two days later, Miranda began vomiting. The night was long and relentless. She vomited more than Micah. I was without rest and beginning to feel completely defeated. I did not see any way to beat the spirit of infirmity. It was beating me. Micah had vomited for about 16 hours before quitting. Miranda had been vomiting for about 24 hours and did not seem to be letting up. I was concerned she would dehydrate. I gave her a suppository and called Kevin. He came home from work and held her on the couch. I went up to her room and confessed over and over, "I have nothing to fear. I have nothing to fear. I have nothing to fear."

Her body calmed down and the vomiting quit. A few days later, I took her urine. I felt confident she was in cycle. After all, she had gained weight and had infection.

We went to the pediatrician for a recheck. Miranda's weight was back down, because she had lost weight while vomiting. I still felt confident her urine would be high. She had been so sick. The cortisol must be high. When I received the normal result again, I was shocked. How could this be? When would it ever come back high? I had no answers. I simply had to trust God and keep going. The darkness grew.

During the middle of May, God began working on my heart. He showed me I was not completely surrendered to His ways. I realized I had been stubborn in my ability to yield to God's way. I always did whatever God wanted, but not completely committed. I always had a "back up" plan in my mind, which I called plan "B." For instance, I would "think" I will do this, but if something goes wrong, I will fall back on my own plan. God wanted me to get rid of my plans and surrender to His no matter what. I repented and told God I was His however, whenever, whatever He wanted. My pastor confirmed what God was revealing to me in the message he preached on May 14, 2000. He taught on submitting to God completely to walk in the 100% power needed for results. I knew God was preparing me for the miracles we needed.

Miranda began to have pain in her right side on a regular basis. She complained and grabbed her side in desperation. I was helpless. I could not make the pain go away. Miranda was crying and saying, "Mommy, Mommy, help me!"

I was unable to help, and the feeling of helplessness was so difficult. Her symptoms began to get more evident. She had blurry vision, weight gain, headaches, acne, swollen face, swollen tummy, irritability, and a variety of other things. Daily her problems would vary, but it was obvious something was wrong. I requested another urine test. Her cortisol level had to be high. We took the test, but would not get the results until the first of June 2000.

It was time to take Micah to Nashville and get direction for our son. A few nights before we left, I was up all night. I spent time seeking God about our situation. My heart was broken, and my despair was without words. But God was there, and He directed me. He reminded me about the time when Miranda had the chicken pox. She was just over a year old, and Micah had just turned three. Micah was determined he would not get them. I was positive he would. One day in the shower God moved in my heart to pray Micah would not get the chicken pox. I felt it was ridiculous to ask God to keep Micah from the chicken pox. As far as I was concerned, chicken pox was a part of childhood. After all, everybody gets them. God continued to impress upon me to pray. Finally, I agreed, but I told God I only had enough faith to pray. I was not telling anyone I believed Micah would not get the chicken pox. I prayed in the shower a very short and simple prayer. Micah daily confessed he was not getting those bumps on him. I watched and waited. Time proved Micah's confession to be the truth. He never contracted the chicken pox. I was amazed. I knew it was a miracle. According to the world, it is inevitable that a person will get the chicken pox, if they are exposed to the virus. Micah proved the world to be wrong.

God spoke clearly to me NF would be no different. According to the world, if a person has NF - they may have tumors, but Micah would once again prove the world wrong. He would never suffer from this diagnosis. I prayed a simple prayer, and trusted God was in charge. God said, "It will never touch him."

I did plead with God to please not put us through any testing at this time. I did not feel like I could handle it. Miranda's constant tests were a drain, and I knew I did not have any strength to begin going through similar things with Micah. A friend was going to go; however, the night before, she ended up not being able to go. It was not easy, but Kevin took off work to go with us. Immediately, we knew he needed to go with me. In my heart, I was reminded of the scripture in Proverbs, which states even accidental things are ordered by God. I felt confident God wanted Kevin there.

Micah, Kevin, and I headed to Nashville, TN. We stayed in a Ronald McDonald house, which was located just beside the hospital. Even though God had prepared me, I was still unsettled by the entire situation. I wanted to run away, but there was nowhere to run. I had to go through to get to the other side and going through was painful.

We went to our appointment with the genetic doctor. It was amazingly pleasant. A very kind woman came in first and asked us loads of questions. We were even asked if we were cousins, which, of course, we were not. I had figured that would come up. I almost found it funny. I must say I was thankful to know Kevin's mother was born and reared in Oregon; therefore, making it impossible for us to be blood related. I was from Tennessee. His mother had moved to Tennessee and met Kevin's father. His father was of no relation to my family either.

They took lots of notes and said the doctor would be in shortly. Micah sat on the table and played his hand-held game, while we waited. The doctor came in and immediately connected with Micah. He was wonderful. He played with him and totally put Micah at ease. He checked Micah from head to toe, counted and measured Micah's cafe-au-lait spots, and noted the freckling in the groin. Kevin and I watched and waited.

The genetic doctor then turned his attention to us. He began to go over information about NF. We listened. He explained all the criteria and went over a list of things to watch for as Micah grew. He said now he was not going to do further tests. He simply wanted us to keep an eye on Micah, and for us to bring him back in a year. I was excited, because this was the best news I had heard in a long time. I felt very peaceful. The genetic doctor told us he would send a letter to Micah's regular pediatrician as well as to us. He told us, "Don't lose any sleep over it."

I felt as if God, Himself was telling me everything was fine. We left the office and headed home with good news.

My parents had invited us to go to the beach with them as we did every year. I was not sure I wanted to go. We were waiting on a UFC result, and I did not want to leave town if Miranda was in cycle. I wanted to be ready to go back to the NIH whenever her level was high. I prayed about going to the beach. I pressed God for direction, and Saturday night, May 27, 2000, God spoke to me. He said, "Donna, go to the beach. You need the rest. The next thirty days will be difficult."

On Sunday, a woman I did not know came up to me at church after the service. She asked me how Miranda was, and I answered as usual. She again questioned me and then went on to say God had sent her over to me with a "message from God." She told me God was going to make Miranda whole and for me not to back up. I had no idea what we were going to face. God was preparing me for a difficult month.

Very reluctantly, we went to the beach. Micah went on Monday with my parents. Kevin, Miranda, and I went Wednesday night after church. While we were getting gas to leave, Miranda had to use the bathroom. I took her inside and Kevin pulled the van up to the door. We came out to get in the van when Miranda looked down by her door. She picked up something and said, "Mom, I just found $100.00."

I asked her to let me see. To my amazement, she had just found a one-hundred-dollar bill. There were no other cars around or people. Miranda declared God had given it to her. She was extremely excited, and I was confident God was looking out for her. It might sound silly, but I saw it as hope. Hope was hard to come by, and Miranda was blessed, which gave me hope.

The beach proved to be a wonderful rest. We spent time with Ginger and her family as well as my parents. Miranda had a wonderful time. It was as if she was graced to be there. She had little discomfort and lots of energy. I did feel rested when we came back home. Miranda began feeling poorly Sunday. She was extremely emotional and had a horrible headache. She described it by saying she felt like "horses were trampling my brain." We came home Sunday afternoon. I felt ready to face whatever the next test result would bring. I was just sure she was in cycle, and we would move towards a diagnosis.

Monday morning, I called Dr. Endo #1's office. A male nurse called me back and said everything was within normal ranges. I wanted to know the exact number, but he did not know it. I told him Miranda was not well, so I wanted a blood test. He called me back within five minutes and said the blood test was ordered. We went to the office at 1:30 p.m., and her endocrinologist met us there. I told him she had not been well. Her weight was up to 90 pounds, and she was symptomatic. They drew blood, and the doctor said we would talk more on next Monday at our scheduled appointment. I was frustrated. He acted as if there was nothing wrong with Miranda, and I was over-reacting. I wanted to get her help, but nothing helped.

Miranda continued to complain about her headache. Feeling desperate, I cried out to God. Where was He?

I was distraught to the point of making myself sick. I recall standing in the kitchen and gagging. I hung on to the kitchen counter, so I would not fall. I was devastated by the constant persistence of her physical problems without any answers. I told God I could not keep on taking her urine without results. I begged Him to end this nightmare. I told God I would do anything to save my daughter.

I cried until I fell into a heap in my kitchen floor. My nose began to bleed, which I experienced on a regular basis. I assumed it was because my sinuses were swollen and raw due to all the tears I had shed throughout the year. I pulled myself somewhat together and held a tissue over my nose. My heart was broken, and it appeared as if everything I believed was a lie. My God was nowhere to be found. After some time, I called a dear friend. She was a blessing as always. She encouraged me by just being herself. We talked for a while, and after I hung up I had the strength to face another day.

I requested another urine test. Miranda had to be in cycle. Why else would she have so many symptoms? I felt confident we would catch it. I took her urine and turned in the jug. We waited. Kevin was not doing well with the entire situation. A nurse at the doctor's office told him we should just give up. Miranda's tests were all normal. They could not find anything, and she would probably just die anyhow. He told Kevin he did not even understand why we would even test her. Kevin was tired of the uphill battle. We talked, and decided we would quit if this cortisol was low. After all, she had symptoms. If she had Cushing's, then her cortisol level would have to be high or something else was her problem. Right?

Often, I spent time "surfing the Internet" to see if I could get any more information. I felt confident answers were somewhere. That night I went to the Cushing's bulletin board, and a woman had posted an article about Intermittent Cushing's. I downloaded and printed it. The article was extremely interesting and stated that a man who was 70 years old took his urine every day for two consecutive years. He had Intermittent Cushing's, and his cycles were completely unpredictable. He had symptoms all the time, even when his cortisol was normal. When his cortisol was high – it was not high every day. In other words, during a "cycle" his cortisol could be high for a day and then low for two days and then high again. I found this article to be very informative. If this man could have wild cycles, so could Miranda. I also felt resentment. Why did the doctors only take her urine once a month? How in the world would we ever catch this thing with a hit-and-miss method?

A friend and I decided to take the kids to Dollywood on Friday. Just before I left the house a nurse called and reminded me we had an appointment with the endocrinologist on Monday. During the phone call, he told me her blood test was normal. I was used to the normal results, but this call was odd. I felt the presence of God while he was speaking to me. I hung up and felt confident God wanted me to go to the appointment. I had been considering not going and only getting the results. If they were low, we were quitting. I rationalized there was no reason to go and be asked if I had "seen a dietitian" yet again.

I was so tired of feeling the blame for her problems. But, I could not deny how God moved on me during the call, and I wanted to discuss the recent article I had found.

While at Dollywood, God gave me a scripture:

Isaiah 35:4

"Say to those who are fearful-hearted, "Be strong, do not fear! Behold, your God will come with vengeance, with the recompense of God; He will come and save you." (NKJV)

I knew God was telling me He was coming, but I did not know when. Sunday morning at church during praise and worship I had a vision. I saw myself on a path. My feet were attached to the path, and the path was moving. The path moved me by an operating table, and then I saw a healthy little girl playing in my yard. I knew immediately God was showing me the way for Miranda's healing was through surgery. Just after the vision, Amy, a friend of mine, came up to me to say God told her to tell me, "Faint not."

I must say; I was bothered. I knew "faint not" meant to wait. According to the Bible, they that wait upon the Lord shall renew their strength. They shall run and not be weary. They shall walk and not faint. Not fainting meant waiting. I was upset by the thought of more waiting. Had I not waited long enough? Why was God drawing out this process? When would it ever end?

I knew immediately this also meant her UFC would be low. I began to think it was useless to even go see the endocrinologist. A friend of mine was planning to go with me. I called her Sunday night and told her I did not know if I would go or not. She said to just let her know. I prayed when I lay down God would give me direction. I really did not know what to do. I slept well and woke up early. As soon as I woke up, I knew I should go to the appointment. After all, I could say I had done everything humanly possible if I were not the one who closed the door.

My friend drove Miranda and me to the appointment. We did not wait long before they took us back to see Dr. Endo #1. Miranda had gained another pound since we were there the previous week. The nurse took her height and blood pressure then placed us in a room. The endocrinologist came in to see her. He was very nice. He checked her out and talked to me. I was shocked to hear him say we should quit testing her. He did not think she had Cushing's and was ready to release her back to her regular pediatrician. I told him I too was frustrated by the low test, but had found an article I thought was interesting. I asked him if we could do some consecutive tests, and he agreed. We decided on four days, and I took home the jugs. However, the endocrinologist made it clear to me if these tests were normal, he was releasing her.

As bad as I wanted this nightmare to end, I could not believe it would end like this. God had said we would go to the other side. Surely, we were not there yet. These tests would have to show something. We needed a miracle, and I knew it.

During the next staff meeting, my pastor came over to me and prayed for me. It was unusual, because we do not pray for each other during staff meetings. It is a time where we went over current events and the work of the ministry. Pastor prayed for a fire to burn in me, so I would not give up until I reached the other side. I knew it was profound and from God. I just did not know how difficult the journey was about to become.

We successfully took Miranda's urine and turned in the jugs. I was just positive at least one test would show high cortisol. After all, God had promised me a doctor with a diagnosis and this was the last opportunity for tests to reveal the truth. Days passed, and we began to get the results. One at a time they came back. Every result brought hope and devastation. I would hope it would reveal something, but each time darkness grew. They were all normal. The endocrinologist released her. Now, I had no one to help me.

I assumed the NIH would quit since we could no longer test her and show cortisol levels. My false expectations devastated me. I was without direction and extremely angry at God. Where was He? He had promised me a doctor with a diagnosis. He told me we would go to the other side. He told me I would know Him as Healer. What kind of cruel joke was this? Why had all the doors opened for her and now closed?

I found myself in great darkness. I found myself hopeless and in grief. The only good thing I could think of was the fact – we would not have to catch urine anymore. I watched Miranda and my heart ached. She needed help. I could not help her, and God had failed me. He had lied to me. His promises were broken. I hurt so much. I cannot even express my pain. I felt betrayed by the One in Whose hands I had placed my very life, and Whom I served without reservation. I never wanted to use the doctors. I had wanted God to just heal her. I had prayed. I had fasted. I had believed. I had fought. I had submitted to His way. I had trusted Him. Where was He? Why did He not rescue me?

Sunday morning, June 25, 2000, I went to church because I felt I should. I did not want to be there, but I had to go and fulfill my obligation. I stood at the beginning of praise, but after a few songs I sat down and placed my hands over my face. Anger and bitterness were swelling inside me.

As I sat there with my hands over my face, Cara came up beside me and sat down. She was praying in the spirit. I wanted her to leave. I personally did not want to hear from God. He had not done anything He had said so far. Why should I trust He would do anything she might say right then? Cara prayed for a while before she began to prophesy. Then she said, "A refreshing is coming to you. God is the lifter of your head. He will come and save you. On wings – He will come. Things have not happened the way you thought. Hard walk. Sacrifice received up in Heaven."

I began to cry. I wanted God to save me. I was desperate for Him to save me, but He did not show up. What was I to do? Where was I to turn?

At the end of the service, my pastor had an altar call. I did not go up to the altar, but I did respond. I told God I needed direction. I wanted to hear something by Friday. Even if it meant waiting, I wanted to know. I went home and decided Miranda's endocrinologist could quit, family could quit, friends could quit, the church could quit, and Kevin could quit, but I could not. She was my child. I recalled God saying to me at the beginning of the journey, "You are her advocate, and I am yours."

Also, God continually told me throughout the year 2000, "Donna the answers lie in you." Somehow or someway, I would find the answer.

Miranda did not have a voice for herself. I had to be her voice. I had to find someone to help her. I went on the internet and found out information about pituitary centers. It was clear Miranda's pituitary gland was the source of her problem; therefore, I needed an expert in Neuroendocrinology to help her. I found phone numbers to three centers, and decided I would call them Monday.

I was only able to get through to one center, which was located in Boston, Massachusetts. I left a message and a number. To my surprise, the chief resident of pediatric Neuroendocrinology called me back. She was very kind. I explained our situation with the test results. She knew Dr. Endo #2 very well. They apparently worked together and communicated often. I told her Miranda had a positive CRH test, and she told me Dr. Endo #2 had developed the CRH test and stands by it 100% of the time. If a person tests positive, then they have Cushing's. I was surprised to hear that information. I told her Miranda had suppressed her Dex test. She said people with Cushing's suppress that test all the time. She encouraged me to talk to Dr. Endo #2 and see what he was going to do. She offered to see Miranda if I wanted her to, but told me if Dr. Endo #2 could not help, she did not know what she could do. He was the best.

I was amazed by our conversation. Yet again, I was directed to Dr. Endo #2. He had been the only human who had made me sense hope. But, I knew the NIH questioned greatly whether Miranda had Cushing's. They wanted test results, and now no one was testing her.

God had often spoken to me test results do not order her steps. He does. However, the NIH wanted test results. After some thought, I wrote Dr. Endo #2 a letter. I told him in my heart I believed Miranda had Cushing's. I realized she could not be diagnosed based on my heart; however, if we continued looking for the root of her problem, we might find it. I requested a couple of tests. I told him I did not wish to waste his time, so if he believed she did not have Cushing's to let me know, and I would go another route. I faxed the letter on Tuesday.

Wednesday night at church, God moved in my heart. He gave me specific instruction. I recall God telling me, "Don't let Satan see you squirm."

I was greatly encouraged after the service. I knew I needed to get back into a routine of spending time confessing the Word, scripture, and being on the offense spiritually. I had been so battered by the battle. I was weary and needed refreshing, but that would not come. I needed to do my part. I needed to go back to the basics. Time in prayer, praise, and the Bible were the key to walking in victory. I needed to rise up and press on.

Easier said than done. However, I felt inspired again. I could feel the fire Pastor had prayed for me being ignited. I could sense my fight returning. Friday arrived, and I had not heard from the NIH. I had pleaded with God all week for an answer by Friday. I felt a nudging from God telling me to call Dr. Endo #2. I had his number, but the thought of it brought me fear. I sat on my bed and battled fear for about fifteen minutes. I was so afraid he would drop Miranda and give up. As I sat there, I realized my fear was without logic. If he was going to drop her and give up, I needed to know. Then, I could look for help elsewhere. If God had chosen him to help her, he would not be able to drop Miranda. Finally, I picked up the phone and called him. He did not answer, so I left a message. The message was simple. I asked him to let me know if he was going to continue with Miranda or quit.

I had to run some errands. I was gone for about two hours. When I came home, I had several messages. Dr. Endo #2 had returned my call. He was very compassionate with his tone. He said he had received my letter, and the tests I requested would not indicate a hormonal imbalance. He was not sure what might be going on with Miranda. However, there were constant medical research breakthroughs.

Dr. Endo #2 was correct, it would take a medical research breakthrough to help Miranda.

He went on to say he wanted to keep close contact over the next three months and maybe bring her back up to the NIH for a re-evaluation.

The message was not what I wanted to hear. Three months seemed like an eternity. However, God had answered my prayer. I had direction. Dr. Endo #2 had not given up even though he was not sure what her problem was at the current moment. He made no promises, but maybe bringing her back was better than never. I was going to have to trust God to order her steps.

Revelation 3:8

"I know your works. See, I have set before you an open door, and no one can shut it; for you have little strength, yet you have kept My word, and have not denied My name." (NKJV)

It would take a miracle for the NIH to bring Miranda back. It would take a miracle for her cortisol level to be high when we went. It would take a miracle to find the tumor. But God had promised me just that: a miracle. I was willing to wait.

CHAPTER 14

BITTERNESS REVEALED

Well, the last few months have proven to be adventuresome, to say the least. I was able to "put Miranda's miracle on a shelf" and focus on other things. I worked diligently at the church during July and August. Micah and Miranda had pneumonia in July 2000, and Miranda had another urinary tract infection in August. God was faithful as always. The week Miranda became sick with pneumonia, I received two cards with a total of $300 in them from people in our church who wanted to encourage me. Neither of them knew Miranda was sick. Also, during an intercessory prayer meeting, a woman in our church gave me a ring. She said God had moved in her heart to give me that particular ring, because it had every gem in it and represented a rainbow. In the Bible, the rainbow represented a promise God gave to Noah. She told me God had a covenant with me and never forget it. Deuteronomy chapter 28 is like a contract between God and His children. He was going to make Miranda whole.

Even with God's continual faithfulness and encouragement, my heart was broken. Inside I still felt as if God had failed me. I kept myself busy on purpose, because I was running from the disappointment and pain in my heart. My pastor was led by the Holy Spirit to initiate a twenty-four-hour-a-day prayer push for seven days. It was called 24-7 prayer, and our entire church joined the effort. Personally, I did not want to pray. I had lived a life of prayer to no avail. I was still going to church and working, because I did not know what else to do. But, my heart was crushed by the feeling of hopelessness.

Tuesday was my day to take care of the prayer room. I felt obligated to go and pray. As I entered the room, I was frustrated and out of sorts. I could not stay in there, so I left and worked some more. Later in the afternoon, I went back to the prayer room. Again, I was frustrated and unable to pray. As I sat on the floor in the prayer room, God spoke to me, "You are bitter." I did not feel attacked. I felt revealed. I left the prayer room and went to another classroom, I cried out to God for a long time. I cried and expressed all my hurt to Him. I do not recall repenting for bitterness, but I did tell God I wanted to be free from the anger and hurt.

We serve an awesome God. He knew I was broken-hearted by the delay and was not going to let this destroy me. God always reveals our sin to help us. He wants us to be in peace and fellowship with Him. Sin separates us from Him and His peace.

On Sunday morning, August 20, 2000, during the next church service, the praise music was awesome. I ran to the altar in a song about miracles. I was praising God with all my might. I began to say over and over, "Miranda needs a miracle." As the song ended and another song began, I felt I needed to get on my knees. As I knelt there, God began to speak to me. He said, "You have to fight for her. Give Miranda to another doctor. It is time to test her again. It will be quick."

I was devastated by the words. I did not want to "give" Miranda to another doctor and test her some more. I had decided in my mind unless the NIH called back, I was done. No more doctors looking for a problem and certainly no more tests. They had never helped so far. I sat on the floor at the altar and cried desperately for God to change this path. I felt sick when I stood up, and the color was drained from my face. Several people asked if I was okay. I just tried graciously to leave the church.

Leaving, I saw a friend of mine who was the doctor God had placed in my heart. She and her husband had gone to our church the entire time she was in medical school. The month I conceived Miranda, she and her family moved away for her to serve in the military. They moved back to Tennessee and came back to our church the month the endocrinologist released Miranda, exactly seven years from when they left. We had talked some about Miranda, but it had never gone through my mind to use her as Miranda's pediatrician. I was satisfied with the group I was using, and I never considered changing pediatricians. I stopped her and asked her if we could meet. She suggested we get together soon. I told her I would call her.

That afternoon, we met at the church. I took everything I had. Miranda's medical record, this book I had been writing, and pictures of Miranda. I told her we were looking at an impossible situation. Miranda needed a miracle. Her response amazed me. She and her husband had been praying for Miranda during the entire ordeal. She said, "I knew when we moved back I would be a part of helping Miranda get her miracle."

She seemed positive God was going to move for Miranda – full of faith. I was still without hope. I just looked at her in amazement as she felt confident we would get through this; however, the darkness for me was without any glimmer of light.

She was going to read everything and contact the doctors. She was now fighting for Miranda. It was as if someone was on my side. I had an ally in the medical field. I felt as if a burden had been removed. I did not want to test Miranda, but at least I was not the one who was going to have to deal with the medical end any more. I could relax and trust her. I knew she loved God and was led by His Spirit. We decided I would bring Miranda to her office in a week, which would give her time to get a handle on the situation.

The very next Wednesday, she walked up to me at church before the service began. She was not kidding about getting Miranda help. She had already contacted several specialists and was plowing ahead quickly. She told me she had talked to Dr. Endo #2. He would need another high UFC test before he would bring her back to the NIH. She went on to tell me she was going to look at every avenue and not just Cushing's. She said we would test her, and if we could not find anything, then we would take her urine until it revealed itself. She seemed so determined to get to the root of the problem. I felt hopelessness grip me when she told me what Dr. Endo #2 said. Just the thought of taking urine was overwhelming. I did not think I could do it anymore. It never helped! How much pee do you catch before you give up?

Seeing the hopelessness in my eyes, she calmly put one hand on each side on my face and pulled my head up to look her in the eyes. As soon as she touched me, I felt the power of God surge through my body. She said, "Donna, you can do this. You can catch her urine."

The church service was beginning, so I went to my seat for praise and worship. I had a hard time getting through church. I wanted to run out. I could not believe Dr. Endo #2 needed another high UFC. It was impossible to catch her in cycle, and I knew it.

After the service, she caught me in the hall and said she wanted me to take Miranda to an eye doctor for a check-up. Miranda had double vision as well as blurred vision. She gave me the name of a doctor and told me her office would set up the appointment. Also, she said we should do a full MRI of Miranda's brain. A brain MRI had never been done before, and it was possible the problem could be outside of the pituitary gland. I agreed. This doctor, my friend, was the first person to look outside the box of Cushing's and suggest the entire brain. She was led by God! Also, she thought we would need a medical research breakthrough to help Miranda.

On Tuesday, September 5, 2000, we saw my friend, and now Miranda's new pediatrician in her office for the first time. It was pleasant, and Miranda was peaceful. A friend met me after the appointment to take Micah and Miranda home with her. I had gone to the doctor for a physical at the end of August, and he said I should take a stress test for my heart, due to the pain I had been having. I felt confident the pain was from stress. My chest would hurt when I dealt with stress. The doctor wanted to be on the safe side and test me. I had a little bit of time to waste, so I went to a craft store to walk around. As I was looking, I began to feel the burning sensation I get when something is not right. This is an odd and personal way the Holy Spirit gives me discernment. Just after my burning sensation, my cell phone rang and it was Miranda's new doctor, my friend. She had set up the MRI for September 21, 2000. I was excited. I felt the timing was perfect. We had already planned to go to Atlanta from September 15-20, so it would be fine with me to come home and do the MRI. I hoped it would end our nightmare – they would find it. I completely ignored the warning from the Holy Spirit. I left the craft store and went to the doctor. I did not do too well on the heart stress test. My heart beat was too fast, so my internist put me on medication. I was bothered, but not much. I knew my heart would be fine when this ordeal was over.

Wednesday night, Kevin went to church with me. My pastor kept talking about having joy. The presence of the Holy Spirit was strong. My pastor called a woman down to the altar who needed healing in her body. While they were praying for her, I felt God wanted me to squat down where I stood. I obeyed, and he reminded me of Naaman in 2 Kings 5:1-11. Naaman was a great man in the land of Syria. He became sick with leprosy. He went to the prophet Elisha, who told him to go dip seven times in the Jordan to receive his healing. Naaman was angered by the directions of the prophet. He felt that Elisha should just come out and *"wave his hand over the spot and cure me of my leprosy."*

God made it clear to me that obedience would bring Miranda's miracle. An altar call for people needing healing was given, I went forward. Some friends of mine went with me and brought Miranda from the children's ministry in the church service where I was. We both received prayer. I declared my heart beats for Jesus, and I received an assurance I was fine.

The next morning, September 7, 2000, I took Miranda to the eye doctor. He said Miranda's eye muscles were weak, which caused double vision. He thought her blurred vision was caused by migraines. He gave a prescription for glasses, and we left. Miranda was flushed and swollen. She did not look well. I called her new pediatrician, and she suggested we do a UFC test. I agreed and had great peace in my heart. I picked up the jug, and we went home. During the night, Miranda woke up with a rash on her legs. It was exactly like the rash she had in May. I called her pediatrician, and she met with me to look at Miranda's rash. It had spread to her tummy and back. Miranda was not feeling well. She was tired and irritable. The doctor said, "We'll just have to wait it out."

All day Saturday, it was on my heart to do another UFC test. I thought maybe the rash was an indicator of cortisol. The new pediatrician called to check on Miranda and suggested we do another test. I was amazed and explained to her I had the same thought. Sunday, September 10, 2000, we tested again.

Monday, Miranda was still not doing well. I took her in the office for the pediatrician to see her. We ran a strep test just to rule it out. On Wednesday, I was at the church when a woman from our church called me. She felt God wanted her to take my family to see a famous evangelist known for supernatural healings, in Charlotte, NC. I was not on the phone with her long, but I did accept the invitation. I told her Kevin could not go, but I would go with Miranda. Then, I received a call from the pediatrician. Miranda had strep throat. Micah and I were feeling poorly, so we too went on antibiotics. I was angered by the entire situation. I felt as if it would never go away. I spent my time running to doctors, and our money paying doctor bills or prescriptions. My emotions were drained. I stopped by the church in between doctors' appointments, and I unloaded all my frustrations on my pastor. She was wonderful. She said she would keep praying.

Saturday, we left town. I was so excited. We were going to visit Ginger in Atlanta. On the way, we were going to stop at Babyland General Hospital for their Fall Festival. I love Babyland, because we have so much fun there. Ginger and her family met us. The kids had a great time. Ginger and I went on into Helen, which is small town nearby and shopped. It was the most fun I had experienced in a long time. No doctors. No tests. No results. Just fun.

The next morning, we all went to church. I did not really want to go to church. I did not want to hear from God, and I knew God was at Ginger's church. I told God to please not talk to me. I wanted to forget my life for a few days and just have fun.

Before church, I walked by a woman in the hall. She spoke, and I responded. The church service began, and I enjoyed it. Praise was sweet and the message from the pastor was good. When the service ended, the pastor gave an altar call. Kevin went to get the kids, and I waited in my seat for Ginger to finish ministering. Ginger was praying for people who went to the altar to receive prayer.

Ginger came over to me and told me Mona wanted to pray for me. Mona is one of her friends who is very sweet. I said it was fine and Mona took my hands. She prayed a precious prayer, which brought tears to my eyes. Just as she finished, Ginger said a woman had a word for me. Immediately, I put up my defense. I did not want a "word." I had made that clear to God. As far as I was concerned, I did not want to hear from Him again until He proved Himself faithful with Miranda.

This woman began to prophesy to me. I felt the presence of the Holy Spirit. She said when she looked at me she saw anger. She went on to say I felt as if God had failed me, and God wanted me to know He loved me. She hugged me, and I walked away. We left and went to eat. After lunch, Ginger asked me to ride back to her house with her. We went alone in her van. She asked me what I thought about the "word." I told her, if I was angry – I felt I had a right to be!

She kept pressing me. As she pressed these words fell out of my mouth, "I do not believe He will heal her. I don't believe it. I just don't." I was shocked to hear myself. I knew I was angry at God for not just making the entire thing disappear, but I did not realize I had lost my faith.

Over the next several days, the story of Naaman began to give me more insight. I was just like him. I was angered by the directions from God to go use doctors and take urine again. I wanted someone to just lay hands on Miranda and make "it" go away. I justified my thoughts, because I felt I deserved an easier route. I had loved God and served Him without reservation. I felt He should move my way. I was in sin. I realized my anger was not justified or even warranted. He is God. I am a piece of clay. He saved me. I am a sinner. He made the way. I can only walk in it. I had pride due to my obedience to Him, and God wanted me to rid myself of it. I was no better than any other sinner. I had to surrender to Him regardless of any service I had ever rendered. God was not going to heal Miranda or give her a miracle because of me. He had already made the way for her at Calvary. He had already ordered every step. He was going to make her whole because of Jesus. Jesus paid the price at Calvary with His shed blood. I soon realized due to Galatians 2:20, it was not even "my faith" that would cause her healing manifestation. The Word declares the faith of the Living Son is in me, because I am crucified with Christ. I knew God was showing me clearly: It was up to Him, and it would happen His way.

We did the MRI and again nothing showed up. The pediatrician and I met and decided to take 24-hour UFC test every Monday as well as keep a close check on Miranda. Monday, September 25, 2000, I took her urine. I continually cried out to God, and was praying for God to "end this!" Before I ever went to the NIH in Bethesda, Maryland, God had promised me, "It would end."

On October 9, 2000, I took Miranda's urine. It was the fifth urine test we had done since the new pediatrician had taken her case. I was up all night praying. I knew October 9th had always been a pivotal point for Miranda. Her first dietitian meeting, her second time with high cortisol, and the day she was dedicated to God was all on October 9, 1994. But in my heart, I did not expect this one would be. However, I kept praying. During the night, God once again took me to the story of Naaman. I was reminded he dipped seven times. I knew seven was prophetic for completion. All year I had been standing in faith, Miranda would be whole by her seventh birthday, which happened to fall on the seventh day of February. I realized I would be taking the seventh urine on October 23 & 24, 2000. Then, the Holy Spirit reminded me of the faith offering I had sown for Miranda back in March 24, 2000. I went and looked at the date. I knew it had been profound. The Holy Spirit had made it clear to me, I had to sow the offering on the exact day I went. I was shocked to realize October 24, 2000, would be exactly seven months from the date I had sowed $1,000.00 on Miranda's behalf, and the seventh urine test would end that very morning. I knew it was God. He had so ordered every step. I knew in my heart, I would be finished with urine tests for now, maybe not forever, but a break was coming. During my prayer time, God impressed upon me to sow another $1,000.00. I told God I would, but I did not have the money. I asked Him to provide it.

Tuesday, October 17, 2000, I turned in the sixth urine and told Miranda's doctor I was only willing to do one more. I had already settled it with God in prayer. I knew seven was it. No matter what it showed or did not show – I was released. In my heart. I knew seven was enough. I could stop, not because I wanted to, but because God said I could. I did want to stop. I wanted the entire situation to simply go away!

I left the office and drove to church. On my way up the church driveway, God reminded me of how seven of us prayer warriors walked around the church seven times and declared victory.

I knew God was confirming for me it was over, even if it was a temporary break. Whatever the tests showed. It simply did not matter. I was going to get a break, and I needed one!

The woman who had offered to take us to a Christian conference called me to complete our plans. We were leaving on Wednesday October 25, 2000, to go to his meeting. I knew the timing was God. I explained to her about sowing a faith offering and how it would be seven months on October 24. I told her I knew we were getting our breakthrough. She amazed me by offering to match my faith seed. I told her it was a large sum of money, and she did not care. That very day, which was October 17, 2000, she came to the church and sowed $1,000.00 as an offering for Miranda's miracle. She brought me some minerals and calcium for Miranda to take as well. I knew it was directly from God to help heal Miranda's body. I was completely blown away. I knew God was moving. He had told me another offering needed to be made and provided the offering through this incredible woman. I knew He was watching, and I had a strong sense nothing was going to stop what He had pre-ordained for Miranda.

I took Miranda's urine on October 23 and 24, 2000. I turned it in, and we went to a Christian conference. We were going to get our miracle!

CHAPTER 15

VICTORY IS IN THE WALK, NOT THE END RESULT

Well, it has been a year since I last wrote. I have put off writing for the past few weeks, because it overwhelmed me to try to think of all that has occurred. God is so good. I am truly amazed to think about how much my life has changed in the last year.

Miranda with her Daddy

I had a great time at the Christian conference. The family who took us were such a blessing. They made the entire weekend a gift. I felt the love of God through them in every situation. The meetings were wonderful. During the first meeting, a woman received a supernatural healing. While the woman was testifying, a different woman beside me asked me what was wrong with my daughter. I explained to her Miranda had a tumor, which could not be found. She said she had a word from God for me, "Take her back to the doctors and have them test her again."

I was shocked, but wrote it down. At the last meeting, the evangelist laid his hands on everyone in the room. Just before he prayed for me, I heard the Holy Spirit say, "You will walk through the valley of the shadow of death and fear no evil."

The presence of God was so strong in the room, and Miranda was amazed by the demonstration of power. At the end of the meeting, a complete stranger came up to me and asked me if Miranda was my daughter. I answered, "Yes." He went on to tell me he had a word from God for me. The first words out of his mouth were, "Lighten up."

Immediately, I became offended. Who did this guy think he was? He had no idea what I had endured. How was I supposed to lighten up? Even as my mind was spinning, the Holy Spirit arrested my thoughts and said, "Listen, Donna."

So, I concentrated on the rest of what he said. The man went on to say people had criticized me, and he listed specific people in my life and then said, "Criticism will fall off of you and both of your children will be healthy and whole." As he finished, I knew it had been God, but I was not sure what "lighten up" meant. During the night, I lay in the bed and tried to figure it out. But, it was a waste of my time.

We came home from the meetings, and Miranda's last UFC was normal. I went to my pastor and told her what the women had said about going back to the doctors. She told me if I was to go back, I would know and for now to follow peace. I knew in my heart not to bother testing further, and I had peace about no more testing.

Within days of being home, a friend of mine asked me if I would be interested in going to Atlanta to an evangelist conference in November 2000. I said no at first, but later in prayer the Holy Spirit spoke to me to go. So, I went with my friend to the conference. It was a tremendous blessing. The evangelist taught on walking in the fruit of the Spirit. I needed to hear her practical teachings. I had lost sight of how to live for Jesus. I needed to be reminded of daily application. The teaching was refreshing and for the first time in almost two years, I was desiring to press into my Christian walk again.

December 2000, proved to be a rough month. Miranda was sick as usual. She was gaining weight and tests showed her to have yet another urinary tract infection. I felt compelled by the Holy Spirit to pray. I diligently prayed over Miranda during the entire month of December. I cannot put into words the depth of prayer I experienced – except to say over and over I declared, Miranda will live and not die. Just before Christmas, I had a release in my spirit, and the praying ceased.

The last week of December, I was excited. Nothing good had happened. I just could not wait for the year 2000 to end. I had no word from God, just a desire to get out of that year. I wanted January 1, 2001, to come more than anything. The year 2000 had proven to be the darkest year of my life. To even recap at this point makes my heart race and my stomach hurt. Nothing could have prepared me for the emotional pain I endured concerning my children.

At the end of the year 2000, God spoke to me, "Donna, you have the Miranda Right."

I had no idea what God meant. So, I asked Kevin if it made any sense to him. Kevin told me the legal words a police officer reads to a person who is being arrested are called the Miranda Rights. In other words, God told me I had the right to remain silent. This particular key helped stop the false accusations. I only talked about our situation in places where I knew I was safe from judgment and criticism. The journey was hard enough already. Being silent is sometimes your best defense!

On January 3, 2001, I was shopping when the Holy Spirit led me to look at some diet books. I had been so stubborn concerning diets with Miranda. I knew her problems were not caused by overeating, or the amount she ate. I was defensive, and only God could reach me in the area of diet. I picked up the book *Protein Power* by Michael R. Eades, M.D. and Mary Dan Eades, M.D. to look at it while I was shopping. When I began to read a couple of pages, light began to shine. The book made perfect sense to me. I had studied the endocrine system, but this book gave me revelation about metabolism which made perfect sense. I bought the book and read it immediately. The book tells how sugar is the hormone which stores fat. As I read, I knew I had found a key to Miranda's health. I bought Dr. Atkins' book as well and read it within days. By Micah's birthday, I had decided to try Miranda on the high protein/low carbohydrate diet. I spoke with her pediatrician, and she said it was okay with her, but she was skeptical.

On January 9, 2001, Miranda began the diet. She was not thrilled at first. The first two or three days were hard, but at the end of one week we could note amazing changes in her. She lost three pounds and appeared to have more energy. By the end of two weeks, she no longer had daily pain in her stomach, and the headaches were gone. She lost another two pounds in the second week. I was excited, but at the same time fearful. Deep in my heart, it was hard for me to believe she could ever really be okay.

The last Sunday in January during praise and worship at church, God spoke to me. He said, "When Miranda is not spilling ketones she is in cycle."

I just wrote it down. I really did not think about it too much. Miranda's new diet puts her body in an induced state of ketosis, which means her kidneys were spilling ketones in her urine. Miranda continued on the diet until her seventh birthday. She had lost around seven pounds, and her health was improving daily. On her birthday, she went off the diet and ate a piece of cake as well as some french fries. The results were unbelievable. She became sick within twelve hours. A bad rash broke out on her back, and her emotions were completely out of control. It was as if we had never dieted one day. It took almost two weeks back on the diet to gain the lost ground of one day off. I was shocked by the drastic change. Obviously, Miranda was unable to process sugar.

Miranda's diet consisted of meat, eggs, cheese, and vitamin supplements. She consumed less than 15 carbohydrates a day. The main drink she had was water. The diet affected every area of our lives. This diet allowed for no cheating. The absence of sugar caused her body to go into induced ketosis, and every night I would check her urine to see what level of ketones she was spilling. She had to exhibit self-control by denying her food cravings and chose only the allowed foods. It became evident Miranda was graced by God to walk this walk. I battled with feeling sorry for her, but quickly realized my pity would not benefit her. We had to do whatever it took for her to be healthy.

The spring was busy. We took a family vacation to Florida, and both of Kevin's sisters were married. I went to a part-time status in the church, because our lives were becoming increasingly busy. My pastors agreed it was the best situation for all. Miranda and Micah were both in the weddings. Due to the diet and continued weight loss, Miranda was able to wear regular little girl dresses in the weddings. I was excited, because her body was beginning to work properly.

Miranda loved horses

Right after the last wedding, Micah had an appointment with a genetic specialist. Our new pediatrician had changed us to a doctor whom we could see in the local area, so we would not have to travel to Nashville. Micah had developed more cafe-au-lait spots, and his diagnosis of Neurofibromatosis Type I was confirmed. Because Micah walked on his toes, an MRI of his brain was ordered to rule out tumors. The MRI was completely normal. As I sit here typing, I think back to those days in awe. God carried me through. I was peaceful and confident of the outcome. I knew Micah would be diagnosed, but deeper yet was the confidence in my heart of the covenant I had with God. I knew then, and I am even more confident now NF will never touch Micah. I know Micah will grow whole!

January to May 2001, had been amazing. This year was so much better than last. Miranda's health was improving daily. Although, I did not like the diet, it was working. She weighed 98 pounds when the diet started and at the end of May, Miranda weighed 82 pounds. Not only the weight had changed, she had changed. Her emotions were under control, and the constant sickness in her body was helped by the diet as well. Miranda seemed almost like a normal child, which was wonderful.

We went on our annual beach trip with my parents and sister's family at the end of May. The trip was a struggle to say the least. Miranda had been in a relatively protected environment with her diet until we went on vacation. Kevin, Micah, and I did not tempt Miranda by eating foods in front of her that she could not have, so being with others who ate carbohydrates was not easy for her. On Wednesday, Miranda became blood red. Her entire body appeared to be badly burned. Time would prove it was not the sun, but just her own body struggling. She became extremely upset and emotional. Fatigue set in her little body, and she was difficult to handle due to her emotions. Her urine showed no ketones, which meant something had caused her body to break ketosis. I left on Friday, and on Monday I took Miranda to see her pediatrician.

I remembered what God had spoken to my heart about ketones. The theory was simple, and it seemed extremely logical to me Miranda was in cycle. Cortisol causes the human body to produce the hormone insulin, and if Miranda was not taking in any foods which would raise her blood sugar, then her pituitary gland must be releasing cortisol. I questioned her pediatrician, and she agreed. So, we took her urine. I was just sure this was it, and they would finally get to the root of her problem. However, by the time I took her urine. She was beginning to spill about 5 ketones, and I wondered if it would be accurate. Because, it takes about 24 hours to get into ketosis. So, the cycle may not have lasted long enough to show up.

My sister Ginger called me on the morning of the urine test with a word from God on June 5, 2001. "No longer strive with me for the plan of her life for I have all things in My hand, and I am the author of the plan. Do not forget I execute judgment and righteousness in the earth. She is my daughter, and the seed of My birth. I am her Father. Do not fret and do not doubt for the path you walk will come out as a victory to My name. Guard your tongue. Guard your mouth. For it is your words that I will watch to see if you truly will agree with Me. For nothing is too difficult and nothing is too hard. For I temper, and I form in the fires of life to produce the choice gems of My heart. Miranda Audrey-Ruth is Mine, and see to her I am. I will arise with healing in My wings to execute the plan! Do not strive – but rest and know she is Mine, and I will fight her foes for victory is in the hand of the Lord. I will perform the acts that fulfill My purposes and plans. Rest Donna, and fear not for you are seeing the salvation of the Lord. Love Me. Love Kevin. Love Micah. Love Miranda. For this reason, were you created, and you are seeing truth is greater than fact, and My word is greater than man, and it is I alone who orchestrate the sons of man. Grace I impart this day. Strength to run the race. Joy in the face of pain, and daily you are to stand and say: I love you Lord! I love you Lord! I love you Lord!"

The tests were normal, and I was bothered. Miranda had been doing so well. The diet had helped so much and now once again, we faced an unseen foe. Even if the theory was correct, would she ever be in cycle long enough to prove it? I struggled.

A woman in our church knew I was having difficulty. She said God laid it on her heart to research Miranda's name. Remember when we found out we would have a baby girl, Kevin and I had trouble agreeing on what Miranda's name would be. God had spoken to me before I had even conceived Micah and told us what to name him. But not with Miranda – it took several months for us to come into agreement. Finally, at a basketball game I was reminded of a little girl I had taught during my student teaching who was named Miranda. As soon as I suggested the name, Kevin loved it. I had always thought we were both just being stubborn, but when I found out what her name meant it was obvious God had named her.

Miranda:

Admirable; perfectness; render complete; free from imperfection; unblemished; sound, in perfect condition; intact; harmless; complete; come to a head; go whole length; be all and end all; whole in trunk, tissue, mass, lump, bulk, torso; whole in body; all put together; in the lump, in the mass, in the gross, in the main, in the long run; on the whole body, every inch, goodness; to stand the test; stand the proof; virtue; strength; heaven-born; angelic; genius; jack of all trades; no broken bones; live to an old age.

My heart cry to God in prayer was for Miranda to be whole. When I read what I was saying each time I said her name, I had a renewed confidence in God, and His ability to perform His word. I was amazed at the reality of the meaning of her name. Prophetically each time someone called her name, they were literally saying, "Miranda - whole in every aspect . . ."

It was as if the truth of the meaning of her name brought a deeper level of peace and rest to my soul. The summer proved to be challenging. Miranda's ketones were up and down. Her symptoms would come and go. I wrote Dr. Endo #2 at the NIH about my theory. My theory was simply when Miranda stopped spilling ketones, I believed her pituitary gland was releasing cortisol, which was elevating her blood sugar. But, he did not get back to me. I assumed he did not think it was credible.

In August, 2001, in prayer, I began to sense my season on staff at my church was coming to an end. One Sunday morning, a man in the congregation said he had a word from God for me. I was skeptical, but agreed to hear it. I do not remember it word for word, but basically, he said... "I see you standing and your feet are in cement buckets. This is not a bad thing, but a good thing. You are fixed in Him. Although the storm has blown, you have stood. You have been in a season of training which is coming to an end. You are entering a new season. There is one area in your heart – painful area – God is moving on your behalf. You will not even recognize your life in six months. I see a piano in your future."

In prayer, I became more convinced my season on staff was over. It was not easy. I was accustomed to being on staff and all my responsibilities at the church. I loved both my pastors and felt such obligation to them. God continued to impress upon me to resign. He would simply say "I needed to track with Him."

I had a wonderful opportunity to look at myself in a mirror, let go of position, and pride attached to working on the staff. I had to obey God and resign. I turned in my notice, and my last day was October 1, 2001, which was definitely God. The pastors released me, so I knew in my heart it was time for me to go. Everyone blessed me as I stepped down. My heart was pleased to see other people in the church fill my position with excellence. I knew it was the right timing. Including my first year as a volunteer, I had served for seven years to the month. Seven is often completion – my season on staff was over.

One service in October 2001, God spoke to me. He said, "Doors will begin to open for Miranda in the spring." I simply wrote it down, and shelved it in my heart.

Daily my walk with God was growing. My thoughts were consumed with Him again. I woke up happy and went to bed peaceful. I was truly peaceful with my life. I no longer was striving with God concerning my circumstances. Peace and joy became my fruit. Even as I type tonight I am in awe of God and His graciousness. He has not removed me from my circumstances, but changed me despite them.

I believe the miracle of my heart change, and the ability to be happy in the midst of adversity is truly a reflection of His awesome power and might. Before this walk even began, God had clearly spoken to me, "Victory is in the walk, not the end result."

I had victory and clearly understood what God had meant. To enjoy the day and walk with Him regardless of the circumstances is truly victory.

On Sunday, November 18, 2001, pastor released a word from the Holy Spirit over our church. He said, "The Spirit of Supernatural increase is on our church." He went on to say he had spent much time in prayer. The pastor declared, "The Spirit of God is stirring the water." These words caught my attention. I knew we were in a season for miracles. I had been waiting for the angel of the Lord to stir the water at Bethesda ever since I had studied the passage. I was amazed at my pastor declaring the season was upon us. I listened to my pastor's message with excitement in my heart. At the end of the message, he had an altar call. During the altar call, he said if there were any sick in the nursery to go and get them. I left the sanctuary and struggled in my heart about whether or not to get Miranda. Clearly, the Holy Spirit spoke to me, "Do you want her whole?"

My heart cry was, "Yes!" So, He told me to go and get her.

When I came back, my pastor had just finished praying for the last child. He saw Miranda and said to bring her up to him. I walked up with her. My pastor wrapped his arms all the way around her and prayed for a long time. He took authority over the spirit of infirmity, but the words that caught my attention was at the end of the prayer. He said, "I see a tumor." He declared, "it" has to go in the name of Jesus!" I felt weak in my legs, like I could faint. The word tumor had not been used in many months. An altar worker looked me in the eyes and said, "Fear not." When my pastor was finished, a woman felt she had a word for me, saying that she believed I would walk through the water and not be overtaken.

I was grieved in my heart when I left church. Miranda had been on the diet for ten months, and although she was not whole, she seemed so healthy. I had put thoughts of tumors and traumas out of my mind. I suppose I began to think if she just eats meat and cheese forever, she will be fine. God was reminding me of the battle we were in, and it was not easy to accept.

Someone gave Miranda a piano, just as the man had prophesied, and I was amazed. God was constantly moving in the hearts of people on our behalf and blessing us. He had removed responsibility outside my home from me and yet increased us with financial as well as material things. I felt in my heart, He was setting us up . . . for a miracle.

During the next few days, I began vomiting and was very sick. I physically struggled as my spirit was grieved. Finally, after about a week I sought God. He led me to Daniel chapter seven where Daniel too was grieved at the word of God. I found peace in the passage.

The next day was Wednesday, and I sensed God's presence all day. I knew He was going to minister to me at church. That night my pastor preached on the ABC's of faith. He reminded us that we must be in agreement with God. I knew God was speaking to me. I did not want to agree with God concerning Miranda. A piece of me still wanted the entire ordeal to just go away. I had even cried out to God and told Him I would rather be wrong, but my heart knew the truth.

During worship, the Glory of God filled the sanctuary. God did a supernatural work in me. He spoke to me, "You are now walking through the valley of the shadow of death. Your journey began the day your pastor prayed over Miranda. Every step is ordered. Money will find you. You will fear not.

Your confession will now be "Miranda is whole." Regardless of circumstances, confess "Miranda is whole."

My heart received the revelation. As soon as worship ended, God sent a woman to bless me with money. I knew He was moving on our behalf. I just was not sure how it was going to unfold.

In December 2001, just after Christmas, I went to visit Ginger in Atlanta. During a church service, she received a word from God concerning Miranda. She said, "God will open the doors, and it would be quick. Don't cry."

I really did not give much thought to the word. I had learned by this point to simply receive whatever God wanted me to know and trust Him to unfold His plan His way. I had learned to control my thought patterns and just stay submitted to the plan of God one day at a time.

In February 2002, we went to Disney World for two weeks. The first week Kevin was with us, and Ginger came to visit with her children. The second week, some of our friends stayed with us. By the third day of our trip, Miranda began to have symptoms. She was gaining weight and was extremely irritable. She was fatigued easily and cried often. Her difficulties concerned me, so when we came home, I called her doctor. She instructed me to bring her in the office and mentioned the possibility of sending Miranda to another endocrinologist. I was stunned at first. Miranda had been under her new pediatrician's care for eighteen months without any endocrinologist involved. I had no desire whatsoever to go back to another endocrinologist. However, I prayed about it and felt God wanted us to go.

I took Miranda into the office to see her pediatrician. She just lay on the table sucking her thumb. She was extremely fatigued and her face was flushed. The doctor could not find any infections or reason for her symptoms. However, it was noted Miranda was not spilling ketones in her urine. The doctor asked me if we would consider going to an endocrinologist, so I told her it was fine. Kevin and I had peace about it. She referred us to Dr. Endo #4 who was an adult endocrinologist, but willing to take Miranda's case. His office is about one hour from our house. The appointment was set for May 13, 2002.

On April 14, 2002, at church my pastor had an altar call. He said he wanted to pray for people who needed divine direction. I felt the Holy Spirit moving on my heart, but I hesitated about going down to the altar to receive prayer. I left the sanctuary and went to the bathroom. God asked me if I wanted to walk the next nine months on my own or with divine help. I wanted help, so I went back into the sanctuary and went down front for prayer. The experience was awesome. As soon as my pastor prayed for me, I felt the presence of God flow through my body. I knew God was doing a work in me. All I could think in my mind was: "I can do whatever it takes. I can do it."

Miranda at Disney

On April 17, 2002, Miranda had an appointment to see her kidney doctor who was wonderful. While at the visit, he said he knew we had been referred to the adult endocrinologist. He encouraged me to wait on the pediatric endocrinologist who would be joining their practice in July 2002. Even while he was talking, the Spirit of God spoke to me, "Go see Dr. Endo #4." God's voice overrode the words of the doctor. I simply thanked him for his advice and left. I felt excited God had given me clear direction. I did not know Dr. Endo #4, but I knew he was the man God wanted us to see.

During prayer God told me I could trust Dr. Endo #4, and we would have the first confirming test by June 21, 2002. He also moved on my heart to go to the appointment prepared and single-minded. As easy as that may sound, it took faith and trust to line myself up with God. As much as I wanted Miranda whole, I did not want to believe she really had a tumor in her brain. I knew I had to be her advocate and walk this process out God's way. One interesting point: sometime in February 2002, I was in a church service, and realized I was in unity within myself. My fear and my faith had become one. I knew by faith God was going to make Miranda whole, and I feared the process ahead of us.

On May 13, 2002, my mother and I took Miranda to see Dr. Endo #4. He was wonderful and seemed very interested in helping Miranda. He appreciated the information I gave him, and I could tell he listened to me when I spoke. He simply ordered one urinary free cortisol test and blood to be drawn when the test was done. He instructed me to take the test when Miranda was sick. I told him I had no idea when that would be and he simply replied, "That is why it is called Intermittent Cushing's."

When we left the office, I was in shock. The appointment was easy and peaceful. The doctor was kind and seemed determined to help Miranda. I struggled for a couple of days about opening the "door" again. Our lives had been so peaceful since we had not been testing or looking for the root of the problem. I was not sure I wanted to open the door again. Also, how would I know when to take her urine. Within three days, I had settled it in my heart. I would simply trust God to let me know.

Micah, Miranda, and I went on our annual beach trip with my family on May 26, 2002. We were gone about four days when Miranda stopped spilling ketones. I decided to stay the rest of the week and hope when we arrived home she would go back into ketosis. We came home on Sunday, June 2, and we restricted her diet even more to regain ketosis. On Tuesday June 4, the children were playing with friends at their home. I was ready to leave, but they wanted to stay and spend the night with each of their friends. I was concerned about leaving Miranda due to her diet, but eventually decided to let Micah and Miranda spend the night. As I was leaving I recall thinking: "Yes, Micah has Neurofibromatosis, and it will never touch him. No, they cannot find Miranda's problem, but I believe they will. What are You going to do God to reveal this thing?"

I had been home for about an hour when the phone rang. My friend said Miranda had an accident, and we needed to come. She was on a diving board at their house when she fell. The injury was serious, so after Kevin and I arrived at their home we took Miranda to the hospital. She had surgery during the night to repair her body. I was amazed at the grace of God on my life. I was completely peaceful through the entire ordeal. We went home from the hospital the next morning.

By Friday, I was beginning to wonder if Miranda was in a Cushing's cycle. She was still not spilling ketones, and she was oddly well. Her reaction to her injury was too good to be true. For some reason, she did not feel the pain a normal person would have felt from the trauma to her body. It was almost as if she was on a medication or something. I recall looking out our kitchen window and thinking, "Is this it?"

I decided if she was still not spilling ketones on Monday, I would take her urine. Monday, June 10, I called Dr. Endo #4's office and told them I would be taking her urine and turning it in on June 11, 2002. They said that was fine, so we tested. I was again amazed. For the first time, I truly did not care what the results were. I realized my trust was totally in God. I no longer felt Miranda's life was based on the doctors helping us. I truly believed God would make her whole, and it took the stress out of the testing.

On June 20, I received the call. Miranda's urine cortisol level was elevated. We now had our third high test. God had told me we would have our first confirming test by June 21, 2002. He was right!

CHAPTER 16

DOORS OPENED MIRACULOUSLY

After we received the high UFC on June 20, 2002, I was just sure this would bring it to an end. I was wrong.

Dr. Endo #4 contacted the NIH about Miranda's high cortisol test. Dr. Endo #2 told us to continue taking her urine. We would need three more high test to confirm a hormone imbalance, in other words, the doctors wanted six total abnormal tests, before they did anything. Miranda already had three, so we would need three more before medical intervention would occur. Honestly, I was peaceful with Dr. Endo #2's decision. I wanted God to prove to me beyond a shadow of a doubt Miranda needed the doctors' help before I consented. I had memories of our last visit to the NIH, and frankly, I did not want to go back unless it was the only way.

I went to visit my sister in Atlanta. At a church we attended, they prayed for Miranda. The pastor said he heard God saying, "No more opinions." I knew God was speaking to me, but I was not sure what he meant.

During September God dealt with me about fear. I went on a three-day fast. I knew I was afraid. God showed me how my fear hindered His ability to move. In my opinion, God should just heal Miranda without the doctors or the pain. While I was seeking Him, I realized due to my opinion, I was hindering Him and not submitted to His way completely. I thought I had been surrendered to God. But, when the door was opened again, I realized I was not wanting to go through this one. I wanted to get out! I surrendered in prayer. I asked God to help me let go of my ideas and truly trust His way. As part of aligning myself with God's plan, I was led to pray "Miranda's pituitary would reveal itself."

Miranda began going in and out of ketosis, which was really frustrating. Because, she would only stay negative for about 24 hours. By the time I knew she was out, it was too late to take her urine. After five weeks, I decided to take her urine. I turned in three urine collections even though she was spilling around 5 ketones during the test. I knew in my heart they would all be normal, but I wanted to just take them and be finished testing. All three tests came back normal. I struggled with my faith. I went to God in prayer, and let Him know I loved Him regardless of any miracle. I wanted to quit.

I let God know I was finished. I had done all I could do and nothing ever helped. Anyhow, I had always wanted God to just heal her, and now He would have to, because the doctors could not find the problem. God was not the least bit moved by my quitting. He kept me up all night on October 14, 2002. I kept telling Him I was finished, but He would not leave me alone. Around 3:00 a.m., I had a vision. Every time I said I was done, I saw dirt being flung by a shovel. Finally, I asked God what the vision meant, and He showed me. The dirt was being thrown on a casket, which was six feet in the ground. Then God spoke to me, "If you quit, she will die."

Around 7:00 a.m., I surrendered. I wrote Dr. Endo #4 a letter expressing my frustration in trying to catch her urine, while she was not spilling ketones for an accurate test. I asked him for one more urine order, and stated I would wait until she was negative during the entire test before I turned it in for results. Dr. Endo #4 faxed me the order, and I put it away.

Wednesday night, October 16, 2002, my pastor had an altar call for healing. I went down to receive prayer. When she laid her hands on me, I felt the presence of God surge through my body. I did not hear most of what she prayed, except she said, "Things are turning for you."

On Friday, November 15, 2002, God was dealing with my heart. I could hear, "It's been a year." I was not exactly sure what He meant, but I knew He was moving. Because I was spending so much time in worship and prayer, I was drawn to Jesus and enjoyed it. On Monday, November 18, I woke up with a really unsettled feeling. I had to leave the room where I was home-schooling the children, because I was so bothered. I went into the bathroom and cried. I asked God to end this walk with Miranda.

Miranda's ketones had been 160, which is the highest level, for about two weeks. That Monday night when I took her urine, her ketones were completely negative. I was shocked, but really gave it little thought. I just decided to wait to see what they would be on Tuesday.

I was bitten by the cleaning bug. I began cleaning my house from top to bottom. I cleaned light fixtures, windows, kitchen cabinets – you name it, and I cleaned it. Also, I decided to paint Micah's room. His room had not been painted for three and a half years. I was motivated. It seemed as if spring cleaning was in my heart.

I took a break Tuesday from painting and spent some time with God. During my worship and prayer time of about an hour, God instructed my heart. He told me we were in light. He said to trust Him regardless. He would make her whole. He was the Healer. He instructed me to go through.

Tuesday night, Miranda was negative. I was stunned. I really thought it would be like it had been where she went high and low. I called a close friend, and she reminded me I had decided I would take her urine when she was negative for 48 hours. So, I began a 24-hour urine collection on Wednesday. Miranda's ketones remained negative throughout the test. I was shocked. On Thursday morning, I came under a mental attack of fear. I was afraid to turn in the urine. I called a friend, and she prayed for me. I knew to go through. So, I turned in the urine. While I was at the hospital, I felt like I should ask for another urine jug. The lab does not give out jugs unless you have an order for a test. Even though I was nervous, I asked for a jug. The lab tech gave me two and was very nice about it. I felt the presence of God.

That night Miranda was still negative. On Friday, I called Dr. Endo #4 and let him know. I asked if he wanted me to take one more urine. His nurse called back and said, Dr. Endo #4 wants you to take two more urines. I knew God was in charge. I had two jugs and two more test orders. I turned in the last urine on Sunday, November 24. I had complete peace!

All tests came back normal, but I was still peaceful. I knew in my heart, God was ordering her steps. In December 2002, when all tests were confirmed negative, again I thought this time Dr. Endo #4 will quit. All the other doctors did when they could not get the test results they wanted. I was wrong! Not only did Dr. Endo #4 not quit, he told me to take her off the ketogenic diet. I received the phone call just before Christmas, and I was stunned. I did not want to take her off the diet. It was the only thing helping her. I knew if we stopped the diet, she would regress. I was instructed by the nurse to add one new food a week. I responded by telling the nurse, I would begin after the holidays were over.

January 2003, came quicker than I could imagine. I was not ready to take her off her diet. I did not want to take her off her diet until the root of her problem was exposed and removed. I wanted to keep my child safe. And as far as I could tell, the diet was the only thing in the natural world I could count on to help Miranda. I prayed and added back foods, which would not affect her as much, such as green beans. I continued to pray and every time I would get in the presence of God, He would instruct me to give her bread. My reaction was simple: "NO way!" I knew bread would make her swell up and react negatively in her body.

On January 21, 2003, I went to a prayer meeting at the church. At the end of the meeting an elder in our church asked me to get a vision of Miranda healthy in my head. So, I imagined her at Disney World holding ice cream and playing without any symptoms. In my heart, I wanted to take her to the "Not So Scary Halloween Party" this year and a have breakthrough. But I kept this desire to myself. During the prayer, I knew God was dealing with me about allowing Miranda to come off her diet. I cannot put into words how hard this was for me. Ultimately, it came down to the question: Whom do I trust? And the answer was "God," so I began to feed Miranda bread.

Christmas 2002 – before Miranda went off the diet

Immediately, Miranda's body began to react in a negative way. I contacted Dr. Endo #4's office with the results, and on my birthday February 10, 2003, they called me back. On the answering machine was a message to put Miranda on a gluten-free diet – another piece of the puzzle. I had never heard of gluten, but my spirit was excited. I studied and found out gluten is from wheat, oats, and barley, which causes Celiac Disease. Miranda did not appear to have any of the typical symptoms of Celiac, but the removal of gluten from her diet helped immensely. Also, while studying gluten, I found it was helpful for patients with pituitary or thyroid problems to avoid gluten. I knew God had revealed more truth to help Miranda.

In April 2003, we met with Dr. Endo #4. By this point, I wanted to put Miranda back on the protein diet. She was gaining weight and still struggling with other symptoms. Dr. Endo #4 strongly disagreed. He was adamant about Miranda not being on the protein diet. He wanted her on the gluten diet. I asked him how he came up with the gluten diet and his response, "It was a shot in the dark."

Also, Dr. Endo #4 said he did not believe Miranda had Cushing's. I was not even bothered. I had settled in my spirit God was responsible for proving His word, not me. If Miranda had Cushing's, God would have to prove it. Meanwhile, I had to daily enjoy my life and raise this child. A few of our close friends and I continued to pray over Miranda's pituitary revealing itself throughout the year. I had no thought processing as to how God would do it, only that He would.

April to September of 2003 were not the easiest months for me. Miranda continued to gain weight. She went from 78 pounds on our scales to 101. It was discouraging to watch her regress. Many of her symptoms were back. Almost daily, she struggled with headaches. I was peaceful in my heart, but as her mother watching her struggle I did not like the gluten-free diet. The ketogenic diet produced the results on the outside of her body which I could see, but the gluten diet produced results I did not want to see. I often said the ketogenic diet "caged the problem" and almost caused it to be a non-issue, except the diet was a daily walk of self-denial for a small child. I suppose the reason I allowed the gluten-free diet was because I was believing God to make Miranda whole, and if this was the way than I needed to trust Him over my current circumstances. God had instructed me to trust Dr. Endo #4. I simply had to obey.

In August 2003, the Holy Spirit moved in an amazing way in the sanctuary at church. I was so excited. I wanted to see our church explode and reach the people in the region, and this service was the first time I "saw" what I was believing God to do in our church. During the service, the Holy Spirit spoke to me, "Even as you see this movement beginning, they will 'see' the tumor."

I began to weep. I never thought they would see it. God had promised me, they would find it, but I never believed they would see it. At the NIH when God told me it would get darker, but no matter how dark it was, His light would shine, I assumed the doctors would never see the tumor on imaging. However, I did believe they would find it in surgery. So, the revelation of them actually seeing the tumor on imaging thrilled me. This would be a tremendous breakthrough for Miranda.

God kept dealing with me about an MRI. I kept praying Dr. Endo #4 would order one if it was time. But God kept dealing with me. So, finally on September 14, 2003, I sent a short letter by fax asking for an MRI. I was completely peaceful. I truly only wanted the MRI if it was going to show the tumor. So, I asked God to only have Dr. Endo #4 order the test if it would reveal the root of the problem. We were scheduled to go see Dr. Endo #4 on October 29, 2003, so I was not sure if he would respond to the letter or wait till the appointment to discuss it.

On Wednesday night at church, I had a vision. In the vision, large, white, feathery wings wrapped around me. I was completely covered. I saw something fall that landed on the wings and did not even touch me. And then the Holy Spirit spoke to me, "Do not be overwhelmed. The burden which is about to drop on you, is not yours. It is mine."

On Friday, September 19, Kevin told me to make plans to go to the Halloween party at Disney World. I called to get our tickets and make our hotel reservations. I was excited. All year I wanted to go and now it was official – we were going. We would go see Dr. Endo #4 on October 29, and leave for Disney on October 30, 2003.

Sunday morning, September 21, 2003, eight months after the prayer at the church meeting, God spoke to me in the church service saying, "You are in light. You will walk through the valley of the shadow of death and fear no evil."

I had another vision. In the vision, I saw my path where my feet were melted in the walkway. But this time the walkway opened, and I saw Miranda on her own path. I knew by this vision, God was simply reminding me every step is ordered. Miranda and I had our own paths.

Monday, September 22, 2003, I received a phone call at 3:00 p.m. in the afternoon. As soon as the phone rang, I knew it was good news. It was a nurse from Dr. Endo #4's office. She asked me where I wanted the MRI done, and then called back to tell me it was set for Friday, September 27, 2003.

I was so excited. I knew in my heart: "This is it!" They will find it. They will see it. This is Miranda's breakthrough! The excitement overtook me. I had never felt excited over an MRI. I had never believed they would see it. But this time was different. We had been praying for a year over Miranda's pituitary revealing itself, and in the last few weeks God had been dealing with me. This MRI was different. This MRI was ordered by the divine mandate of God. This MRI would be her turning point.

I praised God as if the MRI was already finished and the results revealed the root of the problem. I was in awe of the faith in me. I was determined in my spirit. I knew God would keep His promise, and it was her time.

Romans 4: 20-21

"Yet he did not waiver through unbelief regarding the promises of God, but was strengthened in his faith and gave glory to God, being fully persuaded that God had power to do what He promises." (NIV)

Isaiah 40: 31

"But hey that wait upon the Lord shall renew their strength; they shall mount up with wings as eagles; they shall run, and not be weary; and they shall walk, and not faint." (KJV)

I had waited. I had stood. I had not given up. This time was it. This time would reveal the truth. This time, God would come and rescue us. I knew it.

Well, I was wrong - dead wrong! The MRI came back normal. I was angry and frustrated. What was God doing and what was He thinking? A close friend encouraged me to not give up. I simply felt shock and anger again.

> ➢ This is added after the journey ended – the MRI taken on September 27, 2003, would eventually be read three years later by a neurosurgeon and reveal truth. It was on the MRI, just as God had said, but the people looking at the MRI did not know how to read it accurately. God did not lie, but it would be three long years before I found out.

Two days after receiving the MRI results, a door opened an opportunity for me to go on an Emmaus Walk, which was God for me. There, I could lay Micah and Miranda at the altar of God. The entire weekend seemed to be tailored for me. I am sure it was that way for all who went. God is faithful, and He loves us all the same.

I was especially touched by a testimony given by a mother who had to wait for 12 years to get her son diagnosed. I had never met anyone who had struggled like I had for a diagnosis. She and I had the chance to talk, and she greatly encouraged me to not give up.

Wednesday night during worship at church, God moved on my heart that things were about to begin for Miranda, and I needed to play praise and worship music. He impressed upon me to set my face like flint and be full of faith.

The next morning, October 9, 2003, I called a Boston Hospital just to ask a question. I was immediately put through to Dr. Endo #5, who took Miranda's case on the spot and gave her an appointment on October 17, 2003. I was shocked. God had quickly opened a door for her. October 9 had great significance in Miranda's life. She had been dedicated to God on October 9, nine years previous to that date. And, the phone call was made at 9:00 a.m. God opened a door for her. The number nine in the Bible means "divine intervention." October 17 was also significant for Miranda. We had sown a financial seed of $1,000 on October 17, 2000. I knew God had opened the door. Even the doctor told me it never happened this fast. Usually, there was a six-month waiting period. I love the number nine.

My dear friend, Miranda, and I went to Boston on October 16, 2003. We drove the entire distance and stayed with a wonderful family. They were a part of a medical program to house people who brought children to Boston for medical help. Before we left, several people gave us money to help pay for the travel, which was a blessing. God provided for everything.

I took praise and worship music with us and played it when I struggled with my faith. We were blessed during the entire trip. We met with the doctors, both Dr. Endo #5 and #6 on October 17, 2003. The second doctor, Dr. Endo #6, entered the room and said, "Does your daughter have Cushing's? Probably. Can we catch it? I don't know. Will we remove her pituitary? No, I don't think so."

Miranda in Boston

I was stunned at her candor. I was not ready to remove any part of Miranda's pituitary gland. I wanted more tests to confirm the diagnosis. The doctors were very kind. It was decided to test Miranda while we were there. They ordered lots of tests, but all tests were outpatient, which was a blessing. We would go to the hospital early in the morning for Miranda's medical tests and take the rest of the day to see Boston. We stayed a week.

While in Boston, I had a dream: We were camping at a beach on an island, which looked like Edisto Beach. Kevin, Micah, Miranda, and I were all together. Suddenly, a large wave began to cover the island. Then, I looked up and saw more waves. They were coming from all around the island. I grabbed a float and hung on for my life. Kevin, Micah, and I found each other and floated together until the storm stopped and the water receded. In the dream, I thought Miranda had died. But as the water receded, she was standing on the shore line with a woman behind her. The woman was wearing a white dress and looked angelic. Miranda was completely fine. It was as if I knew she was whole. The dream was odd, but I knew it was from God. Even more strange, two days after we were home from Boston, Miranda had the exact same dream. She came and told me. She had no idea about the dream I had. It was definitely God!

A few weeks later, I received a written report of the visit, which read they wanted to help "establish" the diagnosis. Boston requested the NIH reports from the year 2000. Within a few weeks of receiving the report, the Boston doctor emailed me saying, "They agreed with Dr. Endo #2 that Miranda may in fact have Intermittent Cushing's."

She said a lot of other things, but I was stunned to see the words as if it was a fact. I decided to not push it. I did not want anything else to happen. I wanted the entire ordeal to just go away. So, I did not respond to the email.

Several weeks later in a Wednesday night service God gave me a vision. I was sitting in a boat holding my oar. He told me to put the oar in the water and push the boat forward. He said, "Fear not, fear not, fear not, fear not." I just began to cry. I did not want to push the boat forward – I did not even know how. I asked my pastor to pray for me, which he did. He prayed the right tests would be ordered.

The next day, I contacted Boston and took Miranda to see her new pediatrician here in Tennessee. We had to change to another pediatrician who was already extremely familiar with Miranda and Micah's case, because she had treated them in the past. My friend who had been Miranda's pediatrician for the past three years was too busy and rarely saw us personally. She had joined another practice and was teaching at the local college. She had been a tremendous blessing and provided faith when mine was gone, but we now had needs she could not meet. I wanted a person who would see us every time and follow Miranda's case closely. I was very content with going back to this particular pediatrician, who was a Christian. The visit was extremely peaceful. At the office visit, we discussed possibly taking more urine tests, Miranda's heart pain, and rapid heart rate.

The new pediatrician was going to talk to the doctors in Boston and obtain an appointment for us to see a heart doctor. We saw the pediatric cardiologist in April 2004, who ordered a heart monitor for Miranda to wear for the next thirty days. They were testing Miranda for SVT. I was peaceful about the test, and it was easy.

The heart test came back with some problem, but ruled out SVT. The decision by the pediatrician as well as Boston was to wait and watch Miranda grow. I was not pleased with the idea of waiting, but honestly, I was tired of testing. So, I just agreed.

Also, the decision was made to send Miranda to yet another endocrinologist. This would be Miranda's 7th endocrine doctor. I was fine with it. By this point, I was numb to the doctors and their words. My trust was totally in God's ability to perform what He had promised, and His ability to solve this impossible situation.

We met with the new endocrine doctor two times in the year 2005. I liked him both times; but, I gave the visits little thought. I simply did what I had to do and went on living. I do remember he constantly told us to feed Miranda vegetable, which we did. I was so very tired of doctors telling us what to feed her. I was sick of doctors always believing food or Miranda over eating was the issue. I knew her diet was not the root of her problem, but I had come to the place where I simply listened and did not react. I knew it would be up to God to reveal the truth.

Also, my sister encouraged me to know the Word over the circumstances. My heart was greatly discouraged by the natural circumstances. It seemed impossible to get Miranda help. My sister had received a prophecy which stated, "God was an impossible problem solving God."

I hung on to those words!

CHAPTER 17

THE TWIST!

2 Kings 20:05
"I have heard your prayer, I have seen your tears: surely I will heal you." (NIV)

I was in the shower in the fall of 2003 when God spoke to me, "2005 will bring new life." I was excited. New life…that had to mean Miranda would get her miracle. It had to mean good things were coming. I called a close friend, and she said next year is 2004. I thought for a moment and said well at least it is on the way!

Throughout the year 2003, I would hear God tell me I was a very healthy woman. I was not surprised by these words. I never thought I was sick. Of course, I had dealt with the flu or normal viruses, but nothing I thought was serious. In December 2003, when God moved in my heart to begin "The Word Works" ministry, the timing stunned me. We were on our way home from Florida, and I was sitting in the back seat with Miranda. She was not feeling well and had a nosebleed. We passed the exit to Jekyll Island, and I recalled how God had instantly delivered me when I received prayer. While I was thinking, God instructed me it was time. I needed to step out in faith to begin my ministry.

I came home and prayed. First, I asked Kevin and his response stunned me as well. He said I should do it. The reason I was so surprised is Kevin still had issues with God about our children, and I was not sure our family was ready to step out. Whenever you "step out" for God adversity comes against you. I continued to pray. I went to my pastor, and he agreed I should begin. So, December 10, 2003, Donna Renfro Ministries was born. I prayed over every aspect and asked the people God would put in my heart to join me in having conferences. We set dates for 2004 and began to move forward. Although I had never birthed a ministry on my own, I had served my entire life in a church and was well aware of the adversity I would face.

Adversity was my best friend in the year 2004. As we moved forward with the ministry, I was attacked on every front. I continued and was relentless. I set my face like flint as God had trained me and went forward in love regardless of how any person or circumstance treated me. It was truly amazing. We began with pennies and managed to pay in cash for every conference and even went on the radio by March 2004, only three months into the ministry. Jealousy came at me through others as well as false accusations, but I held my tongue and continued to trust God to calm the hearts of others. We had a conference in March, and my expectations were high. I wanted lots of people to come. I was frustrated when our average per session was only 35-40 people. God had given me a big vision, and I thought it would happen overnight. God impressed upon my heart to believe Him to bring 200 people, so I did. My last meeting was on October 17, 2004, which was held at a Methodist Church, and I gave my personal testimony. The entire church was full, approximately 200 people. It was an incredible start for a baby ministry. We did four conferences, were on the radio weekly, and had a large meeting all in our first year. It was obvious God was blessing my obedience.

We received our federal approval for a non-profit organization the first time we applied, which I had heard was nearly impossible. With God, all things are possible! We received the confirmation on the date of our first conference. By October 2004, each person who had ill feelings towards the ministry had realized I was simply obeying God. They began to support me. I was blown away how very fast God had worked. His hand was on the ministry. We paid cash for everything and had no debt. He blessed what He had started.

The year 2004 proved to be difficult for me physically. In January 2004, I had sudden horrible pain in my right side. The pain was so bad I literally crawled on the floor to the bathroom. I found lots of blood and the pain would not ease. You would think I would have gone to the hospital, but instead I went to the couch to lay there. Not very intelligent, I know. But, honestly, I thought I was healthy, and it would just go away. Denial is a powerful tool.

The next day when I continued in such horrible pain, I went to the doctor. They ran a lot of tests on me, even a colonoscopy. The test showed nothing wrong. So, I just tolerated the pain. I had thought it might be my gallbladder, but the ultrasound did not show it to be a problem. The doctors did find kidney stones, but said they could not be the source of my pain; because, they were not moving. I refused further testing and went home. I figured it would heal and go away on its own. I justified my actions, because God had told me I was a healthy woman.

By June 2004, I began to realize I was having debilitating headaches more often. I had headaches my entire life, but they were getting worse. Also, at night I would stand up and sometimes my feet were numb. It was odd, but again, I did not give it much thought. I had been taking medication for my heart ever since 2000. My heart rate was extremely high and skipped beats, but I credited it to all the stress from dealing with the children. Whatever symptom came my way, I had a reason for it. Or, I simply ignored it. Truly, I gave it no place. I just kept going and doing what God had put before me.

In October 2004, I had a dream. I was standing in my kitchen, and I saw a storm headed towards my house. I was all alone. The storm took form, and I could tell it was a tornado. There was no time to react. The tornado picked up my house and twisted it around and set it back down on the foundation. I was horrified. When the storm passed, I ran outside and the sky was blue. I was terrified by the storm. I ran back inside to find my family. I could not find them. I ran to the walls to check the plumbing, and it was fine. I ran up the stairs to my bedroom, and the only things out of place were the pictures of my children's dedication outfits. In 1999, I had their dedication outfits reserved in shadow boxes, which hung at the end of my bed. I simply reached up to each one of them and fixed them by adjusting the way they were hanging on the wall. Then, I ran out of the bedroom and down the first flight of stairs. I opened the basement door with my right hand and ran down the second flight of stairs to the basement. When I landed in the basement the entire Body of Christ was there as well as every person I had ever known. It was odd, because during the storm I was alone, but in the basement of my house there were hundreds of people praying for me. Then God spoke; "Now it is time to pay off your house."

I woke up absolutely scared to death. I knew the dream was from God, and I was extremely concerned about whatever was headed toward my house. Of course, I thought it was going to be about Miranda, but Miranda was not in the dream. I was.

I went to church in the morning and was told by a friend about a woman I had prayed for seven years prior was pregnant. I had seen a vision where this woman held a baby girl. I knew she would have a little girl. When, I heard the word she was pregnant, I began to cry, not because she was getting her promise, but because I was so concerned about my dream. I struggled for two weeks and then settled it with God. I decided I would handle whatever this storm was like Jesus had handled storms. Jesus slept during the storm. I told God I would trust him totally concerning whatever was coming my way.

Donna weeks before the car accident

I must interject here in my worst nightmares I could not have imagined what lay ahead for my family and me. December 23, 2004, I went to the post office to check on the ministry mail, and we had received some financial gifts. I was so thankful. I was thanking God for all He had done in such a short period of time. I was overwhelmed with how fast He had begun and built the ministry as well as bringing such faithful people along side of me to carry the gospel. I was in amazement. I pulled out from the post office to go to the grocery store. It was two days before Christmas, and I needed to get groceries for the big breakfast we do at our house Christmas morning with our family. I was sitting at a red light in the far-right lane. In Tennessee, right on red is okay, so I was looking to see if any cars were coming. My neck was twisted as far to the left as it would go. Suddenly, horrid pain rushed through my neck and shoulders all the way down to my hands. I did not know what had happened. I began to cry and instantly I knew to go to the hospital. At that point, a very nice man approached my window and said, "Are you okay?"

I was still crying and feeling horrible pain in my neck. I asked what had happened, and he said he had rear-ended my car. He was so kind and very apologetic. I stepped out of the car and looked at the back. There were only a couple of scratches on my bumper. His car had more damage to the front, but not too severe. A police officer saw the accident and had us pull into an empty parking lot. By this point my neck was beginning to feel numb. Even though I had felt such horrible pain, I decided to not go to the hospital. I wanted to get the groceries. All I could think about was Christmas for my kids. The officer took our information, and we left the scene. I did not listen to God and go to the hospital. I should have, but I thought I needed to go and get the groceries. This decision would prove to be wrong.

As the day progressed, I became worse by the hour. I had unbelievable pain and my hands were going numb. I still refused to pay attention to my body, even though it clearly needed help. I went on to bed. When I woke up on Christmas Eve, I prayed in the shower and asked God to please not let today be about my neck. I wanted my children to enjoy Christmas Eve. I was unable to turn my head, but managed to sit through Christmas Eve morning at my parents and endure Christmas Eve night at Kevin's parents. By the time we arrived home, I was scared. It was becoming increasingly more difficult for me to breathe. I felt like I was suffocating. I called a nurse service, and she said to go directly to the emergency room. So, Kevin took the kids to his parents, and we went to the hospital. They ran several tests and found no broken bones. The doctor did say she thought I had bulging discs. She sent us home with a pain medication and muscle relaxer. We did not get home until late. Kevin picked up the kids and put them in bed. Christmas morning was difficult. I was in a great deal of pain even on the medications. The nightmare was just beginning. It is difficult to even recall the year 2005 for me. Words simply will not be able to infuse into anyone how horrible, excruciatingly painful, and scary it was to go from being a full functioning individual to bed ridden in relentless pain. I hope as I write you will grasp the depth of the nightmare and intense horror of the walk.

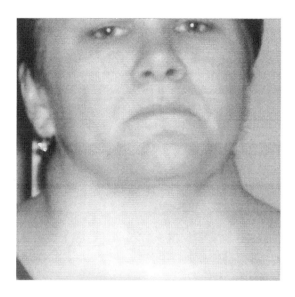

Donna's pain is evident days after the accident

Within days of the wreck, it was evident I was not okay. The pain levels continued to elevate and my hands were numb more often than not. My doctor ordered a CAT scan to see if anything else would show up, and it did not. So, he told me to take the pain medication and muscle relaxers. He thought with time I would simply heal. Whiplash is painful, but will heal. The pain grew worse, and I went back to my doctor within a couple of days. I told him I could not feel my hands and the pain was getting worse. He told me it was probably an emotional response, because I had been through a trauma. His response brought out anger in me. It was not an emotional response. I could not feel my hands. I argued with him, and he ordered an MRI and an EMG. I left the office frustrated and angry. I was so tired of doctors thinking things were in my head! I had trusted my doctor for years. He is a great man and proved to be my advocate all year, but he hit a painful place in my heart when he suggested my hands going numb was due to an emotional reaction. I knew I could not feel my hands. I had been accused so many times with my children this time it was the last straw. I prayed over my doctor and asked God to show him it was not emotional. God clearly spoke to me, "I will."

I had a wonderful doctor! He was an internist, who had been my primary doctor for five years when the car wreck happened. So, he knew me and the situation concerning my children. He was a Christian and proved to take great care of me through the entire nightmare. No human could have known what my body was about to do. My doctor was led of God at every turn no matter how horrible or impossible the situation. He was a blessing.

While we were waiting for the MRI dates, my doctor sent me to a physical therapist. I went to a chiropractor too. The physical therapist knew something was terribly wrong with me, and he expressed it every time I went in to see him. The chiropractor was a Christian, and he told me something I would keep in my heart throughout the entire journey. He said healing will take, "God, time, and patience!"

During this time of extreme suffering God would continually tell me, "Donna you will be better at the end of this than you were going into it. And, be thankful you are not paralyzed." The MRI was extremely painful for me. The MRI machine vibrates and the vibration sent my body into unexplainable horrid pain. I lost feeling in my entire right arm during the testing. I had peace in my heart, but constant pain in my body. During the night, I slept little because of all the pain. I was on painkillers, but they did not help. The medications made me sluggish and not myself, but did not take the pain away. During the night while I was up I would pray. The day before I received the MRI results God spoke to me. He said, "You will need a neurosurgeon, Dr. Neuro #1." God gave me the specific name of a doctor without me knowing him prior to the accident. Yes, here we go again with lists of doctors! Buckle up – it is about to get very interesting.

I wrote down what God had said and thought nothing of it. I simply thought I had bulging discs like the emergency room doctor had suggested. My doctor called the very next morning and said, "Donna, you have a cyst in your neck, and I am sending you to see Dr. Neuro #1 as soon as possible." Amazingly, Dr. Neuro #1 was the exact doctor God had told me to go and see. I hung up the phone and was in shock. What kind of cyst? What could the problem be? My mother came over to take me to physical therapy and the chiropractor. I was crying, and we prayed together. I decided to stop the physical therapy and chiropractor treatments until someone knew exactly what was wrong with me. It was strong in my heart for no one to touch my neck. I had to wait for a week to get into to see Dr. Neuro #1. It seemed like eternity. When you are being sent to a neurosurgeon, you do not want to wait.

Before I saw the neurosurgeon, I had the EMG test. A neurologist performed the test. It is a painful test where the doctor sends electricity through your arms, shoulders, and neck to see if you have nerve damage. They jab a needle into your nerves and move it around to see the extent of any nerve damage. My Mom took me and sat in the corner of the room. She had a look of horror on her face as she watched this doctor torture me. I was already in so much pain. The test just magnified it. At the end of the test, the doctor concluded I had carpal tunnel in my right hand. I thought she was wrong. How could I have carpal tunnel? I had never had any problems prior to the wreck. She said my neck was not the source of my pain. At that point, I simply thought she was wrong and dismissed her diagnoses as well as her opinion. My neck was swollen and had to be the root of the pain in my opinion.

The day finally arrived to see the neurosurgeon, and I thought they would do surgery on me that afternoon. I was in so much pain and unable to tolerate another day of the intensity. I was just sure they would help me immediately. Kevin, Mom, Dad, and best friend all went with me to the doctor's office. Kevin and I went back to the treatment room. We did not even see Dr. Neuro #1. Instead, we saw a physician's assistant. Apparently, it is normal for the first visit to not see the doctor. He looked at my MRI and walked into the room. He was very calm and seemed kind. He told me I had four bulging discs and a syrinx in my spinal cord. I had never heard the word syrinx. So, we asked him to spell it for us. He said I had a bad case of whiplash, and I needed to go home and lay still till March 2005. He did not offer any other help. I was devastated. The pain in my body was unbearable. Now, I had to go home and lie still for months. It seemed so insane to me. Why would they not help me? Kevin, my parents, and friend were as shocked as I was. I recall walking up the stairs to my bedroom when we arrived home and hearing God speak. He said, "Just be patient."

I cannot even describe the next few weeks of my life except to say torture looked good to me. Pain shot throughout my body like bolts of electricity while I had constant pain in my neck. All my right side neck muscles were torn and had to heal while my nerves were damaged. The medications made it difficult to have bowel movements, and I had to literally crawl on the floor to get to the bathroom. My body was ravaged with pain from my head to my toes. I was bed ridden and desperate. Nothing took the pain away day or night. I would listen to worship music, and it would help my body relax. But, nothing stopped the pain. My eyesight would come go, and my ability to hear was less every day.

My bedroom quickly became like a hospital room with medications and special neck pillows to support my body. I thought about how God had told me to just be patient. So, I decided to look up the word patient. I always thought it meant to wait, but it means much more. To be patient is to endure all the pain without complaining. Honestly, I thought that was a lot to ask of me.

We met with the neurosurgeon again in March, and it was evident to me I was not improving. If it was whiplash, I should be improving. I made such a scene in the doctor's office the physician's assistant went and found Dr. Neuro #1. He came in the room. I had studied about the syrinx and had even sent my MRI to the National Institute of Health for another opinion. Both Dr. Neuro #1 and the NIH agreed to do nothing about the syrinx, and I did not have Chiari. Chiari is a brain malformation, which can cause a syrinx in the spinal cord. Dr. Neuro #1 said he wanted me to see a pain specialist and keep a close eye on my case. So, he sent me to a pain specialist in his office. I saw the pain specialist within a couple of days, and he suggested trigger point injections in my back. I agreed. I would have agreed to allow them to cut my head off. The pain in my body was relentless. The specialist did the injections in the office, and I went home. Within hours I was in worse pain, which continued to grow worse by the hour. I literally thought I would die. I went back to the office and the specialist was surprised. He had never seen a reaction like mine. He gave me stronger pain medications. Also, he ordered another MRI and EMG test for me to endure again. I simply felt desperate. I agreed to anything they asked of me. The pain specialist lifted my head and looked in my eyes. He said, "Donna, give the syrinx no place, you will get better!" I wanted my life back.

Every day, all twenty-four hours of the day, I suffered without relief. My neck was swollen, and my body ravaged with pain – pain I cannot put into words. My personality was altered because of the pain and medications. I was miserable without a break. I wanted to be well again. I would think about the dream God had given me and focus on the fact at the end of the dream I was okay.

Even though my body was in pain, I went ahead with a scheduled conference in March 2005. Foolish, I know, but I felt I had to do it. I taught "Just Be Patient." The conference was for me. It was God preparing me for the year ahead. I recall a man from my church sitting beside me between sessions, and he said over and over in his heart all he could hear was, "and it came to pass." In other words, whatever we would go through would pass. It was only temporary.

April came and it appeared as if I was getting better. I recall on April 17, 2005, I did not have to take a pain pill. I thought the entire nightmare was over. I lay on my bed praising God I had endured, and my life was coming back. He spoke clearly to me, "Donna, you will always go the hard way, but you will always overcome!"

Those words might have bothered someone else, but not me. I saw the good. I heard the fact I would always overcome. Life presents pain for all. No one is exempt. I had the knowledge no matter what came my way, I would overcome.

To me it was a blessing.

Also, in April, I kept sensing something was headed our way in the fall. I prayed often. It was as if I saw a semi-truck headed to our house. I prayed it would be over before we even knew what had happened. I was also led to pray it would end with me before it began with Miranda. I had no idea what my future would hold. But, I trusted God held my future.

Just a couple of days later, I developed a cough. In my heart, I knew it was not good. Believe me, you do not want to cough when you have a neck injury. I called my doctor, and he called me in a prescription. A horrid headache quickly followed. I was up in the night vomiting. I knew I needed to go to the hospital. I woke Kevin up, and he suggested I take medication. I continued to vomit. I called my friend, and she suggested the medication. But, my heart knew I needed to go to the hospital. I woke Kevin up again, and he took me. We were not even thinking clearly. We left the kids in the bed and went to the emergency room around 3:00 a.m. We lived next door to my Mom and Dad; so, the kids were safe. The drive to the hospital is only three miles, and Kevin had to stop several times for me to vomit on the way. The horrid pain in my head was without words. I was admitted immediately. As morning approached, we called my Mom to get the kids, and a friend came to help me.

It is difficult for me to recall the week. I was medicated severely due to the intense pain. I do recall pulling my hair out and literally digging holes in my head, trying to relieve the pain I was enduring. The vomiting would not cease regardless of their medications. I was tested for everything and the only thing which showed up was my gallbladder. Also, I was told I had cirrhosis of the liver, which considering I did not drink alcohol was odd. But, there was confusion concerning what exactly was the root of the problem, and if it would even benefit me to remove my gallbladder. Finally, on Friday, I was dismissed from the hospital. I was still very sick, but left anyway.

Friday night late Kevin ended up taking me back to the hospital. While we were sitting in the waiting area I heard God say, "Right time, right place, and right people."

Then, I was taken into the emergency room and was immediately signed up for gallbladder surgery that afternoon. So, they removed my gallbladder, and I thought I would get better. I went home the next day and did not recover well. It became difficult to walk. I did not mention it to the doctors, because I thought it was simply my body was so weak from the traumas I had endured. Gallbladder surgery is usually an easy recovery, but my body did not bounce back.

I went ahead and met with Dr. Neuro #1 again about my right hand. I decided to go ahead with the carpal tunnel release surgery in June 2005. I was not able to use my right arm much since the car wreck and by that point I thought maybe the neurologist was right. So, I had carpal tunnel surgery. But, instead of improving the opposite happened. I became worse. My right hand pain increased severely, and my ability to use my right arm went to almost zero. Still, I thought with time my right hand would just heal. Two weeks out of the carpal tunnel surgery, the nurse was removing my stitches and said I would need to come back in four weeks for follow-up. At that moment in time, it hit me. It was not over! Something else was lurking around the corner. I felt sick to my stomach. I was scared. I left the office feeling in shock.

Six weeks out of surgery, I met with another physician's assistant at Dr. Neuro #1's office. He was shocked at my inability to use my right hand. My right hand had drawn up and basically had become paralyzed. He went out to look at my MRI's, and I could hear him arguing with the pain specialist about my syrinx and the location of it. Apparently, it was located in a place in my neck where the ulnar nerve is connected. He was saying the ulnar nerve was damaging my arms. I sat inside the room alone and scared. I knew in my heart it was not over, but what was I going to face. What else could possibly happen?

CHAPTER 18

HORROR BEYOND HORROR

After leaving the neurosurgeon's office, again I felt shock. I knew deep in my heart it was not over, but what else could possibly go wrong?

During the entire month of June 2005, the car insurance company which represented the man who hit my car, and began the nightmare for me, said they would settle with me for the entire policy limit. His personal limit was only $25,000. I agreed to settle even though at the time my medical bills were already over $55,000. I did not want to get a lawyer, nor did I want to sue. I simply wanted the entire ordeal to just go away. I wanted it over and settled. I wanted my life back. Money had never motivated me. I simply wanted my bills paid and my life back.

Just after I found out about the ulnar nerve being pressed on by my syrinx, I received a call from the auto insurance company. They offered me $1,000 for pain and suffering as well as refused to pay my medical bills. Of course, this offer was given after they had already agreed to settle for the entire policy limit of $25,000. They reversed their original decision and gave me no reason why. Just when you think it is over or cannot get any worse, it does!

I was again in shock, and just kept saying over and over to the representative I could not believe what I was hearing. She told me I could talk to anyone in the company, but the decision would stand. I was hurt, angry, and frustrated by the entire ordeal. The pain in my body was enough to deal with in my mind – I should not have to deal with all the medical bills and insurance companies. Due to the fact, my personal health insurance wanted to be reimbursed for the money they had paid on my behalf since it was an accident, I was caught in the middle and tried to settle. But, the insurance companies would not settle, so I was forced to get a lawyer.

Getting a lawyer was one of the hardest things I did. I did not believe in suing, especially as a Christian. Before I hired the lawyer, I called every supervisor in the car insurance company. I spoke with the man who hit me and told him what his insurance company was doing to me. He said he would help, but the next day called and told me he was instructed by his insurance company not to talk to me again. I was devastated. I could not get the insurance companies to just settle and could not believe this part of the nightmare was so very difficult. It should have been the easiest part. My bills clearly passed his insurance limit, and I was willing to settle for the limit, but no one else would. So, I prayed and Kevin obtained the name of a lawyer. I went to see him and handed him my case. My case was probably the easiest case he ever received. I had kept excellent records, pictures, every bill, and pain diaries. Now, once again we would be robbed. The accident had robbed my physical body, my relationships with family and friends, my time, our money, my children did not have their mother, I had no life at all except to lay in a bed suffering in extreme pain, and now we would have to pay a lawyer as well as spend time dealing with the entire lawsuit issue. I cried and prayed. I studied in the Bible to find answers and realized taking a matter before the judge was done all the time. It changed my thinking. Suing is not ungodly; sometimes, it is the only way to settle a matter. I did give my word to the man who hit my car I would not come after him personally. We would settle for the insurance policy.

The money part of the entire ordeal was as difficult as the physical part. All year I had to borrow from Peter to pay Paul. We took out a second mortgage and opened credit cards, which we did not have prior to the accident. Our debt soared and increased which meant instead of getting out of debt any time soon as God had promised us, our debt was increasing. Every day we would receive bills and insurance information. This pressure took its toll on my body, mind, and soul. I was desperate for it to end. Yet, no end was in sight.

In September 2005, I went to hand therapy. I had the most wonderful therapist. It was evident to her something bad was wrong with my hand. During the three weeks that I went to therapy, my health went drastically downhill. My left hand began to draw up as well. Her advice to me was surgery. She said it was obvious I was going downhill and fast. I recall the day well, because I was no longer driving, a friend had dropped me off for physical therapy. I had to wait for her to pick me up. I recall leaning against the brick building outside and crying. I kept thinking, "Oh, my God! What is wrong with me?" I knew I needed a miracle. Even Miranda's life-threatening problems had to be "shelved" while I was fighting for my life. Miranda continued with severe symptoms and even gained a new one. Her big toe on her left foot had multiple black spots, but we simply could not deal with it yet.

I went back to Dr. Neuro #1 and expected he would do surgery immediately, but I was wrong. He decided he wanted a second opinion. Again, I was shocked. My hands were drawn up, my ears had a ringing sound, making it very difficult to hear, my eyesight would come and go, and other motor skills were deteriorating daily. Why would he wait? In my heart, I knew to follow his instructions, but it made no sense. Logic appeared to be, the sooner they operated on my spinal cord the better my chances would be, but logic did not prevail. I was sent to a neurologist to have several painful tests. I had more

EMG's and two SSEP tests. Both of these tests are painful and require the patient to be electrocuted. During the SSEP test, I had to lay completely still for twenty minutes per each leg and arm while the test sent electric shocks through my body from my head to my leg or arm, depending on which limb they were testing. The test did reveal the syrinx was "catching" in my spinal cord. When I left the hospital after the SSEP test, I could not walk. By this point, I was walking with a cane daily, but this test put me in so much pain I was simply unable to walk at all. This was my first ride in a wheelchair.

I went back to Dr. Neuro #1, and he was still not satisfied with the second opinion. We were all in shock. What else could it be if the syrinx was not the problem? My husband suggested to Dr. Neuro #1 that they should check my brain, but Dr. Neuro #1 wanted another neurosurgeon to check me out. My body was rapidly deteriorating, so I needed fast answers. We left the office in shock, but had plans to go to Florida that afternoon. Our children's best friends were moving to Florida for the winter, and they had invited Micah and Miranda to come down with them as they went. Kevin and I agreed to let them go. So, they had left for Florida, and now we had to go pick them up. Therefore, we left Dr. Neuro #1's office and headed down the road to Florida to pick up Micah and Miranda.

Two hours into the trip, I received a call from Dr. Neuro #1's office saying I was booked to see a neurosurgeon in Memphis, Tennessee, on Monday. Even though it was Thursday afternoon when the receptionist asked me if I could make the appointment, I said, "Yes." I hung up and felt panic. How was I going to get from Florida to Memphis? I was wheelchair bound and had difficulty doing anything for myself. By this point, I had to eat with plastic forks and spoons, because regular silverware was simply too heavy for me to lift. I called a friend who said she would take me to Memphis once we returned home and not to worry. She said she would work it all out. Kevin and I continued our trip to Florida.

Friday, while in Florida, I received a phone call from the Chiari doctors in New York. I had filled out papers to go and be evaluated online back in January right after the car wreck, but really did not expect anything to come of it. I had retrieved their information on the internet when I researched about the syrinx. Chiari causes most syrinxes, but every neurosurgeon had told me I did not have Chiari Brain Malformation, so I had let it go. Anyhow, I received a call stating they could see me in December. I told the receptionist I was going to Memphis instead, but I appreciated their offer. I did not give it another thought.

We picked the children up in Florida and headed home on Sunday. When I pulled into the house after 10 long hours in a car, my parents were in the house.

My Dad helped me fill out the paper work for social security disability before I left for Memphis. Needless to say, it was all overwhelming. I climbed into a car with my friend, and we traveled another five hours towards Memphis. My body was in great pain, but I had no choice except to breathe in and out to endure the ride. The next morning, we woke up early to drive the additional hours to Memphis. We arrived in time for my appointment. We met with the new neurosurgeon, and the encounter was a nightmare! The man came into the room and checked out my body. He left and was gone for a while. When he returned, he was cold and distant. He told me to go back home and have an MRI. He also suggested I go on anti-depressant medication. Again, shock filled my head. All I could say was, "You think I am depressed?"

I clearly angered this neurosurgeon as he responded with contempt for my question. He went on to say if I was not depressed I should be, because I was going to die. I just sat there in disbelief. He was not going to help me. He did not offer anything except another medication, and took what little hope I had away. I was going blind, deaf, and paralyzed extremely fast. It was as if someone hit me with a stun gun. I was unable to talk or even process words through my brain. I was barely able to breathe. My friend took me out of the office in my wheelchair, and we returned to the hotel. We were both devastated, so we sat on the beds and ate chocolate. When all else fails, eat chocolate!

After completely eating an entire bag of chocolate covered turtles, I began to talk. My dear friend simply listened. I was beginning to think maybe this was my "new life." After all, God had told me 2005 would bring new life. I just thought it would be a good thing. I was beginning to think I was wrong. I even suggested maybe this neurosurgeon was right, and I was just going to die. With great authority in her voice, my friend declared, "No way, that is not how this story is going to end!" God gave this precious friend to me to walk through the valley of the shadow of death and keep me sane.

After our chocolate, we went to a local clearance store and bought bathing suits, because the hotel had a jacuzzi and I was cold. I thought sitting in the tub of hot water would help my body. We bought the bathing suits for $2.00 and they were laughable, to say the least; but, we needed to laugh. The day had proven to be a nightmare, and we needed to let it go. Anyhow, we went back to the hotel and put on our suits. We went to the jacuzzi, and the water was not even hot; it was barely warm, which was a perfect ending to a horrible day. We began to laugh and just make fun of the entire ordeal. Laughter is good medicine – in my opinion, much better than anti-depressants.

The next morning, we were leaving and my friend wanted to stop at a grocery store. While she was in the store, the Holy Spirit reminded me of the

Chiari doctors and told me to call. I thought how can I call them, I do not have their number, and then I remembered the receptionist had called my cell phone, so it was in my caller ID. I simply called the number, and a woman answered. She told me they just had an opening come up for October 21 and 24, 2005, so she asked, "Could you be here in ten days?" I said, "Yes!"

We confirmed the plans and when my friend came out of the grocery store, I was now headed to New York for help. Within less than 24 hours God had opened another door. Hope was not over yet. But what lay ahead was definitely uncertainty.

We drove home from Memphis and began to plan a trip to New York. Kevin and I had no money. The entire year had been a terrible financial drain with no end in sight. I simply prayed and gave it to God. I was in so much pain and unable to do anything about the situation except trust God. I consumed my time listening to praise music. The music eased my physical pain and increased my spiritual strength.

I knew New York was going to bring answers from God, but I had a lot of concerns. These specialists were not on our PPO for our medical insurance. In other words, they were out-of-network; therefore, Kevin and I would have to pay the bills. However, every part of me knew New York was the right place to go.

Back in January, February, and March, I would lay in the bed and think of things I wanted to do when I was well. Things I had wanted, but never had or done. One of the things was to go to New York, which was an odd desire, because prior to the car wreck I never wanted to go to New York. The other thing I wanted to do was see a Broadway play. Because of all my pain and suffering, I would daydream about receiving a huge settlement from the car wreck insurance. I thought people injured in car wrecks were compensated for all the medical bills, pain, and suffering – I was wrong. In my day dreams, Kevin would take me to New York. He was dressed in a suit, and I was dressed in a beautiful dress. We went to a jewelry store and picked out a beautiful marquee ring, ate dinner, and ended the perfect day with a Broadway play. I had always wanted a marquee diamond ring. I thought we would have plenty of money to pay our debts off and see New York City. Plus, buy me the diamond of my dreams. Obviously, I was wrong. Not only would we not receive a fair financial settlement; we were drowning in debt worse than ever. My dreams appeared to be destroyed.

My reality was horrid. I was growing worse daily. I had difficulty speaking, seeing, and hearing. I was in a wheelchair or confined to a bed. I had little to no use of both hands and no answers from any doctor. My prognosis was grim to say the least!

My dear friend and I left for New York. On October 21, 2005, I was tested at their diagnostic center. They ran a battery of tests on me. Tests I had not had prior. They ran a CINE MRI, which gave them a much better assessment of my condition. They did x-rays, CAT scans, and other tests. I handled the testing okay. I was in pain, but pain was my constant companion throughout the year. Pain was my new normal.

God miraculously provided the money for the trip. He moved on the hearts of several different people to give to me. God opened a door for us to go and see a Broadway play. I was excited and thrilled. In my dreams about seeing a play, I was dressed up, and it was all romantic. The reality was quite different. I was in a wheelchair, and I had to wear lounge wear. Because, I was unable to button clothing. We did get great seats, because I was able to sit in the handicap area. Imagine that, sitting in the handicap area when just months prior I was completely fine. This was not exactly how I thought it would go, but nonetheless God gave me the desire of my heart and allowed me to see a play. Things just were not the way I imagined them at all. However, the experience was blessed, and holds a very special memory for me in my heart.

On Monday, October 24, 2005, the bomb finally dropped. First, I met with a young woman who took my medical history. Then, I met with the neurologist. Finally, I met with Dr. Neuro #3 – he was my third neurosurgeon. He told me a lot. I had multiple diagnoses. He said I had Syringomyelia, Chiari 1 Brain Malformation, ligamentous injury, retroflexed ondontoid with pannus formation, flattened pituitary, low-lying tonsils, decreased posterior cerebrospinal fluid flow and anterior cerebrospinal fluid flow, just to mention a few.

Dr. Neuro #3 went on to tell my friend and me about a surgery, which could help me. There would be two parts. Part one would consist of the doctors placing rods in my head and pulling my head up with weights. I would remain conscious; so, I could communicate if the stretching of my neck was helping me. I would be in this traction for 48 hours prior to the next surgery. The second surgery would consist of the doctors taking rods and attaching them to my skull and down my vertebrae to support my neck. The car wreck had ripped out all my ligaments; so, my head had no support. The rods would need to be on both sides of my head and down both sides of my spine. The doctors would literally screw the rods to my C2, 3, 4 and 5 vertebrae. The rods would permanently hold my head up, but I would lose the mobility of my neck forever. Also, while in the second surgery they would cut out a section of my skull and shave off the bottom of my brain. The skull would then be replaced with a metal plate.

He explained why I felt like I was suffocating all year. The bone, which your head pivots on, was bent in my body. When the car wreck happened, my retroflexed ondontoid was pushed into my throat. With the surgeries they offered, my bone would be pulled to a different place in my neck, and I would be able to breathe better.

Truly, as Dr. Neuro #3 spoke I was not alert or aware. I was in horrid pain. I had a headache and was almost completely blind. It was also difficult to hear him. My dear friend asked a lot of questions. I only asked one. Simply, I asked Dr. Neuro #3 if he could fix me. He replied, "Yes!" He also said, "Donna, you are a very sick woman!"

Dr. Neuro #3 went on to tell us I would be the 111th person to have this procedure done in New York with this Chiari doctor, and only two people had not done well with the procedure. Dr. Neuro #3 then hugged me. When he pulled back, I saw the tears in his eyes. He was an incredible man. He had the best spirit about him, which made me feel safe. Finally, someone was going to help me, and someone knew what to do. Finally, I had answers!

As Dr. Neuro #3 left the room, he turned to me and made the strangest comment. He said, "Merry Christmas!" This comment was embedded in my mind from the moment I heard it. I knew there was significance to it, but not exactly what.

As soon as we left the office, I called Kevin. He was upset. I then called my pastor. He too seemed bothered. I called my parents, and then talked with my sister. Everyone seemed upset about the information. I, however, was not. I did not see the bad. I saw hope for the first time. I saw help for the first time. I was not in denial. I knew I would suffer and surgery would be painful, but finally there was help. In my heart, I knew I needed a miracle. Now, I knew I would get it. Not because of a doctor, but because God had revealed the root of the problem. Hosea 4:6, *"My people are destroyed for lack of knowledge."* (KJV) I would no longer perish, because these men had knowledge and could help me.

God had begun preparing me at least a decade before the storm. But I had spent the entire year in the bed listening to praise and praying. I was walking closer to God than ever before. I knew His leading, and I knew this was my way out. I also knew I could do whatever it would require of me. I was determined to be well! I was determined to live! I was determined to testify!

My friend and I left early the next morning and drove all the way home. I was in pain and not doing well at all physically. I was trying to comprehend what had been explained to me by Dr. Neuro #3. The ride was long and it rained the entire way, which was fitting considering the personal storm I was enduring. Once I was home, I received a call, and the dates for surgery were set for January 21, and 23, 2006. I was devastated. I did not want this nightmare to go into 2006. I recall laying my head on my desk and crying. I was desperate. I did not want to wait. It was difficult to survive in my body much less think about what the doctors were going to do to me. As I was crying God spoke to me, "Donna, it will be okay."

I thought, "No, it won't! It is not okay. I am not okay. This is not okay." Over and over God comforted me until finally I worked through my disappointment and decided God was in control. My steps were ordered. If January was when I was to have surgery, then I would simply wait.

My body grew worse daily. In November 2005, I was having a very bad day. A friend came over to pick the children and me up to come to her house. My heart was racing out of control, my legs would not work, my hearing was almost gone, and my sight was extremely dim. When we reached her house, I waited until the children stepped out of the van and told her I needed to go to the emergency room. The pain in my body was too great to endure. I needed help and fast. She made sure the kids were fine and took me to the emergency room. I told her on the way not to let them admit me. I only wanted them to help me get through the pain. The pain caused my blood pressure to be sky high and make my heart race. I was dizzy and not completely conscious of my surroundings. We called Kevin to meet us at the hospital. She explained to the emergency room doctor my diagnoses and surgery was planned, but I needed immediate help. The doctor had such compassion for me. The emergency doctor kept me for several hours and administered pain medications through an I.V. I have no memory of leaving the hospital, but Kevin said he had to carry me out. It was that day – I realized I would not live until January.

I would be dead if they waited until January 2006, to operate on me. My body was shutting down and fast. It was not able to take much more. In my heart, I knew I needed miraculous intervention.

Two days later, I was on my bed praying and asking God what to do. I knew immediately to email Dr. Neuro #3, and let him know what was going on with my body. Kevin emailed him for me, and he immediately emailed me back. He said his assistant would call me and set up another date. The next day I received a call and surgery was set for December 14, 2005, and December 16, 2005. I agreed with the dates, but was not satisfied at all. These dates would mean I would miss Christmas with my kids; yet, another sacrifice for my family and myself. I had no choice, but to accept the dates. Death would be the only other option.

I cried, prayed, and begged God to move the dates earlier, but they did not budge. I was bothered and frustrated, but was simply left with no options. Once again, I submitted my will and embraced my reality. We decided to celebrate Christmas on December 3, 2005 at my house, because per to the surgery schedule I would not be back in town until at least January 3, 2006.

My sister was led of God to do a fundraiser for my medical expenses. I was not too happy about the whole idea. Does anyone ever want to be the picture on the glass jar sitting inside the local gas station asking for donations? I certainly did not want to be the poster child for all diseases hosted in my body, nor did I want my church, family, friends, much less the entire world to know about the horrid situation we were facing. I wanted the whole thing to simply disappear. I wanted to wake up from my nightmare, but instead found myself slipping farther downhill and farther into debt every day.

My parents, pastors, and friends all thought the fundraiser was a God idea. I did not! I struggled and made my frustrations known. I did not want to be where I was. My parents and I fought over the entire ordeal. My Dad was the one who finally reached me. He began to cry, and it broke my heart. He said there was nothing else he could do to help me. He just wanted to help, and I would not let him. I heard his heart cry and agreed to the fundraiser, but was still bothered. I am sure it boiled down to pride. God was continually peeling back layers of my heart. It is extremely humbling to receive help, whether it is money, food, assistance in walking, being driven from place to place, or a variety of other things. I had gone from a completely independent woman to a completely dependent woman in less than a year. I had lost my dignity, and this was just another level of letting go and asking for help.

My family sent out letters requesting help, and money came quickly. People were eager to help us. My Dad was humbled by the entire ordeal as well. He handled the finances, and the burden of the medical bills began to lift. I would simply give him the bills, and he would pay them. As hard as I fought against it, truly, it was a blessing. Kevin and I needed the help.

I do not have much memory of the last emergency room visit until December 3, 2005. On December 3, 2005, we celebrated Christmas at our house, because Kevin and I would have to leave on December 9, 2005, to go to New York for the surgeries. Even as I write, my emotions overwhelm me. It was difficult and a blessing, all at the same time. We woke up just like it was Christmas morning and opened gifts. The kids had fun, and I savored the moment. Life and death make you appreciate things usually taken for granted. I did not care about receiving any gift. Simply, I wanted to bless others and watch them be happy. Our year had been so devastating with horror beyond words. My children had grown and changed, because of the trauma to the entire family. I wanted them just to have fun and enjoy the day. I was heartbroken we would be gone for Christmas, but there was no option.

I opened my gift last, and I was stunned. My husband, Kevin, gave me my dream ring. We had a local jeweler who was a friend of ours. Kevin and this man designed a marquee diamond ring set in a unique setting just for me. It was one of a kind. I was shocked and blessed. I made the joke just before opening the present that I did not want it unless it was my diamond. Kevin told me to just open the gift. Although, I could not even see the ring I knew it was the marquee, because I could feel the shape. I was shocked. Miranda did not miss a beat. She ran across the room and shouted, "When you die, I get that ring!" Miranda was precious and funny. She was only ten years old, and not aware of how very sick I was, or the possibility I may not live.

I asked Kevin if it was real, and he said, "Yes." Then, I asked Kevin if it was paid for, and he said "Yes." Apparently, our local jeweler had helped Kevin make my dream come true. I was blown away. Later, that day I asked him if there was a money back guarantee just in case I died in surgery. He said, "No, I figured I would give it to my next wife." He was joking. I quickly responded, "I'll haunt you day and night if you give this ring to another woman," and we both laughed.

Our families came to our home, and we all ate breakfast together. What a blessed and happy memory in the middle of a nightmare! I would carry this memory in my heart as I went to New York. Decisions were made about the children. They would stay with Kevin's parents while we were gone and spend Christmas Eve night at my dear friend's house. She was going to make sure they had a wonderful Christmas Day. I was determined for them to have a blessed

Christmas. Their hearts were already broken, and I could do nothing about it. But, I could make sure they were in a safe place with people who loved them deeply.

My son Micah had one request before we had Christmas at our house on December 3, 2005. He asked me to save something special for them to receive on the real Christmas morning. I told him not to worry. He would be blessed.

Both children had wanted laptop computers. Micah and Miranda were home-schooled; so, they did all their school work on computers and laptops would be more convenient than desktop computers. I had promised the kids when we received our settlement, we would buy them computers. Well, that was before I knew the truth about the car insurance. So, God moved on the hearts of two separate people to buy laptop computers for Micah and Miranda to receive Christmas morning. We left the laptops for Christmas morning. Several other people gave to our children as well. To be honest, I do not even know all they received. But, I did know before we left town, they would have a blessed Christmas – even if we were not there.

CHAPTER 19

GOD IS AN IMPOSSIBLE PROBLEM SOLVING GOD

Kevin and I were preparing to go out of town. We did not know exactly how long we would be gone. The estimated time was a minimum of seven days in the hospital after the second surgery with four more days staying in a house beside the hospital. We expected to be gone a minimum of three weeks.

During the days leading up to our departure, God kept working on my heart concerning the man who hit my car. Truly, I was not angry with him. I knew he did not mean to hurt me. It was an accident. But, the reality of the pain and suffering the accident had caused me was a daily reminder of the situation. God kept pressing my heart to keep my word. I had promised the man we would settle for the insurance policy limit and not come after him personally. Well, when I promised him, I had no idea how bad the situation was or how bad it would become. We were now looking at over $500,000 in medical bills and using specialists who did not take our insurance, which was overwhelming. God continued to press into my heart to keep my word and release the man. This pressure made me certain our lawyer was going to call, and sure enough, two days before we left town to go to New York the phone rang. Our lawyer said his insurance company was willing to settle for the entire amount of $25,000. I was irritated to put it mildly. Of course they would settle, our bills greatly exceeded their limit. They should have settled with me back in July. But no, I had to hire a lawyer and pay a lawyer. The fun did not end there because my personal health insurance wanted to be reimbursed part of the settlement, due to the fact the accident had caused the medical bills.

By this point, it was evident the car wreck had not caused all the problems in my body. However, the wreck had caused the physical conditions in my body to activate and created a new world for me, which was full of constant pain and suffering. Actually, the car wreck had revealed the hidden things in my body which were killing me.

Really, I only had one choice. As hard as it was, the only choice was to settle and forgive the man. Also, I had to forgive his insurance company for treating me so horribly. Forgiveness is a powerful tool. I needed my soul ready for the battle ahead. I needed to go into this surgery emotionally well and spiritually strong. So, Kevin took me to the lawyer's office, and we signed all the papers, which released the man who hit my car from any financial obligation. I was blind, so the lawyer and Kevin had to put my hand on the papers and say sign. I was not doing well physically, and my lawyer was shocked at the deterioration of my body. He said, "Donna, you are dying."

I said, "I know."

I came home, and with the help of a friend filled, out a Christmas card for the man who hit my car. Then she took me to see him the next day. I told him it was over. I told him Kevin and I signed all the papers, and we would not take him to court. I told him I kept my promise to him.

He did not even recognize me. It was evident he was shocked to see me, especially in my physical condition. He asked me if his insurance helped at all, and I told him no. Our bills far exceeded his liability limit, plus we had to pay a lawyer as well as our health insurance was to be reimbursed for their costs. I really had no idea how car insurance worked in this country until I was in the middle of a mess.

As hard as it was, I knew I had done the right thing. I would have to trust God to pay our bills and fulfill His word. I knew our bills were about to skyrocket, but with God all things are possible.

Kevin and I left for New York. We drove to Pennsylvania and slept. The next day we entered the city and went to the house for Chiari patients. The Variety House is a house beside the hospital where Chiari patients and one caregiver can stay for free if you qualify financially. My friend and I had stayed there on our first visit to New York, so I was familiar with the house. This was a blessing and gave Kevin a close place to stay, while I had surgery.

Kevin took me to the hospital on December 12, 2005, for our preadmission. It was awful. The pathways in the hospital were made of bricks. I was riding in a wheelchair, and my body was in horrid pain. Every bump caused me significant pain throughout my entire body. By the time we arrived at the admitting office, I had to go to the bathroom and vomit from the pain.

I was clearly the worst patient being admitted. It is interesting to sit around a waiting room and know you are the worst patient, by that I mean in the worst medical condition. I did it all year. I would go from doctor to doctor and know I was in worse pain than any other person in the room. I would even think to myself, "Why are some of you here?" I do not know why I thought about it, except it gave me something to think about besides the reality I was facing.

Anyhow, I was checked thoroughly by a doctor and given orders to return on Wednesday, December 14, 2005, for the first surgery. We left the hospital. I do not recall the rest of the day. I was in too much pain.

My parents and sister came to New York to help Kevin take care of me. On Tuesday before the first surgery, we all went into New York to see the Christmas tree at Rockefeller Center. I have little memory of the experience, although there are pictures. My body was in so much pain and apparently dying. It simply could not handle the trip. My family drove by Ground Zero and saw Lady Liberty, but I do not recall any of the events.

Tuesday night I was lying in the bed, and I was reminded of something God had spoken to me in the year 2000. He said, "Donna, all the answers lie in you."

Of course I interpreted it to mean somehow I would find the answers for my children and help them. But suddenly, everything made perfect sense. Every medical condition my children had was literally in my physical body. Miranda and I had the same symptoms, and Micah had Neurofibromatosis. So, I wanted him evaluated as well. I knew these doctors could be the ones to help Miranda. I knew I needed to let them know about our children and take them to New York for tests. I knew in my heart, finally after all these years, answers were upon us. I had peace.

That was the moment, when I realized the root of the problems were within me, and it overwhelmed me. My mind raced back to my childhood. I had suffered with leg issues, headaches, sick pregnancies, right side pain, and numbness in my feet, and a variety of other medical issues. My flat pituitary gland was most likely the cause of my loss of appetite when I was diagnosed with anorexia. It was never mental, instead it was a physical problem in my body. During my childhood and early adulthood, there was not enough medical knowledge.

I had never connected the dots. I never thought I was sick, even till that very night. Even though I was being diagnosed with so many physical conditions, I continued to simply think I was injured – not sick. The car wreck did destroy the ligaments in my neck, but it brought to light all the other physical conditions my body hosted. That night, December 13, 2005, was when the light of the truth shined so brightly I wanted to close my eyes. It was the knowledge I had been searching for throughout Miranda's life. It was the knowledge that would lead us to life!

Wednesday morning I was awakened by a phone call from the hospital stating I was supposed to be there already for the first surgery. My paper work had clearly stated the surgery would be at 3:00 p.m. and for me to arrive at 1:00 p.m., but apparently, somebody goofed. I told them the earliest I could come would be around 11:00 a.m., because I had to get ready and inform my family. So, suddenly we were on our way.

Let me interject here, I had purposefully not thought about the surgery or the suffering. I refused to let my brain go there. I made up my mind, I could and would do whatever it took to get through this nightmare, and I would live. I would testify. My mental state going into this situation was simply God had made a way, and He was faithful. He had created me, and I could do it!

Determination is a huge key in facing adversity. It is not what you face, but rather how you face it. I was determined to live. I was determined to go home to my children. I was determined to walk through the valley of the shadow of death and fear no evil. I was determined!

Kevin took me to the hospital, so my parents and my sister met us there. We only waited a couple of minutes before they took me back to a surgery holding room. Kevin was allowed to go with me as they prepared me for the surgery. I had to put on a gown and take off all my jewelry. Kevin was given all my belongings. We sat in the room in silence. At this point, what is there to say?

Kevin kissed me goodbye at the corner. Then, I was rolled away from Kevin into a waiting room and taken to an operating room. When Dr. Neuro #4, another Chiari doctor, entered the room, I began talking and fast. I told him all about my children and their diagnoses. I wanted to be sure the doctors knew to help my children before I was put to sleep. He listened. Finally, somebody listened.

He said he wanted to see them in the clinic, and I had peace. He asked me if I was ready, and I said, "Let's get this show on the road."

Let me interject here, I told the doctors about my children before they put me under anesthesia just in case I died while in surgery. My body was weak, and I knew it.

While I was in the first surgery, a medical technician took the paperwork to Kevin for the kids. Kevin had no idea I was going to tell the doctors about the kids and apparently, it was extremely difficult for him to receive the information while I was in surgery. When I told Dr. Neuro #4 about Micah and Miranda, I did not expect an immediate response, but it was definitely directed by God. I knew these were the doctors to help us, and finally answers were being found in me to help solve the problems in my children. I must say this is not the way I would have fixed the medical problems, but whatever it took, I was willing to do it.

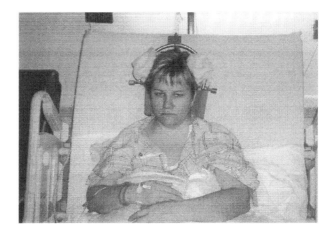

When I woke up from surgery, I was still in the operating room. The rods were literally installed into each side of my head just above my ears. The rods were attached to a metal band that went across my head. At the top of the metal band was a hook, which had a rope attached to it. The rope was pulled by weights, which pulled my head off my neck. Even though it sounds barbaric, it brought relief. It relieved pain instantly and made a huge difference. The doctors asked me how I felt, and I asked them to add more weight. They kept adding weights until I felt significant relief.

I was sent to intensive care. It was a unit where only curtains separated you from the next patient over. It had a large nursing area in the center, which I could see from my bed. I asked for Kevin. I was uncomfortable, but all and all I felt better than before the surgery. Kevin came in for just a few minutes, and they made him leave. When he left, the woman on my left went into trauma. I could hear the entire ordeal, which was horrible. I felt so alone. I asked for my husband, but they would not let him come back in the room. The trauma of the woman beside me was more than I could take emotionally. I shut down emotionally and really do not remember much past that moment.

I do recall being on the floor of the bathroom vomiting during the night. My sister took the night shift. She was with me and praying diligently over me, "I would live and not die." She was fighting in the spirit world, and I was fighting in the physical one. She told me later she was led to call an intercessor/prayer warrior at her church to pray for me as well. The woman stayed up all night and literally took on the intercession of my condition as she prayed. My sister said I vomited one more time, and my body calmed down.

I recall using the bathroom with the metal device attached to my head, and my Mom trying to lighten the situation by comparing me with a reindeer. I laughed. Also, I asked Dr. Neuro #3 to please not take the weights off again. The original treatment plan was the rods were installed into my skull. My head would hang for three hours with and three hours without weights. When the weights were removed, the pain was more than I could bear, so I would become extremely sick. When I asked Dr. Neuro #3 to please not take the weights off again, he agreed and the weights remained on until the second surgery.

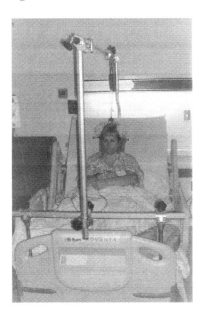

I wore the weights and rods for two days and have only the limited memory, which I have written about. I believe when I experienced the trauma of the woman beside me in intensive care, my emotions and mind shut down. Also, pain is difficult to take, and I had so much it makes it difficult to recall details, which I would rather forget anyhow.

December 16, 2005 the main surgery was performed. The doctors opened the back of my head and neck about one foot in length. They put a plate on each side of my skull and attached a rod, which went down to my C2, 3, 4 and 5 vertebrae. The rods were screwed into my bones all the way down. They cut the section of the back of my skull out and shaved the base of my brain. They covered the hole in my skull with a metal plate. The doctors did other things inside my body to help correct the rest of the issues as well. The surgery took about eight and a half hours. I was then sent to intensive care, and my family was told I would be there all night. They were not allowed to stay with me. They were allowed a brief visit, but not long.

I woke up in intensive care, a PACU unit, in excruciating pain; the type of pain I cannot put into words. Pain I truly hope no other person on the planet ever experiences. I argued and cursed my nurse. I made her life miserable. She would not listen to me when I told her my pain medication was not working. She ignored me, which of course made me even angrier. I was so difficult they decided to send me back to my room five hours earlier than they had planned. I assumed they were sick of listening to me fight with them over my medication. They did not even bother to call my family and let them know I was back in my room.

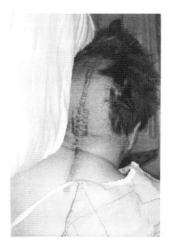

Kevin woke up early and called to check on me. He found out I was in my room and rushed over. He found Dr. Neuro #4 to check my pain medication pump, and sure enough the pump was broken. It appeared as if the medication was going into my veins, but it was not. I had no pain medication for the first thirty-six hours after surgery, which words cannot adequately describe! The pain was unbearable.

I had pushed the pain pump 144 times and received no medication!

The pain medication was adjusted, which did help, but still the pain was great, much greater than I expected. My head felt like it weighed a thousand pounds. I would command it to sit up in the "name of Jesus," and my body would obey. I was amazed at how my spirit dominated my flesh. My body was extremely weak and in extreme suffering, yet my spirit remained calm. My determination remained strong. I fought hard, and my family helped me greatly.

I do recall one day when my brain was swelling out of my eye. I was unable to see anything in the natural. I was lying on my left side and saw the angel of death. It was odd really. I did not sense fear. I simply rebuked the angel and proclaimed out loud I would live and not die. The angel of death was not scary or evil, just strange. The angel had dust it was trying to throw on me, but I continued to rebuke it until it went away. Then, the next thing I recall seeing was the Lion of the Tribe of Judah. He was glorious in ways words cannot describe. The colors were magnificent, and His glory filled the room. I saw Him three separate times. I knew this particular battle for my life was over. I would live through this pain.

There are not words to describe the events or the horror of the suffering. I simply kept my "head" about me and was determined to do whatever the doctors said; so, I could get out of that hospital as soon as possible. I recall one day Dr. Neuro #3 came in the room. He grabbed the back of my neck and massaged it roughly. He showed Kevin and told him to do this for me. I thought I would die. The pain that surged through my body as he grabbed it was unthinkable. There was no way I was going to let Kevin or anyone else do that to me again. I adored Dr. Neuro #3 until that moment. My mind changed immediately, and I told him, "I used to like you."

He made it into a joke and had me say it over and over while making fun of my Tennessee accent. I did not have the knowledge or wisdom he had. As painful as the massage was, it was less painful than the muscle spasms I was going to face. He knew the surgery would cause the spasms and the massaging would ease the pain. All I knew was he caused me great pain. But, time would tell his wisdom would prevail and Kevin, Dad, Mom, and whoever else was near massaged the spasms out of my neck over the next six weeks.

I was told prior to surgery I would spend a minimum of three weeks in New York, and there was no way I would be home for Christmas. Although, during the days and weeks up to the point we left I kept hearing the song in my heart, *I'll be home for Christmas*. Well, that would take a miracle!

Monday morning a medical technician working with the Chiari doctors told me I might get out of the hospital on Wednesday. I was shocked. I still could not walk around the hallways. I could barely get to the bathroom. But, I felt in my spirit it was God. I kept hearing, "There is nothing more they can do for you."

On Wednesday, December 21, 2005, I was released from the hospital. It was only five days after the surgery and well before the projected timetable. Dr. Neuro #3 cleared me to go home. As he headed out the door he turned and said, "Merry Christmas!" I recalled these words from our first encounter. It was definitely my time to head home.

I wanted to surprise my children and be home on Christmas. I knew it would mean the world to them. Micah and Miranda were staying with Kevin's parents, while we were in New York. I was unaware, at the time I was released from the hospital, but Miranda had written a letter to Santa at her Mamaw's, Kevin's mother, while we were in New York. Simply, she wrote, "All I want for Christmas is my parents' home." At the bottom of the note she wrote in big letters, "I BELIEVE!"

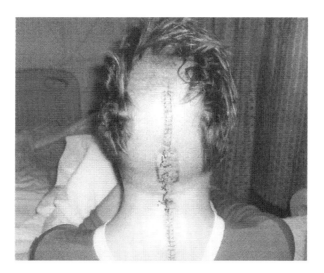

I was not aware of the letter or her heart's cry, but God was, so He put the determination in me to get home. It was difficult, to say the least. My body was riveted with pain, and I was vomiting constantly. I was not mentally alert in a moving vehicle at all. The medications I was taking made me unconscious of my surroundings and difficult to deal with per Kevin and my parents. I truly do not recall most of the ride home. I only recall the determination to get home.

I wanted my children to know their Mommy was okay, so they could enjoy their Christmas. They were the force, which enabled me to fight through the pain and stay focused on my goal. We did not tell the kids we were on the way home. On Christmas Eve at noon, I was sitting on a couch in my house. My sister brought over my children as well as my niece and nephew to see me. It was a priceless moment, and one I recall well. I recall the surprise in Miranda's face, and the relief in Micah's eyes. Mommy was home. She was not well yet, but she was home. The children went on to do the prepared Christmas events and had a ball. It was worth the pain and suffering to give them peace. I always say, "You can't buy peace."

God was faithful and miraculously brought me home for Christmas. I was unable to do the normal festive events, but my family could with the knowledge this part of our journey was over. Now, all I had to do was heal.

Donna's Medical Diagnoses during the year 2005:

Heart Arrhythmia
Kidney Stones
Kidney Cyst
Cyst behind heart
Whip Lash
Four Bulging Disks
Degenerative Bone and Disk Disease
Both Hands Numb and Becoming Paralyzed
Syrinx/Syringomyelia
Dead Gallbladder
Cirrhosis of the Liver
Hearing Loss/Completely Deaf at Times
Eyesight loss/ Completely Blind at Times
Right Hand Carpel Tunnel
Ulnar Nerve Entrapment Bilateral
Lung Lesion
Hands became paralyzed
Legs became paralyzed
Chiari 1 Brain Malformation
Retroflexed Ondontoid with Pannus
Decreased Posterior Cerebrospinal Fluid Flow
Decreased Anterior Cerebrospinal Fluid Flow
Ligamentous Injury

Flattened Pituitary
Bifid C1
Positive Tinel at Both Wrists and Elbows
Severe Sensory Loss in the Lower Extremities in A Peripheral Neuropathy
Pattern
Indented Foramen Magnum and Supraoccipital
Volumetrically Small Posterior Fossa
Low-lying Brain Tonsils
Hypertrophy of Styloid Process

CHAPTER 20

TOUGH TRIALS NEVER LAST...TOUGH PEOPLE DO!

God is a miracle working God! I was a dying woman and did not even know it. I had multiple physical conditions in my body that were destroying my life, and I was completely unaware. God in His grace and mercy revealed the hidden things to save my life, and He truly gave me a "new life" just as He promised.

I recall during the entire year of 2003 each time I entered the shower I would hear God tell me, "Donna, you are a very healthy woman."

Honestly, I did not think twice about it, because I thought I was a well woman. I did not think I was sick or had multiple medical conditions. When I met Dr. Neuro #3 he said to me three times, "Donna, you are a very sick woman."

I questioned God about His view versus Dr. Neuro #3's. He simply told me He was telling me the end from the beginning. I am well – regardless of medical conditions and reports. God wanted my mind to dwell on being whole and well, not sick and diseased, even while I suffered in great pain. His ways are not mine, but His ways are the best.

I truly do not recall much after we arrived home. I was on a lot of medication, but I had been on medication all year. The only difference was the medication, I was now daily taking, made my brain mush. I saw people who were not there and things that did not happen. I have no true memories of the first few weeks I was home. I do know I continued to have horrible night terrors, which are often associated with traumas. Night terrors are outrageous nightmares, which feel real. I would wake up and try to flee in the night. More than once, Kevin had to catch me. I was trying to run away from the horrible dreams. In some of my dreams there were men with guns chasing me or horses on the ceiling. It made no sense. These days and weeks were much harder on my family than me. I had prescription medications. They had reality.

I had made reservations back in June of 2005, for our entire family to go on a Disney Cruise. I thought the insurance company was going to settle, and the entire ordeal was over. Obviously, I was wrong. Anyhow, Kevin's parents, sister, brother-in law, and baby were going, as well as a family whose children are my children's friends. Also, Kevin's brother-in-law's parents were going. So, there was a huge group of us traveling to Florida to cruise the Bahamas together. My children had looked forward to this trip for six months. Now, I was placed in a very difficult position. The cruise would depart exactly four weeks after my surgery. I was not well and taking many medications, but made the decision to go anyway. I simply could not take anything else away from my family. I wanted them to have fun, regardless of the cost to me physically.

We traveled to Florida a couple of days prior to the cruise leaving. Honestly, I do not even remember the ride. Somehow, when a vehicle was in motion my brain was dead. I did not know what was going on at all, and I hallucinated a great deal. I saw all kinds of interesting things. It was flat weird, but I could travel. I recall stopping the first night at the hotel on the way to Florida and Kevin's mother said something. I completely freaked out. I asked Kevin if he heard his mother's voice. He calmly answered, "Yes, Donna, she is in the back seat."

I felt a sense of relief that he heard the voice as well. I never knew what was real or imagined. It was a very scary sensation. I hated it to be honest.

Anyhow, we arrived in Florida, and I stayed in the hotel bed the entire time. The family spent time going to Disney World and Sea World. My children played with their friends and things seemed okay, until I was left alone. The day everyone went to Sea World, a couple tried to rob the bank across the street from the hotel. Unbelievable! I was alone in my hotel room. The manager of the hotel did stay at the check-in, which was located in the front lobby. The police cleared the road for a mile each way and everyone was evacuated, but I was unable to go. I had to be in bed. Kevin had left for some reason. I really do not know why, but this standoff with the robbers and the police went on for hours. It was intense, and I was right in the middle of it. Kevin and my brother-in-law finally walked over a mile behind buildings to get to me. I called Dave, my brother-in-law who lived in Georgia, to ask him to pray because I was alone, hungry, and scared. When Ginger, my sister, returned home she did not believe I was telling the truth because my hallucinations had been so severe. She thought I was making the entire thing up. The national news proved I was telling the truth; so, they did pray for me. I was entirely safe throughout the ordeal. However, leaving a woman on the medications I was on for a long period of time was dangerous. I was not lucid most of the time.

My husband thought it was a great adventure to be across the street from a bank robbery. We have all kinds of pictures of the swat team, police, snipers, bank robbers, and any other thing dealing with the robbery. However, Kevin neglected to take any pictures at Disney World or of our kids playing with their friends. It was shocking to me to see the pictures when they were developed. You would think we went to Florida to see a bank robbery.

We left our hotel on Thursday and boarded the Disney Wonder. We were the first family on board. Our family was chosen as the "Disney Family" for the trip. We received all kinds of free gifts and blessings. I had to ride in a wheelchair and spend the majority of the time lying in the bed, but the kids and Kevin had a great time. I could go to supper, which was wonderful. Although I do not have many memories, we do have good pictures. The last night we were aboard the ship a tropical depression hit the Bahamas, and our boat had to go through it. It was quite the ride: a perfect end to a stormy season in our lives.

When we returned home, I still had to spend most of my time in the bed. I made the decision to go off one of the medications. I was now five weeks out from brain surgery and wanted to regain my mind. After two days off the medication, I was feeling better than ever. I could think clearer, and the hallucinations were ceasing. I woke up early one Sunday morning and was walking in my house. As I was walking to try to build up my strength, I had to stop and rest for a moment. As I laid my head against the refrigerator, I heard the voice of God saying, "It is not over yet."

I thought, "Great! What could possibly be left?" Then, I quickly decided to just trust God. He had brought me this far. He had the ability to handle whatever was ahead of me.

At 4:00 p.m. that afternoon, I screamed in pain. Kevin came running. I was standing in the kitchen. It felt like someone stuck a knife in my back. I was bent over and having difficulty catching my breath, due to the horrific pain. Kevin put pressure on my back and the pain eased. We both thought it might be withdrawals from coming off the medication I had just quit. But, later that night around 11:00 p.m., my body began to shake like I was having a seizure. I was aware of the jerking. I yelled for Kevin again. At this point, I felt I should go to the hospital. My body was jerking so violently I was scared. I told Kevin if I was not allowed to ride roller coasters with the rods and screws in my head, I felt sure my body should not be allowed to shake and jerk out of control. He remained calm. He prayed for me and gave me sleeping pills. He kept telling me to breathe in the nose and out the mouth. I fell asleep.

The next morning, my parents called, and I was not lucid. They came over immediately. Kevin had gone on to work. He thought I was simply dealing with withdrawal symptoms. By the time my parents reached me, I was desperate. The pain in my right side was worse, and I was freezing. They took my temperature, and it was over 103. Because I was on a lot of medication, I should not have a fever at all much less run a high fever. I told my parents to call 911 and take me by ambulance to the medical center. My parents did not want to do anything until Kevin came home.

Finally, Kevin arrived and the decision was made to drive me to a local hospital. I was not sure I could even walk down the stairs. I pleaded with my family to please take me by ambulance, but they would not.

I must note here my family had been through a horrible trauma in New York watching me suffer. They did not want me to go back to a hospital. They wanted the entire thing to be over. They had taken all they could stand. However, it was not over.

Kevin drove me to the hospital and literally had to lean me against a wall, while he parked the car. My body was so out of control, a medical technician took me back immediately and put me in a bed. My fever had spiked, and my symptoms were severe. I was unable to hear well, see well, or walk. I had no control over my body, and it continued to jerk and shake. After eight hours and several scans the emergency room doctor told us she could not find the problem. The doctor on call from my group refused to admit me, or even come to see me. So, the emergency room doctor had no choice but to send me home. I could not believe it. She did want to give me strong pain medication before I left. I did not want the pain medication, but after a long conversation, I agreed. The doctor gave me high-powered pain medication. She set an appointment for me to see my doctor the very next day.

We left the emergency room around 4:00 a.m. and went home. Kevin carried me to my bed. I do not remember much until Kevin took me to see my doctor. When I entered the room, I instantly began vomiting. He ordered me to go directly to the hospital and be admitted with antibiotics. Finally, somebody was going to help me.

We left the office, and Kevin was devastated. He had taken more than he could bear. He voiced his frustrations all the way to the hospital, but I remained calm. God had prepared me that it was not over. So, I was ready for whatever lay ahead.

When we reached the hospital, I was sick and had to go directly to the bathroom. I was blind and having great difficulty walking. Luckily the bathroom was empty; so, Kevin carried me into a bathroom stall. I vomited for a while. When I was finished, I heard the door open. I asked if it was Kevin. A sweet woman said no, but went on to ask me if that was my husband with the wheelchair waiting outside the door. I told her, "Yes."

She asked if I needed help, and again I told her, "Yes." She practically carried me out of the bathroom and sat me in the wheelchair. She went with Kevin and me to admitting. They were already waiting on us and told Kevin my room was on the seventh floor. This kind woman kissed me on the forehead, and said she would be praying for me. Then, Kevin took me straight to my hospital room.

Kevin dropped me at the door and nurses lifted me into the bed. Kevin had to go back downstairs to fill out the paper work. Immediately, the nurse began installing the I.V.'s and preparing my body for the tests they would run in the next few hours to find out what the problem was. It was no easy task getting the I.V.'s in my arms. My veins were blown from the previous surgery, which was just five weeks earlier. They sent in several nurses who tried and failed. Finally, a calm and sweet woman was able to insert the I.V. in my left arm for the test. It took her over twenty minutes to get it in, but I remained calm and simply breathed in my nose and out my mouth – just like Kevin had trained me. If I were to move, she would have to start all over.

My parents arrived as soon as possible, and Kevin left. He was exhausted from the previous night in the emergency room, plus he had worked all day. My Dad stayed with me, and my Mom began to line up people to come stay through the next few days.

A surgeon came in and spoke with Dad and me. He said it was probably either a blood clot in my lung or my appendix. I remained calm, but wanted to scream. The thought of another surgery was truly more than I could bear. However, simply I had no choice, but to let them run their tests and find out what was causing so much pain in my body. I needed help.

I was sent down for a scan of my abdomen after having to drink oral contrast. I was told the scan would reveal the problem. If I needed surgery, it would probably be done immediately. I came back from the scan around midnight, and my friend was there. Dad went on home to get some sleep.

I told her we should know within the hour. The surgeon did not contact us; so, no news was good news. We decided to go to sleep. I woke up around 3:00 a.m. in horrible pain. At first I thought I might be back on the cruise ship in the middle of the tropical depression, because it felt like the bed was moving. Then, I felt the horrid pain and thought maybe I was being interrogated. I suppose I was thinking about how in the movies people are tortured to get information out of them – silly I know, but I was on medications. Finally, I said, "Where am I?"

My friend was awake and quickly reassured me. She told me I was in a hospital, and I was okay. I said, "No, I'm not!" and went to the bathroom. The drink they gave me for the scan cleans out your colon. I was at a loss as what to do. How humiliating to have an accident. To make matters worse the hospital was catching my bowel movements, and it smelled horrible. The panties were expensive for me, and I was not willing to throw them away. So, I stood at the sink, holding my breath, bent over in excruciating pain, with a high fever to clean my clothes.

I left the bathroom and told my friend there was a new hospital rule: "I was only bringing 50 cent panties to the hospital, because then if you have an accident you can throw them away without concern." She laughed at me.

My pain was severe, but I refused the pain medication. I would only take the medications I was currently taking. I had to breathe through the pain and simply endure it. I was at a place where I preferred pain to being out of control of my life. When a person is put on the high-powered pain medication, you do not know what you say or do. I did not want that in my life, even if it meant pain.

The next morning a doctor came in and said I had a severe kidney infection, and they would keep me at least twenty-four more hours. The surgeon dropped by to confirm the kidney was the problem. Honestly, it was the best news I had heard in over a year. As painful as the kidney infection was, it was easily treated without surgery. When I was released from the hospital, my Dad drove me home. When my foot hit the bottom step of the basement stair, I heard the voice of God saying, "It is finished, the battle is over."

I know God meant the battle for my life was over, but time would prove I was not yet finished with the medical world. I was going to live, but still had a process to go through to gain quality of life back – a process which would greatly upset me.

I then made the decision to come off another medication. This medication was very dangerous and powerful, and I was on a high dose. I had to wean myself for thirty-six days, and then it would still take time for it to get out of my cells. This medication did carry strong withdrawals. I dealt with pain, hot sweats, cold sweats, fever, difficulty walking, difficulty speaking, night terrors, hallucinations, and other very difficult things. It was a long six weeks, but I remained focused and determined to get off the medication. I wanted to be medication free if possible.

Unless a person has been addicted to a medication or tried to go off one, he truly cannot understand. It was harder than I would have ever imagined. I had to spend much of the six-weeks lying flat in a bed suffering from the withdrawal symptoms day and night without a break. The only thing that would bring me peace was praise and worship music. I would listen to praise, and somehow it would help.

March 4, 2006, was my last day taking that particular medication, and I was thrilled to reach my goal. I still struggled daily for a while, but the further away from that medication – the better I felt. I was still on two medications, but it would be at least June 2006, before I could begin to wean off them. I was almost home free. I could see the finish line, and that is worth a party.

Miranda made the following for Donna in 2006:

The cloth was made in green with gold beads.
Miranda attached the following letter…

Dear Mom,

I love you so much! I hate to see you suffer! I hope you feel better soon.
God loves you so much!
I made this cloth for you. It is not perfect, but I still hope you love it.
Just like God made us.
We're not perfect. But, He still loves us.
Keep this cloth and every time you look at it; be reminded that I love you,
and God loves you.

Green means life.
Gold means God.

Love,
Miranda
I love you!

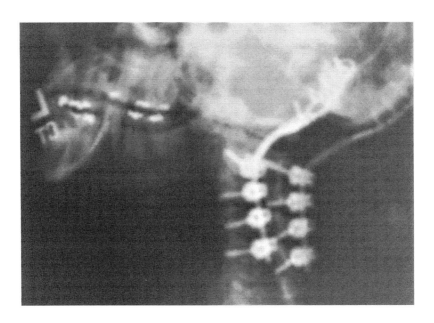

Donna's x-rays taken on March 16, 2006

JOURNAL ENTRY: March 2006

I am beginning to feel a sense of relief. From the date of surgery until now, I cannot say that my life is easy or pain free. But, I am improving and expect to continue improving. I still lay in the bed for most of the day, but I am gaining ground.

It is now the middle of March, and I would like to be further along. But, I am willing to be patient and let my body heal. I did not get this sick overnight and the laws of nature deem it necessary for time to heal my body. I do have time.

Financially, things are still difficult. We have applied for financial assistance in New York. Currently, we owe over $60,000 to our doctors that we do not have. I am trusting God to make a way where there is no way.

Miranda, Micah, and I are scheduled to be seen by the Chiari doctors in June 2006. On June 13, the kids will be tested and on June 14, 2006, we meet with Dr. Neuro #3.

I believe these doctors hold the truth to set our family free.

I trust God and His way is perfect.

CHAPTER 21

NEVER QUIT!

Transition is one of the most painful points of delivery of a baby. However, when you reach transition, the delivery is almost over. This is the point when you want to quit. I remember believing by faith, God would give me the ability to deliver Micah naturally. When I finally went into labor, I was excited. Ignorance is bliss! Anyhow, I had a long and difficult labor. When it came time to push, I was exhausted. I recall after pushing for over three long hours, I said, "I quit!" The doctor said, "You can't quit, it is too late. Push, Donna, you can do it." I remember thinking this is impossible, but I did not quit and pushed. Within minutes it was over. I learned a lot from the experience. Just when you think you cannot do one more thing, push one more time, endure anymore pain, pay one more bill, DON'T QUIT! You can do it. As a matter of fact, you can do whatever you put your mind to – no matter how painful or difficult. You can do it!

On May 1, 2006, I had the best day since surgery in December 2005. The sun was out when I woke up. It was a beautiful day. If you have ever dealt with pain, then you understand the weather affects a body greatly. My neck was strong, and my pain was minimal. I had direction in my heart and excitement about my future. It was a good day. A day I had longed for over sixteen months – a day when I began to think it would end and all would be well again.

In April 2005, I was led to pray diligently. I had no idea of the journey I was going to face during the rest of the year. However, I continually prayed that it would end with me before it began with Miranda. Also, God spoke to me, "Donna, you will always go the hard way, but you will always overcome." I thought I had suffered enough from the car wreck, and it was over. I had no idea what we were about to face.

I did know in my heart I needed to be well before we went forward again for Miranda. On May 2, 2006, I took Miranda to a skin specialist due to a black spot on her toe. They immediately removed the spot and had it evaluated. The diagnosis was bad – either a vascular tumor or something, the dermatologist was not sure. Within two weeks the spot was back, and she had two more. I knew we had our trip to New York planned for June 9–15, 2006, so I decided we would deal with the toe when we arrived home. I did talk to her pediatrician, and she agreed.

We went to Edisto Island for our annual family beach trip. I enjoyed myself. I had looked forward to seeing the ocean for months. There is something healing about sitting on the shore and staring at the ocean. It is so big and always reminds me of how big our God is. While at the beach, my body was showing signs which were bothersome. My legs were weak, and I had great pain in my body. A day before we came home, I had a headache, which made my head feel like it was in a vice grip. Words simply cannot describe the kind of pain I would have with a headache. Usually I would lose my eyesight, be unable to hear well, and often unable to walk. My body regressed more. The travel home caused my legs to almost completely give out. I was upset and for the first time since the car wreck, I felt hopeless and angry. I had been through so much and was doing better. I felt desperate about the regression of my body. I cried out to God. I asked Him to either let me die or heal me, but please do not leave me like this. I had been bed-ridden for practically 18 months. I was exhausted by the pain as well as the roller coaster ride. I wanted it to end.

Several of my close friends felt it was time for people to know we were going to New York to have the kids tested for the same physical conditions which were in me. I let them get the word out, and the response was a blessing. We began getting cards and encouragement from other people. Due to the many prayers, I could tell a greater level of peace invaded my home. Although, I still suffered in pain, I had peace and an inner strength that I could endure this situation, whatever it took.

When I came home from our beach trip, I received another denial from Social Security Disability. I had applied back in October 2005. I had to get a lawyer. It was easier than I thought it would be. Several people gave me the same name for a lawyer, and he met with me the next day. I gave him my case, and let it go. At least, I could clear that off my plate. Plus, using the other lawyer for the car wreck had given me confidence in the system. I did not want to get a lawyer or go before a judge, but I was left with no option. So, I simply did what I had to do.

I received a call from a patient advocacy group just two weeks before we left for our trip to New York to take the kids. Kevin and I had no money, and I kept praying and asking God to pay for our trip. This group connected us with organizations that help families in medical crisis. We received free flights to New York. We stayed at the Ronald McDonald House for a small fee each night. Our car rental was paid for by one of the organizations. Another organization paid for our food. Also, our church family came around us like angels. Several people gave us money, which completely took the financial pressure off us as we went. God paid for everything. We only had to go.

The patient advocacy agent asked me many questions, and after realizing our situation, she said, "If your family is not a humanitarian crisis, I have not heard of one."

That was shocking! I was numb to our difficult situation. But strangers were shocked by it. It was normal for me, but scary for others.

I had not flown in an airplane since the car wreck and had no idea what it would do to my body. We boarded the plane in our local airport and flew to Atlanta to change flights. It was okay until the landing. When the pilot hit the runway, it jerked my neck and sent electric bolts of pain throughout my entire body. I thought I might vomit from the pain. Then, I was taken by wheelchair from where we landed to our next flight. We only had 40 minutes between landing and takeoff, so they pushed me fast over the brick walkways, which took a great toll on my body. By the time we boarded the next flight, I wanted to die.

The stewardess took one look at me and said, "Oh, honey you must be in awful pain. Can I get you anything?"

I said, "Yes, a miracle!"

Kevin helped me into my seat and put my praise music in my ears. I also took some high-powered pain medication. About one hour into the flight, the same stewardess came over to me. She tapped me on the shoulder and asked me what was wrong with me. I quickly told her I had my brain shaved and rods in my neck, and both my children were being tested for the same physical conditions I had. She looked horrified. I put my praise music back in my ears.

A few minutes later, she came back and tapped me on the shoulder again. She said, "I just want to thank you."

I said, "For what?"

Her answer was, "For reminding me I do not have any problems on this planet."

I must say her comment hit me hard. I just smiled and put my music back in my ear and thought, "Well, I am glad I could be of service."

We arrived in New York and Kevin helped me get to a bed. I suffered, but by the next day, I could walk with my cane. We took the kids to Manhattan and let them eat at Bubba Gump's Shrimp Company. They loved it. Kevin drove them around to see different parts of New York. They saw Ground Zero, China Town, the Statue of Liberty, and the street where all the Broadway plays are located. They enjoyed their day.

We went back to the Ronald McDonald House to discover another family had checked in who were also going to the Chiari doctors. She had a son who was 12 and going for medical evaluation, like my kids. I did not know this woman, but she knew a great deal about Chiari. She was one of the first people to have the surgery, and she was highly involved with the Chiari groups. Micah walked by us. She commented, "Your son has a tethered cord." I questioned her, and she explained to me that Micah's toe walking was a sign of a tethered spinal cord. I did not even know what a tethered cord was, but her comment made me feel sick.

When Micah was first diagnosed with Neurofibromatosis type 1, we did a brain MRI on him due to his toe walking, and of course nothing was found.

I did not sleep that night. Instead, I researched online to find out what a tethered cord was. She was right about the toe walking being a sign. Basically, a person with a tethered spinal cord has some extra body tissue wrapped around the cord and pulling on it. The spinal cord is pulling the base of the brain down the back of the neck. The cord must be fixed with surgery or could lead to much more severe symptoms until eventually the person would be paralyzed. I was bothered in my heart, but knew I needed to hold my peace and just wait to see what the tests showed.

The kids saw the intake nurse and the neurologist on Tuesday. The nurse confirmed to me Miranda had Chiari and a flat pituitary. A flat pituitary can cause hormonal imbalances. They could see it in her old MRI's. I was in a great deal of pain, so they let me lie on a bed to rest my back. While I lay there, I thought of all the MRI's and all the doctors – all the times I had asked for help and received none. It was there and no one caught it. I was upset, but held myself steady. A huge piece of me wanted to run to every doctor as well as all the specialist and scream at them. But, I reminded myself the steps of the righteous are ordered of God. If God had wanted it revealed before now, He would have revealed it. I took a deep breath and calmed myself down. I chose the high road of forgiveness and peace when anger would have been easy and satisfied me greatly! Choosing peace was a key throughout the entire process. After seven long years, Miranda finally had the diagnosis, she needed to receive help. Her first MRI was in June 1999, and seven years later in June 2006, the MRI was finally read accurately. It was not that her other MRI's were fine. Simply the people reading them did not know what they were looking for or how to accurately read the images.

Remember how God had me get an MRI of Miranda's brain in 2003, and God said, "They will see it!" Well, "they" did in 2006! A Chiari doctor read the MRI from 2003. Also, do you recall the prophet who said, "Miranda has a pituitary problem? Well, she did. Never Quit!

The neurologist confirmed both children had the eye problems I had, but other than that, nothing really stood out, which relieved me. We completed the day and went back to rest in our room. The following morning, we had to be at the diagnostic center at 7:00 a.m. for the testing to begin. Both children went through a battery of tests, and Miranda had some extra ones, due to the Intermittent Cushing's. I had an MRI of my neck and brain. The MRI was extremely painful, but I took deep breaths and talked myself through it. After the tests were complete, we took the results over to the office to meet with Dr. Neuro #3. At this point, I became nervous. I knew he would tell us the results, and I was concerned for both Micah and Miranda.

We were scheduled to meet with Dr. Neuro #3 individually, but he changed it and had the entire family come in together. He very calmly said both children were carbon copies of me and had all my hereditary diseases. Micah was calm, but Miranda began to cry. Even though she pulled herself together, she was scared.

You must understand my children knew and understood what these diagnoses meant. They had witnessed firsthand watching their mother suffer in relentless pain, be blind at times, deaf at times, and paralyzed at times. They had seen me go through multiple surgeries, seen my scars, and had witnessed my body jerking and shaking. My children knew exactly what these diseases did to the human body. They had seen it.

Dr. Neuro #3 went on to examine each of us. Then, he told us we all three had tethered spinal cords. Mine was the most severe, so I needed surgery as soon as possible on my spinal cord. You could have knocked me over with a feather.

I was prepared for possible surgeries for the children, but I did not think I would have to endure any more surgeries, much less another back surgery. Kevin and I agreed to the surgery for me, and the decision was made for both Micah and Miranda to come back in a year for re-evaluation. Also, Dr. Neuro #3 confirmed diet was a great way to help us. We all three needed to be thin to help our bodies, and Miranda had to lose weight. So, we all committed to an eating plan as well. With our diseases being thin is helpful to our bodies. Extra weight will pull on the back and make it more difficult for the cerebrospinal fluid to go around our brains.

Devastation hit my heart concerning my children. Then, to make matters worse, I was now going to need another major operation, which would involve the doctors going into my back in the L4-L5 region to release a tethered spinal cord. I was in constant and horrid pain, but I thought the pain would go away with time. It had only been six months since my neck and brain surgery. He also said both the children had the tethered spinal cord. Of course, they did – they were just like me!

Dr. Neuro #3 was not satisfied with my neck, and he wanted me in physical therapy, massage therapy, as well as stretching exercises. Obviously, it was not over with me yet. My nightmare had not ended. I thought we were going to New York to end it with me and begin it with the children, especially Miranda. But, I was wrong.

Dr. Neuro #3 said he just wanted to watch the children for the next several years, but my surgery needed to be done as soon as possible. We left the office, and I was emotionally numb. I had just agreed to another operation that would be extremely painful, and there was no hope placed before us for our children. Finally, after years of not knowing what the problem was exactly, we knew. But knowing was sickening, it placed a sense of doom and suffering over my head I could not shake. I had suffered in severe unending, relentless pain for 18 months. My children are now doomed to my existence according to their medical records. My heart was not broken – it was crushed. The reality of the depth of the problem was too big. Numbness became my friend again as I passed the information to the people around us who loved us and cared.

Victory is in the walk! Trust me! Victory is a word to think about. I thought I would feel some kind of vindication when the doctors finally, after years of fighting for the truth found it, but vindication was not the feeling. I thought I would want to go and tell every doctor as well as any other person who questioned or accused me – how wrong they were and how right I was. But that was not the case. When the victory of getting to the root of the problem finally came, the only feeling I had was hopelessness!

I did not even care that I had heard accurately from God. I wished all the "naysayers" were right, and it had been in my head or my fault somehow instead of a reality, which loomed larger than my brain could wrap around. The funny thing is: it was in my head – my brain was too large! And, to give credit, it was my fault – my children were "carbon copies" of me as Dr. Neuro #3 said. I had genetically given my children every malformation and disease I had plus they each had extras! Victory was not the feeling – trust me on that!

Feelings are fickle, and they are best kept under control to the best of our ability. If the Word of God is your mainstay, than the fruit of the Spirit of love, joy, peace, patience, kindness, goodness, and self-control will prevail even in the worst of circumstances. My feelings at this point outweighed my spirit. The truth of the reality of the circumstances was too large for me to bear. I was so angry! Believe me, I let God know!

Anger grew rapidly in my heart. God had promised me it would end. He had even given me a time frame. He told me when Miranda was 6 years old that by the time she was 14 it would be over, but evidently God meant the battle to find the answers would be over by the time Miranda was 14. Well, Miranda was 12 years old and no plans were made to help her. On top of that, my son had the same diagnoses. God had told me it would never touch Micah. I was devastated beyond words.

I came home and caught the flu. It was just as well. I did not feel like seeing anyone or even talking for that matter. I do recall finally losing it and yelling at God. I told Him exactly how I felt, and I left nothing out. As clearly as I had ever heard from Him, He said, "In six months from this day it will be over." God did not promise we would not face other issues; however, I felt He was promising He was going to move to aid Miranda and Micah within six months, but I had no idea exactly what would happen. I went to the calendar to see it was June 25, 2006, which meant six months, would put us on Christmas Day, December 25, 2006. I lay on the bed and cried. Honestly, I knew it was God, but did not believe it would end. I had heard what Dr. Neuro #3 said, and thought there was no way out.

I realize after reading this book to this point you might think, how could I doubt when God had moved so many times? Faith is fragile and needs to be handled with care. I had been fighting for Miranda's life since she was born, and by this point I had been fighting for my life with severe, horrid pain for 18 months. I was on strong medication, but nothing stopped the nerve pain and excruciating headaches. I was desperate at a different level. I recall reminding God how Jesus suffered, but at least He was allowed to die. I just suffered and without an end in sight, and now to KNOW my children were doomed to my life was incomprehensible. These diseases do not just kill you – they make you suffer greatly and for years before you finally die. Imagine lying in a bed with pain shooting through your body. You are unable to move and yet the pain will not go away. The pain is so strong you can barely breathe, but somehow your body won't quit, and you simply suffer minute-by-minute, hour-by-hour, day-by-day with no end in sight. Your bed becomes your life, and medication is your best friend. It is a world in which no one should have to live, and if you have never been there, count yourself blessed!

I have screamed in pain. I have gritted my teeth so hard that I broke a tooth, and the pain in my body was so great I did not feel the pain of the broken tooth. I have been blind. I have been deaf. I have been unable to walk. I have been unable to crawl. I have pulled my body on the ground from my bed to the bathroom just to vomit, and lay there because I was too weak to get back to bed. I have been carried by my husband and friends in and out of cars to wheelchairs and doctors' offices. My entire life was suffering, pain, and losing complete independence. I was unable to even brush my teeth. The first year I handled it with faith and courage. I believed there was a way out. I believed I would live and be well. I believed God when He told me, "You will be better at the end of this than you were going into it." But time, pain, and now heartbreak had crushed my hopes.

I was facing another painful surgery in New York, and even though we finally had the answers to what was wrong with Miranda, the answer was a nightmare! If quitting were an option, I would have taken it. But, I had been trained by my Dad to NEVER quit. I was never allowed to quit anything and always required to do my best. When my faith was crushed, my training took over. I would not quit – I couldn't.

The surgery for my tethered spinal cord was set for August 31, 2006. So, Kevin and I knew we were headed back to New York. I was scared to death. I was so fearful of allowing them to touch me again. I had endured the pain of the brain and neck surgery, so New York was a scary place to me. I was afraid of the pain. Fortunately for me, my body was also in horrid pain without the surgery, so that helped me set my face like flint one more time to face a painful surgery and recovery.

My heart was broken. My children had inherited their health issues from me. My life was unbearable, and I could not see an end in sight. I had prayed, fought, believed, traveled, fasted, endured endless medical evaluations, had four major operations, I had even let men literally screw my head onto me, but now I could not see any point in it. I could not see a way out. Dr. Neuro #3 said the children would need annual evaluations. God had said it would end.

I want to say it was not Dr. Neuro #3 that upset me. Truly, he was a blessing to my family, and I was tremendously thankful for his hard work with treating our diseases. I trusted him totally, and that was another reason I was so upset. I knew he was telling me the truth based on medical evaluations. Where was God? And more importantly, "Whose report would I believe?"

My pastor had prayed years earlier "a fire would burn in me until I reached the other side." His words rose in my heart. I pressed on out of sheer training.

During the weeks, we waited to go back to New York for my spinal cord surgery, I went to an OBGYN doctor. My body was not well, and after much testing, it was decided I also needed a hysterectomy. Each month, during my female cycles, I would go blind and paralyzed. I had other major problems, so to fix it; of course, surgery was the answer yet again – this would make my sixth surgery in 18 months. I just scheduled the hysterectomy for the first of December 2006, and put it out of my mind. After so much, your brain simply cannot take any more, and I was there. I could not handle it, so I did not think about it.

A couple of days before we flew to New York for the spinal cord surgery, I called a man in our church. He was a physician's assistant for a neurosurgeon, so I knew he would understand the tethered cord surgery I was about to have. I wanted his opinion, and I wanted to know how much suffering I was about to face. He was incredible and extremely encouraging. He kept saying, "Donna, I believe this is your answer." Over and over he used those words.

In the year 2000, I continually cried out to God for the "answer." Religious people would tell me Jesus was the answer. Okay, I know what He did for me. I wanted the answer to Miranda's problem, not the story of Christ Jesus. I wanted knowledge and the truth to handle the exact problem I placed before God – not just a blanket answer. Of course, Jesus is the answer to mankind and salvation. I needed the answer to our problem. Knowledge is power, and people perish for lack of it. I wanted to know "the answer." This man was telling me what I had waited to hear for years. The problem was Chiari, which meant Miranda's brain was herniating down her neck and stopping the cerebrospinal fluid flow, but the answer was the tethered spinal cord. I did not understand it all, but I felt hope, which I had lost.

After talking to the physician's assistant on the phone, I had a renewed sense, I could do it. I could do whatever it took. I could endure this surgery. Kevin and I flew to New York, and my sister met us there. Ginger is so strong. She is like a warrior, and she was exactly what I needed in the battle. Neither she nor Kevin let me quit or felt sorry for me. They required me to do whatever I had to do, no matter how painful. They stuck together and required me to rise up and walk! I had much more memory coming out of this surgery. I recall waking up in the PACU unit, which is where you go after surgery, and taking a moment to assess the pain in my body. It was tolerable. In other words, I could handle it. I had the surgery on Thursday, August 31, 2006. Then, I boarded an airplane on Tuesday, September 5, 2006, and went home. I was in unbearable pain on the plane, and I was difficult to deal with physically. Poor Kevin had to try to help me, but sitting is a nightmare when your back has been cut. My incision was probably about eight inches and located in the lower mid back, the

L-4 region. Sitting in a seat was horrid, but I did it. We arrived home, and I went to bed. I had just a few weeks to heal before my next surgery, the hysterectomy. So, I drank water, ate right, and rested. The de-tethering of my spinal cord brought immediate help to my body. My legs were not in as much pain, and I could stand up straight as well as physically hold up my head.

Of course, life cannot ever just be simple. We had been home just a few days, when Kevin received the email his plant was closing in January 2007. In other words, his job was ending. He called me immediately, and I had peace. Of course, medical insurance was my first concern, but at least we had a warning. As I was praying, God moved in my heart to back up my hysterectomy to the first of November 2006, which would only give me eight weeks out of the spinal cord surgery. I called the OB doctor, and he agreed. I was concerned my body would not be able to handle so much trauma in such a short period of time, but in my heart, I knew God was ordering my steps.

Kevin came home from work and said he thought his insurance company would pay for Micah and Miranda's surgeries. I thought he had lost his mind. The kids were not scheduled to even return to New York until next June 2007, and by then Kevin would be unemployed. Kevin said he felt it was from God. I just thought it was not even possible. I just had surgery, and another surgery was planned in a few weeks.

The next morning when I woke up, God gave me instruction to contact Dr. Neuro #3 and let him know about Kevin's job ending. I called my pastor, and he prayed. It was powerful. He prayed we would walk out of 2006 with this entire thing over. I hung onto his words.

Then, I emailed Dr. Neuro #3 to let him know Kevin would be losing his job in January 2007. I wanted to know if Dr. Neuro #3 wanted to evaluate the kids before we lost our insurance. He emailed me back and set dates to review the kids in December 2006, and he went ahead and scheduled both of my kids to have their de-tethering surgeries. Even as I sit here and write, I am overwhelmed at what we endured. Dr. Neuro #3 had just seen the children in June 2006, and now in September 2006, we were planning on their surgeries. I was just a couple of weeks out of my spinal cord surgery and had another surgery planned for November 3, 2006. How in the world could we possibly do this?

I recall getting the email from Dr. Neuro #3 and going to my bedroom. I called my pastors, but they did not answer. I left a message. I sat in my closet for hours and cried. I did not want my children to suffer the pain of surgery. I wanted it over, but not that way. Micah's situation pulled my heart even more, because God had said, "it will never touch him." I had hung onto those words. I knew Miranda needed medical intervention, but I had trusted Micah would grow whole as God had promised. I found myself sitting in the floor crying and unsure of anything I had ever believed.

CHAPTER 22

IT'S OVER!

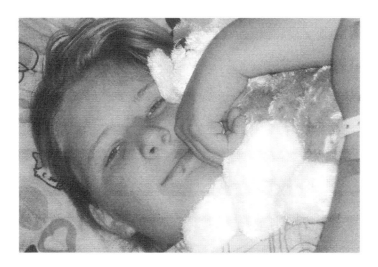

If you have ever ridden a roller coaster then you can comprehend where our family was. We were latched in for the ride. There was no stopping it – only riding it out and getting off as soon as possible. My personal declaration throughout the entire journey was the scripture in Isaiah 40:4.

Isaiah 40:4

"Every valley shall be exalted, and every mountain and hill shall be made low: and the crooked shall be made straight, and the rough places plain. (KJV)

I pulled myself together and set my face like flint. Regardless of the past or future, I had learned happiness in not a place to arrive at, but rather how I daily lived my life. Even though I was in relentless pain and surgeries were being scheduled, I was going to be happy. That was a choice.

We were given a Disney cruise by a friend, which was scheduled for November 31 – December 3, 2006. When we agreed to go, I thought I would be having my hysterectomy the week we returned, but our whole lives had been turned upside down again and our schedule greatly changed. My hysterectomy was scheduled for November 3, 2006. Micah and Miranda would have the de-tethering of their spinal cords on December 11, 2006. We had to be in New York on December 7, 2006, for tests. So, we would have to leave on December

6, 2006.

Kevin and I discussed it and decided it was God for us to go on the vacation. We even lengthened it knowing the children would not be able to physically do much after their surgeries. So, we scheduled to go to Florida the day before Thanksgiving and come home on December 3, 2006. We would then leave for New York on Wednesday, December 6, 2006. I would have two days to get everything ready to go to New York for their surgeries.

We contacted our pastors and elders at our church. We met and prayed over the children. It was odd for me. I had fought this battle for years and the entire time they were praying all I could think is, "It is over." I was not excited by it or even hopeful. It just was. It was over. The children and the pastors talked and prayed. Kevin and I sat there in agreement, but I knew my part was over. I was finished. I had found the answers to the physical problems in our bodies.

> This is added in 2013. This was most definitely a pivotal point in our family's life. The battle to find the root of the problems in Miranda, Micah and myself had ended. That particular portion of the journey was over. However, our war against the physical issues we fought was not over. Simply, the truth to deal with Miranda's physical conditions had been exposed. Knowing what you are fighting is ninety percent of the battle.

I went into the hospital on November 3, 2006, for my hysterectomy. I was nervous. I knew my body was weak. I honestly was not sure it could endure the trauma of another surgery. As always, God brought help, our church pianist was my nurse. She had been Miranda's nurse at Miranda's first MRI, and she was now the head nurse at the hospital where my surgery was located. She stood with me while I lay on the gurney, and she held my hand. She was there when I went to sleep, and she was there when I woke up. It was rough when I woke up. My body did not respond well to the pain medication. I had so many medications go through me it had made my body resistant. She calmly asked me what to do, and I told her to ask Kevin. Kevin always knew what to do. He told her the amount of pain medication I needed, and they gave it to me. It worked. My body calmed down.

By midnight, I thought the worst was behind me, but I was wrong. A friend showed up to take the night shift with me, and within minutes, my brain began to swell. Pain was shooting through my body, and I went blind. I lost the control of my legs. They were paralyzed. I could hear the nurse talking to my friend, but I could not see anything. I was scared. At the same time, the nurse from church called the hospital to check on me. Her phone call gave me peace, knowing God had someone praying. My friend prayed and hung on to me. She kept me going. The nurse gave me shots of medication, and the swelling went down. The next day the doctor released me, and I went home. I was in a great deal of pain, and my body was weak. I had a terrible night again, and Kevin ended up returning me to the hospital. They readmitted me and kept me for the next 48 hours. They put me on antibiotics and high doses of pain medications. I survived, yet again.

My body was so weak when I left the hospital, I did not see any way possible for me to go to Florida by the end of the month. But God!

Days passed, and my body made amazing strides. I was even impressed. I had a vision of God placing me upright on a refrigerator dolly and pushing my body around. I knew it was time to get up and walk on with my life. My physical battle was over, or so I thought. Do not get me wrong, my body had a lot of healing to do, but the war had been won. I simply needed time to heal.

We left for Florida as planned, and we had a blessed trip. God gave us favor everywhere we went. We spent a week in Orlando going to the Disney theme parks, and I did it. I walked through all of them and kept up with my family. I was still medicated, but capable of walking. I even recall the trip. It was great, and I felt as if a state of normal might actually be possible for our family one day. We boarded the Disney cruise on November 31, and we were blessed! They bumped up our cabin to a veranda room, and Miranda was thrilled. They gave us gifts and hosted a VIP party just for our family. Also, they gave us free photos from the pictures taken with Mickey Mouse. The weather was perfect, and the trip was a gift from heaven. I did not want to get off the boat. I would have stayed there forever, but we had to go.

We arrived home late on Sunday, December 3, 2006, and quickly unpacked. The next two days were full of laundry, bills, and taking care of loose ends to prepare for the New York trip.

I had to go to the doctor, because my body was not well. I had extreme swelling, pain, and infection. We all climbed back into our car on December 6, 2006, and headed to New York for the children to have surgery.

We stayed at the Ronald McDonald House on Long Island. The staff was a tremendous blessing to our family. The house provided lodging, food, and a place to do laundry. We arrived Wednesday late and began testing on Thursday. I did not go to any tests or doctor appointments with the children. Kevin took them. I lay on the couches in the waiting rooms. I did not go for two reasons.

One, I was sick. And two, I had told God I could not be the one to push this button. If the children needed the surgeries, then He had to do it. I was staying out of the final inning. I only wanted to watch. I was weary and very unsure of myself. Kevin was strong and very capable of handling the situation. After all, he was their Dad!

Shock riveted throughout my body when Kevin and the kids came out of the meeting with Dr. Neuro #3, the neurosurgeon. Decisions by Dr. Neuro #3 were made, Miranda would have surgery, and Micah would not.

At this point, I want to tell you what the medical records stated for each child. Micah had Neurofibromatosis type 1, retroflexed odontoid with pannus formation, flat pituitary, basilar impression, low-lying brain tonsils – Chiari, meniscus sign, decreased flow posteriorly behind the tip of the odontoid, no lumbarization of S1, conus at mid-L-2, straightened lumbar spine, lateral packing of the roots, EDS, with a tethered spinal cord.

Miranda had Intermittent Cushing's, a flat pituitary, EDS, blurred and double vision, pain, headaches, low-lying brain tonsils – Chiari, decreased flow anteriorly on cine MRI, retroflexed odontoid and pannus formation, conus at mid L-1, straightened cervical spine, as well as a tethered spinal cord.

The decision was made to operate on Miranda and not Micah, which was shocking. Both children had the same malformations and physical conditions, which would require the de-tethering of their spinal cords. Each of them had medical conditions the other one did not have inside their body. My mind began to spin. I was in shock. I had settled in my mind we would do whatever it took to end this, and now Micah's surgery was cancelled. Both children were crying in the car, and I was trying to understand what had happened. Kevin explained Micah had grown four inches in the past five months, and Dr. Neuro #3 did not want to cut into his back at this time. Also, Micah did not meet the criteria for surgery. I wanted this to end. Why not now?

Then, even as my mind was racing, God reminded me of His promise over Micah. God had told me, "It will never touch him." Peace settled in my heart, because I knew it was God who ordered Micah's steps.

Let me say, when you are faced with life and death decisions, you need to know Him for yourself. You need to hear Him when circumstances scream louder than your own ability to think. I knew what God had promised, and the past several months appeared as if the promise was void, but at the last possible minute the promise prevailed. Micah would not have surgery. Micah would grow whole, regardless of the report of the doctors. Regardless of the facts in his body, God spoke and God meant what He said.

Now, our family quickly focused on what lay ahead with Miranda. I was all too familiar with the pain of these types of surgeries. My parents, Kevin's mother, and my friend all came to New York to help us with the caring for Miranda after surgery. It was a journey nobody wanted to take, but necessary to end this nightmare.

Kevin and I took Miranda to the hospital at 5:00 a.m. on December 11, 2006. We did all the preadmission the Friday prior to the surgery. So, Miranda had been on a tour of the hospital and was familiar with the nurses as well as the set up. We prepared her to go into surgery and kissed her goodbye at 7:00 a.m. She was rolled down the same hallway, I had been to suffer the same surgery I had received. I put her in the hands of God. I trusted Him alone to keep her safe during surgery.

Waiting was the next phase. I had not been on the waiting side of the process in quite some time, because during the past couple of years I was the one having surgeries. We waited in the surgical waiting room until they gave us a pager that would go off when the surgeon was going to address the family with the report. After receiving the pager, we went downstairs to get some coffee. The surgery took around five hours. I had perfect peace during the entire time she was gone. As a family, we headed back to the waiting room when it was time for the surgery to end. When the beeper went off, I felt like a robot. I was emotionally numb, but prepared for whatever the doctor would say.

Dr. Neuro #5 walked out to greet Kevin and me. All the family followed us out into the hallway. Dr. Neuro #5 was pleased. He said Miranda was a true tethered cord, one of the worst cases he had seen. When he released her spinal cord, it jumped between two and one-half to three inches. He said Miranda had little to no cerebrospinal fluid flow below her L3 region. He said they took pictures, and he felt confident the surgery was successful. He went on to say, with the spinal cord released, it was their hope her brain would go back into position and her body would be well. There it was! "It" was a tethered spinal cord.

Years of pressing forward. Years of praying God would give us a miracle. Years of believing God would reveal the root of her problem and set her free. There it was. He said it so simply and with such resolve. He had found it and released it. He had made a way for my child to be well. Emotions ran fast through my brain. I thanked him. He went on to say the PACU unit would call Kevin and me soon to go see her.

Remember the PA back home who I called before I had my spinal cord de-tethered. He was right, and his words were prophetic! The de-tethering of Miranda's spinal cord was her answer. With time this could take the pressure off her brain stem, and I was hopeful even her flat pituitary would eventually correct itself!

I turned to my family, and they were all crying except Kevin. He was strong as always. I did not cry either. I simply felt shock. All these years of fighting were over in a second. The root of the problem had been found and fixed, even the report of the doctor said so. We would have never looked in her spinal cord. All symptoms pointed to the pituitary and the brain. Without the car wreck and the surgeries endured, we would have never found it. My fifth surgery was her answer. The number five in the Bible stands for "new life." Miranda would finally be whole. Miranda still had her Chiari Malformation, but this surgery was hopefully going to give Miranda the ability to heal. We were excited. God had made a way – not the way I would have chosen, but nonetheless a way.

I took the medical report of Miranda's toe to New York because, locally, no doctor could figure out what the problem was. She had the black spots cut out through surgery, and they came back. Then we did cryosurgery where the doctors tried to burn the spots off, but they came back. I wanted someone in New York to look at her toe. The physician's assistant asked Dr. Neuro #5, and he said her toe was dying because of the spinal cord not having the cerebrospinal fluid flow. Obviously, he was right. Because within days of her surgery, her toe turned white again and the black spots were gone. We were definitely out of time.

Dr. Neuro #5's words were hard to digest. The thought Miranda had no cerebrospinal fluid flow is unbelievable. How did she walk? How did her bladder ever work? How did she function? Only God! I remembered clearly how in the year 2000, I was told she would die, and there was no hope. Our church fasted and prayed on behalf of our entire family. Miranda regained the ability to walk and her bladder control, which she had lost. I had no idea what God had done in her body, but I knew He had done a miracle. Now a medical report told us why her body did not function. How God kept her safe until the right moment in time is simply grace, and I am thankful from the bottom of my heart.

These doctors and their knowledge – saved our lives. Do you also recall in the year 2000, I was told by Dr. Endo #2 and a pediatrician to help Miranda we would need a medical research breakthrough? Well, we received one!

I was so angry God did not reveal more in the year 2000, but if He had, it would have harmed or possibly killed Miranda. We had to wait for the right doctor with knowledge, and God gave us wisdom through prayer as well as the diet, which allowed for the time to pass. My mind was flooded with the journey we had taken and how all of the sudden it was over. God had kept His word. I also realized if I had known how bad it would get or what I would have to endure before the end, I could not have handled it. God kept me ignorant to keep me safe. It was His love and wisdom not to tell me in advance. I would not have been able to handle it.

I questioned one thing greatly in all the prophecy. Why was the word tumor used when ultimately it was a tethered spinal cord that appeared to be the root of the problem? A tethered spinal cord is where a piece of extra tissue is wrapped around the cord and attached further up the spinal cord, which causes harm. A tumor is simply extra body tissue. Time would tell, but one thing I learned above all else was to let God interpret His words to me and not try to figure them out on my own. I had learned to lean not on my own understanding, which gave me great peace. Whatever the physical problems were, I just wanted both of my children well.

The next step after hearing from the neurosurgeon was getting Miranda through the pain of the surgery. Kevin decided he would take night shifts, and I would take days. One of us had to be there at all times as her advocate. So, I was there from 7:00 a.m. until 7:00 p.m., and Kevin was there the other twelve hours. Twelve-hour shifts are hard, especially on a body like mine, which had just gone through two surgeries in the past four months. My first shift began as soon as Miranda requested us to come to her in the PACU unit, which is the first place a patient goes after surgery at that hospital. Kevin and I went in together, but he left so he could sleep and come back for the night. I sat in a chair beside her bed for about seven hours without a break. The unit was in constant motion with people coming from surgery and heading to their rooms for recovery. Miranda's breathing would not stabilize, so we waited longer than most patients. Grandparents and friends were not allowed in the unit, so I was on my own. It was odd. I had been there twice because of my surgeries, but this time I was there for Miranda. They gave Miranda a pump for her pain, and it did help her greatly. She was upset when she woke up. She was angry, and said we had lied to her. She was screaming at us, because she was in pain. We calmly reminded her no one said it would be pain free or easy. After the pump began to work, Miranda relaxed, but I had to touch her hand continuously to keep her calm.

Finally, Miranda was moved to PICU which is the pediatric intensive care unit. She was blessed to get a private room. For the first 24 hours, a patient must lie flat after the surgery, so it was not too bad. Day two, however, was a different story. Miranda had to stand up, and at that point she was in horrid pain. She screamed and cried, but I knew it was the best thing for her to get moving. So, I knelt down in front of her face and encouraged her she could do it. She could get up. She could walk. She pulled herself together and stood up, which was a victory in the moment. The day went downhill, and she spiked a fever. Her pain increased, and I was exhausted. I left the hospital drained in every aspect. Kevin had my parents stay with me from 7:00 a.m. till 1:00 p.m., my friend and Kevin's mother came at 1:00 p.m. till 7:00 p.m. My body was weak and Kevin knew it, so he did not want me alone. When I left the hospital, and returned to the Ronald McDonald House, I called my pastor and told him about Miranda's day. He said they would pray. I went to bed.

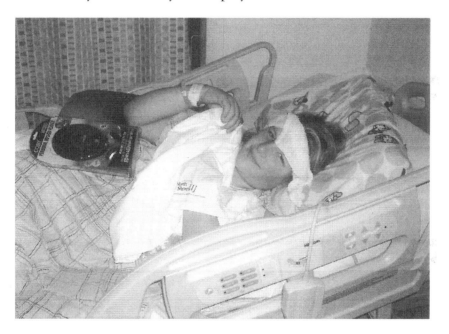

The next day Miranda had improved greatly, and I was relieved. The decision was made to move her out of PICU on the third day into the regular pediatric ward. I was thankful for her body responding well. The pump for pain was removed, and a downward spiral began. Miranda was in extreme pain. Kevin and I had the doctors change her medications. She had difficulty going to the bathroom and refused to sit in a chair. But by the fourth and fifth day, she was gaining ground and even walking. By the sixth day, we could take Miranda out of the hospital to the Ronald McDonald House. We stayed in New York until her stitches were removed to insure she was stable enough to move her back to Tennessee.

We had already celebrated Christmas at our house before we went to New

York, because we did not know when we would be home. We were certain after surgery Christmas would be a great deal to do physically for the children. The Ronald McDonald House gave them a gift, which was so sweet, and Santa visited Miranda in the hospital twice. We were willing to wait to take Miranda home whenever her body was ready to travel. Once again, we thought we would spend Christmas in New York, but Miranda did so well. We had the stitches removed on December 21, 2006, and drove home on December 22, 2006. Just as God promised, it was over by December 25, 2006. We were home for Christmas, but we had already received the best gift we will ever get. Miranda had the ability to grow whole. We thought the battle was over.

Miranda, while in the PACU unit, asked me for a specific toy for Christmas. She wanted a specific stuffed animal called "Cheeky Dog." Well, we looked in New York and it was sold out everywhere. We called a friend back home to see if she could buy it off the internet for us. My friend called me back and said cheeky dog had been retired, and the only place she could find it was online for over $100.00. I told her to let it go for now. My friend sent out emails all over the United States, and a woman named Krista took great interest. She put an ad in her local newspaper in the state of Illinois about Miranda. A very generous man bought Miranda "Cheeky Dog" from online and even more items. The box was at our house when we arrived home from New York. Miranda received her wish!

CHAPTER 23

GAINING GROUND

Miranda and I both continued to heal from December 2006, to the summer of 2007. We spent many hours lying in bed and allowing our bodies to heal. My heart was at peace, and so thankful we had finally conquered the issues in our bodies. God had promised "they will find it." And with time and patience, they did. I would spend many hours reading the book I was documenting about all God was doing to bring healing to Miranda. It was extremely beneficial for me to read through the material I had written from previous years and know all God had accomplished on our behalf. I would have never dreamed I had given Miranda her health issues. I genuinely thought I was completely healthy. Truly, I thought our battle with sickness and disease was over.

Through Donna Renfro Ministries, I held a conference in the spring of 2007, which I titled, "But God." There were just a few people who came; however, the significance was for me. I could stand up and teach a lesson which was amazing considering the previous three years of my life that consisted of lying in a bed and enduring multiple major surgeries. Although, I had regained my ability to walk, use my hands, see, and talk, I was so insecure about my ability to recall facts, read, or make complete sentences with my speech not to mention my physical body. I still did not know if I would be able to stand for any length of time, and the nerve pain in my body was constant and relentless. So, committing to holding a conference where I was the primary speaker took tremendous courage. Ultimately, I was the one who benefitted from the experience. Courage is the ability to go through the fear of a situation and do whatever you must. I learned I could still teach and endure standing long enough to give my message of hope. I came home from the conference hopeful about my future.

In June 2007, Kevin lost the job he received when Micah was born. Kevin had worked for that company Micah's entire life, but the plant was closing. We took the opportunity to travel. Within days of Kevin coming home, we put our suitcases in the car and drove across the United States. It was amazing. We went through all the northern states first. Then, down through California and ended our trip by coming home through the southern states. We were gone for twenty-one days. The kids loved every minute, and my body survived the trip well. I was still on high powered medication, but I was able to go on the trip with my family. Life was good, and we were gaining ground daily.

The fall of 2007 was good. We held another conference which was titled "The Law of Kindness." Again, not many people were there, but my personal insecurities were becoming smaller. After my brain surgery, I had many "mental hurdles" to cross. I feared driving, being alone, talking, walking, physical pain, as well as going back into the public to speak. Daily, I had to reclaim my life. Daily, I had to choose to believe I could do it – whatever it was. At my lowest physical points, I had been trapped in bathrooms blind and unable to walk on my own, so to regain the ability to live again, I overcame many fears. I had to make myself go and do whatever I feared to overcome. I had to overcome my fears; no one could do that for me.

Many people would have seen Kevin's unemployment as a terrible loss. However, perspective is everything, because I saw it as a tremendous gift. I needed him. He made my life normal by being all I could not be physically. For instance, lifting a gallon of milk is out of my ability. But with Kevin around, he could meet all my physical needs, which allowed me to live normally. He drove and did most of the grocery shopping. We became closer than we had ever been. God, through the Bible, explains a man and a woman become one when they are married. Well, Kevin and I were one in a new way. I needed him to physically step in and do for me daily. Deep down, Kevin loved the fact I needed him. It strengthened us as a couple. I had always been so independent before the car wreck. Kevin knew I loved him, but now I needed him at a deeper level.

During the summer of 2008, Kevin had been out of work for a year. He had continued to place resumes in multiple places, but no job. I began searching the heart of God through prayer. As I prayed, I knew Kevin would not be going back to work. This thought concerned me greatly, and I did not think it was a good plan. I was physically disabled. We needed Kevin to gain employment, which would provide insurance as well as income. But deep in my heart, I knew he was home for good. Many people made comments and offered advice about Kevin's employment situation, but I had learned through all our health issues to ignore the words of people, even well-meaning people, and follow God even if I did not understand the circumstances.

In the fall of 2008, I was walking to my mother's house when God moved on my heart concerning a certain medication I was taking for nerve pain. I had thought I would be on it for the rest of my life; however, in prayer, suddenly I had a deep knowledge I could stop taking the medication. This excited me greatly, because the medication made it difficult to recall facts and be myself. So, after speaking with my doctor, I began the process of weaning myself from the nerve medication.

During one of my visits to Miranda's neurologist, a lady in the waiting room came over to me, and spoke with me for a long time. She told me about a program for disabled people called Vocational Rehabilitation. She said it would help disabled individuals go to college and find work they could physically handle. After the visit, I contacted our local Vocational Rehabilitation Services and applied for myself. I wanted to work. I knew, with our ministry, we could help other people, teach, and give our testimony. But, I felt I needed credentials so the Church would take me seriously.

My first encounter with my Vocational advisor was interesting. I walked into the meeting and sat down. Kevin went with me to carry my documentation. The lady was pleasant; however, she took one look at me and said Vocational Rehabilitation Services only take severely handicap people. Because of my personal appearance, she quickly judged me and thought I was an able body individual. I asked her if she would like my documentation. Of course, she wanted to see my evidence. You could literally see the horror in her eyes when she realized what I had endured, my physical limitations, and my permanent disabilities. She was shocked. Just because an individual does not look disabled or sick, they can be in extreme pain, suffering, or fighting for their very life – never judge a person by their appearance.

During my meeting with Vocational services, my advisor told me both my children would qualify as well. So, I immediately had Micah placed with Vocational services. Micah was going to graduate from high school in December 2008 and begin at East Tennessee State University in January 2009. Micah was approved by Vocational Rehabilitation services, and they began helping him in his journey through college, which was a tremendous blessing. I was approved for Vocational Rehabilitation services as well. I made the decision to go to Seminary to work towards a Master of Arts in Religion with a concentration in New Testament.

Since I would always need Kevin by my side to open doors, carry my books, and aid me physically while in school, he decided to complete his Bachelor of Science degree at East Tennessee State University and go with me to Seminary as a full-time student. So, we made the decision to wait until the fall of 2009 to begin. Kevin completed his B.S. degree by July of 2009. We gave Kevin a party to celebrate his achievement in completing his degree. Life was good.

Kevin and I stepped into a whole new world in the fall of 2009. We began our degree program at a local Seminary. We were working on our Master of Arts and Religion. I was excited and nervous about going back to college. Our first day was terrifying. Kevin and I attended orientation the week prior to classes starting. There was a definite realization this academic program was going to be a challenge; however, I wanted a challenge. On the first day of class, we started with Greek. Our professor opened the class with a test. He came over to my chair first and handed me a paper with a list of Greek words on it. My immediate reaction was shock. The professor realized I was overwhelmed by the look on my face. He told the class we could take it home as homework. Many of the students in the Greek class had previous experience with Greek; however, Kevin and I had no knowledge at all. We were overwhelmed. We were assigned five chapters and told to return the next day for a quiz with our homework.

Kevin and I both walked out of the Greek class seriously contemplating quitting immediately. We both wanted to run out of the school. This Seminary had chapel every day; so, we decided to go to chapel to decompress from the Greek class before running out of the building. I do not recall what was said at chapel, but afterwards I did want to go to our Old Testament class. Our next professor taught Old Testament. He was brilliant. I sat in the class taking notes from the moment he opened his mouth until he stopped. The class flew by. Both Kevin and I were intrigued by his knowledge. That night we went home and spent hours going over our Greek to go back the next day to take a test. It was frightening, but we did it. A student in the Greek class took us under his wing, and we began to study with him on a regular basis. Kevin and I both knew we were in over our heads. Honestly, I thought going to Seminary would be easy. I had studied the Bible for over twenty years, but this Seminary was extremely academic and approached the Biblical text in a different way of digging deep into the history, original text, and rigorous study. I was hungry for the truth and genuinely wanted to know the Greek, but was unsure of my abilities to learn, retain, and understand a complex language.

We decided to continue in the program despite much fear, hard work, and intimidation. The other students were younger than us for the most part. Most of them were in their twenties. I was thirty-nine. I could not have endured this Seminary without Kevin. He was my best friend, study partner, and carried all my books. With my neck, I could not even open the doors to the building. We studied together all the time. Kevin could just listen to the professors and understand. I had to diligently take notes, make study guides, and go over the information daily to keep up. I wanted to prove to myself I could recall information. I wanted to know that I had the ability to learn and retain information. Becoming disabled had taken away my confidence. While I was sick and on medication I was not able to recall a lot of my life, and I wanted to know I could build a future. Even when I was a small child, I knew I wanted higher level degrees. However, I always thought I would pursue psychology. Theology was not even a thought. But, God had a different plan for Kevin and me, and His way is perfect.

As I moved through the first semester in this Seminary, Kevin and I diligently studied. We were both nervous each time we took a test. We are both competitive and wanted to do our best. Each test we took, we both grew in our confidence and ultimately made excellent grades. I knew Kevin had the capability of greatness; however, it was a huge success for me personally. Honestly, I struggled with any confidence and only time proved to me that I could learn. My grades reflected my abilities were still intact. Going to Seminary was proving to be educational in the sense we were learning the Biblical text in depth, and our relationship with each other was strengthened. Kevin believed in me. He encouraged me daily. He carried my books, but more importantly, he held my heart. His confidence in me gave me the ability to move forward to accomplish my dream of having a master's degree despite my physical limitations. Once again, Kevin was the strength in our journey. I relied on him completely.

During October of 2009, I woke up in the middle of the night with horrid pain shooting through both of my arms. School was requiring me to use my arms more. I had to write, type, and study, which meant my hands were in constant use. The nerve pain shooting in my body was unbearable. I began to pray about what to do. While praying, I recalled my neurosurgeon in New York telling me I would need both of my ulnar nerves repaired. So, I made an appointment with my local neurosurgeon. He ordered an EMG to be completed on both of my arms. The EMG's were read and the results said the nerve pain was originating in my neck. I was heartbroken with the report. I just sat in the office crying. I have a syrinx in my neck. If the nerve pain was due to the syrinx nothing would stop it. Finally, I pulled myself together and left the office. When I entered the waiting room Kevin, and two very dear friends of mine were sitting there waiting on me. I was unable to talk. I just started crying again and had to leave to spend some time alone. I drove around for a bit. Eventually, I realized I had to simply face the facts. I went to the follow-up appointment with my neurosurgeon, and he disagreed with the findings. He was convinced operating on my ulnar nerves would help me. So, I agreed to the first surgery. We set the date for the first arm after Christmas, so I would be finished with the fall semester of school.

In November 2009, I was sitting downstairs at my computer studying for Old Testament when I heard a loud noise. I went upstairs. Kevin had fallen. He looked a bit dazed. I asked him what happened, and he said he did not know. He just fell. We realized he was not hurt. So, we both went on with our day. Then, a few weeks later he fell again. We were both alarmed, but did not think it was any big deal. Kevin was not in pain. He was beginning to have difficulty walking, but no pain. He said his legs felt numb. My parents encouraged Kevin to go to a chiropractor. So, I took him to be evaluated. The chiropractor took x-rays and said Kevin had a tilted hip. He said with chiropractic adjustments he could help him. Kevin went for several weeks to receive adjustments from the chiropractor and seemed to be improving.

We both survived our first finals week. It was so rewarding to receive our grades. At the end of an academically challenging semester, we both made A's. I was on cloud nine when I received my final test results. I had studied, retained information, and successfully completed a semester towards my master's degree. It was rewarding. Kevin was equally happy. He enjoyed learning all the history and loved the interaction with the other students. Christmas was priceless.

CHAPTER 24

DON'T BE A ROLLER COASTER CHRISTIAN

Isaiah 40:4

"Every valley shall be raised, And every mountain and hill be made low; And let the rough ground become a plain, And the rugged places a broad valley." (Amplified)

Life will take you on a ride if you let it, but God will keep you on flat ground. Through painful experiences such as Miranda, Micah, and my health, I learned to trust God's faithfulness and not ride the roller coaster of life. Peace was a prize I desired; therefore, I put my confidence in the power of Jesus Christ and chose to rest in His Word. Silence can be your best defense during difficult times. Simply choose not to talk about the things you cannot change, and give it to God. At the same time, change the things you can to improve your situation. If you do not know what to do, do nothing. Wait upon God, He will deliver you.

Kevin playing softball before he had Multiple Sclerosis

Our entire life had once again been tossed into a tremendous storm. During December 2009 and January 2010, I had two arm surgeries. In between my arm surgeries, Miranda fell down some stairs at a dance recital she attended to watch

199

her cousin. Kevin was falling and losing more physical ability daily. By January, he could only lay on the couch. I had to meet with Children's Services and discuss the fact Miranda may be facing brain surgery with a fusion, due to a recent MRI and fall she had in January 2010. We received an email from the doctor who requested we have a conference call in the next few weeks to make decisions about Miranda. In February, Kevin tried to go to the Seminary to take a test, and he fell in the bathroom. I stood in shock with my hands on my head in the hallway. All the students who were getting ready for the test walked past me and treated me as if we were an inconvenience. But, there was one Godly man who did not care about his grade. He cared about Kevin. He stopped and asked me if I was okay, and I told him about Kevin. Immediately, this precious young man went to get help, clothes, and another man to aid Kevin. They could get him off the floor and changed him into clean clothes. He was literally Jesus in the flesh for me in the middle of a nightmare. He holds a special place in my heart, and I will never forget his love, sacrifice, and kindness in the middle of a nightmare.

Our life was spinning out of control so rapidly my brain could not keep up with all the issues. Kevin fell at the Seminary on February 24, 2010. However, Kevin refused to go to the hospital. We both took the Old Testament test after he was put in a wheelchair. When the exam was complete, a couple of professors helped put him in my car. Kevin made me take him home. The next morning Kevin tried to walk down our stairs, and he pulled the handrail out of the wall destroying both the sheetrock as well as ruining the wall studs, which supported the handrail. On February 25, 2010, my Dad and I took him to our internist who immediately placed him in the hospital. Within five days, he was diagnosed with Multiple Sclerosis. Then, I had to go to the department of human services to file for benefits for my husband and family. It was a humbling experience. We were going to the Seminary and beginning our second semester towards a master's degree. I thought we had put sickness and disease in our past. I thought we were finished with hospitals, trauma, and life altering information. But, I was wrong. Now we were back in the middle of facing death. When we were first married, working, and living in normal bodies, I would have never dreamed we would, one day, be on food stamps. We were both raised to work hard and earn an education. Our life goes to show you, you never know what a day will hold. Knowing who you are in Christ Jesus will enable you to go through any storm in life. If you get your identity out of being a child of God, then if your body fails you or takes your abilities to work away, you will stay strong in your spirit and have the power to endure. Remember, your worth does not come from your accomplishments, achievements, possessions, or accolades. You are a child of God and are saved by grace, because Jesus paid the price.

The storms of life once again attacked our family. Yet strength, the type of strength which can only come from God, rose again on the inside of me as I faced the unthinkable and the unbelievable. I had spent the past months in hospitals, rehab centers, diagnostic centers, and yet peace remains. I had to withdraw Kevin and me from school and once again placed my desires on the back burner – maybe for a season and maybe forever. However, I know, even though I have been shocked by the reality Kevin has Multiple Sclerosis – God is in control. He knew we would face this situation, and He was not surprised. I find comfort in that truth.

This year, I turned 40 and thought a new decade would bring a new life. I was right. But the new life was not what I expected. Honestly and with my entire heart, I believed sickness and heartbreaking diagnoses was in our past. However, regardless of the blows, which came one right after the other – my heart remains steadfast to the reality of God in me, my Source, my Strength, and my Comforter.

Since December 31, 2009, I have had two arm surgeries. Miranda fell down stairs and was facing the reality she may need brain surgery with a fusion. My son, Micah was falsely accused of a hit and run. My husband was hospitalized and diagnosed with MS – but through it all I have not one time felt alone. My God has sustained me and carried me through. Life is full of pain, disappointment, and sorrow, but God is full of grace, love, and mercy. Regardless of what we face this side of Heaven, joy in us can sustain us through the darkest nights. God is faithful.

On the day, Kevin and I were married nineteen years, he was at the inpatient Rehabilitation Center, because he was wheelchair bound and unable to take care of himself. Kevin was unable to move anything from the waist down. I was spending most of my day trying to make sure Kevin would receive the needed medication, which would cost $3,000.00 a month for the rest of his life. While I drove to the hospital to see my husband, all I could think was: this is not the way I imaged our anniversary. I felt alone and somewhat hopeless. Just weeks prior, Kevin had a limp but was okay. I had no reason to ever think any major illness would strike him, especially with all the physical limitations I daily encountered. I had thought God would keep Kevin safe, and he would take care of me. Now, I was the primary caregiver, and our future looked dim.

I arrived at the rehabilitation center and was sitting in the corner of the room when I saw two women outside the door. Kevin was being examined by another doctor, so I went into the hallway. These women did not know me, but knew of our circumstances due to the Seminary. Kevin and I were students enrolled in a master's program when our life came to a screeching halt on February 25, 2010

– the day Kevin went into the hospital. We had several visitors from the school and tremendous support. But these women would encourage my heart at a level only the One true God could impart.

I had never talked with these ladies or prayed with them, but they boldly told me what God had impressed upon their hearts. One of the ladies had been at their weekly prayer meeting when Kevin's situation was discussed. She said immediately she saw Kevin drowning in water out in the middle of a patch of ice and thought we need to "toss him a rope." She went on to say how God impressed upon her how fireman will not leave a man behind, and Christians should be the same way. She promised me that she would hold on to the rope and help pull us out no matter how long it would take. She told me many others at the Seminary would hang on as well. Then both ladies went on to pray for God to do a miracle for our family.

My eyes filled with tears, and my heart ached. I did not believe we would receive a miracle. All I could feel was the shock and disappointment from the trauma. But her words stuck in my mind as the next days unfolded. Slowly over time, Kevin gained back his abilities. He eventually was well enough to go into outpatient rehabilitation. On March 9, 2010 – my 19th anniversary, I had no reason to believe Kevin would ever walk again. No hope in my heart. But God sent two ladies to hang on to the promises of God for us, while we were too weak to believe.

I do not know where you are today or what you may be facing, but be encouraged. God is faithful. He will make a way where there seems to be no way. My faith was gone, so He sent others to toss us a rope. They refused to let go of us while we struggled. Their faith and hope enabled us to get through. I have had the opportunity to experience the faithfulness of God regardless of my faith. As Christians, we know there is power in numbers. If you are blessed and strong in your faith, then toss a rope to the hurting around you. If you are hurting or fearful, then lean on the faith of your brothers and sisters in Christ. We, as Believers, make up the Body of Christ, and we are never alone.

On March 5, 2010, Kevin was moved to a rehabilitation hospital where he was wheelchair bound. After several weeks, he was released to come home with handicap equipment, which included a ramp being attached to our house for his entrance. Kevin was then scheduled for outpatient rehabilitation services. I woke one morning and was not in the mood to take Kevin to outpatient therapy. It was early, and I wanted to just sleep. However, I did manage to drag my body out of bed and drive him to the rehab center. As I sat there, watching the others – thankfulness grew in my heart. When Kevin first began to learn how to walk, the physical therapists had to use ropes to hoist him up. Kevin could walk today with the use of two canes, and he did well. He is still numb, but his body is learning to move despite the numbness. It was good to see. Just weeks ago, he lay in intensive care unable to move from the chest down. His body was like jello, even if they tried to get him to sit up in the bed.

A man rolled into the rehab facility in a wheelchair with attached oxygen. I immediately was reminded of how God had told me years ago, "Be thankful you are not paralyzed." Back in December 2004, when I was rear ended in an automobile accident. The pain which shot through my body was intolerable. However, pain means you can feel your body. Eventually, I did lose my ability to walk and my hands were paralyzed, but with time I gained back my mobility. Today, as I watched this particular man, my heart was encouraged. His mother did not know me or my story. She simply came over where I was sitting and sat down beside me. She introduced herself and began talking to me about her son. He was 37 years old – just three years younger than me. His car accident was in 2004 just like mine. As she spoke, I knew our meeting was purposefully ordained. God had ordered my steps to meet this lady and hear her story. She bragged about her son. Just recently, he gave a speech at a brain injury seminar. She was so proud of him, and I felt it from her heart. She said he spoke on "Life after Death." This immediately rang in my ears. Over and over, I have had to rebuild my life after a death. Although many normally speak of death in terms of people dying, there are different types of death a person endures and lives through, such as divorce, major illness, loss of a job, or loss of a dream. Redefining a life after major loss and life changing event is difficult, at the least, and with many people, it is impossible.

Honestly, I struggled with God throughout the weeks Kevin was in rehabilitation. Kevin and I were working towards goals, and it appeared our life was back on track. We were living what almost seemed normal. And then suddenly, we were tossed back into the sea of sickness, disease, and suffering. When your life is flipped upside down, you have the opportunity to decide if you will continue to follow Christ. We each have that decision daily, but when life is good – struggles of the heart are minimal, if even there. Today, through a woman who loved God and her son, I saw Christ. I was ministered to at a heart level, which only God knew I needed, and God sent the exact person who could reach me.

Have you ever had the privilege of witnessing a miracle? I have. However, I will say the prerequisite for a miracle is a problem. I have also had my heart crushed by the devastation of disease and sickness. But on April 6, 2010, I witnessed another miracle – Kevin walked without assistance. My husband, Kevin was placed in the hospital on February 25, 2010 and by 11:00 p.m. he had been placed in ICU. The reports indicated he may lose his respiratory system, due to lesions seen on an MRI image. By this point, Kevin was unable to move from the waist down, and we did not even have a diagnosis. Just three weeks prior, he had been up walking and helping me during my arm surgeries.

Our world was flipped upside down. Kevin was extremely sick, unable to walk, and diagnosed with Multiple Sclerosis! Now, I was the caregiver.

Three months later, Kevin walked for six minutes with no cane, no walker, and no wheelchair. Although, I have had the heartbreak of watching my husband lose all control – I have now had the privilege of watching him gain a miracle. Sometimes, we want instant miracles, which I would prefer. But, waiting on "seeing" what you so desire to "see" can make the moment magical when it does occur. This day will forever be marked in my memory as miraculous, and I would have never appreciated it if we had not had the day of doom. If you are facing doom, keep the faith, a miracle could be just around the next corner. Remember: Faith is being sure of what you hope for and certain of what you do not see. (Hebrews 11:1)

Yesterday was Easter, which is my favorite holiday. This year was different. Miranda went to Florida to spend some time with her best friend. So, it was the first Easter without her, and our first Easter with the knowledge of Kevin's diagnosis. I was not sure if I wanted to celebrate with people or just be alone. I must say God was good to me throughout the entire day. I woke up with peace in my heart. We had a good day, even though much change had occurred. If life has taught me anything, it is to enjoy the moment.

Even when you know God, the Bible, spend time in worship, and keep your hope in Jesus, you will face moments of pain and fear can try to torment you. After we were home, fear gripped my heart when I saw Kevin standing in the bedroom. He was not standing up straight, due to muscle wasting, which bothered me greatly. I wanted to shut my eyes and walk into the other room. Although, he has been diagnosed for a few months– it still does not seem real. It is amazing to me how I could spend twenty-two days watching him in the hospital; deal with all the insurances and financial burdens; trade our vehicles; pull us out of school; and, still denial is the feeling I have most moments. I was just sitting on the couch thinking about the reality of Kevin having Multiple Sclerosis. It still seemed unbelievable to me. As I sat there, I realized how very much I have taken Kevin for granted. I truly believed with my entire heart he would always be there to take care of me after my car wreck. I believed he would never be sick even now that he is – it is still hard for me to wrap my brain around. It simply confirms the fact, as people we can sincerely believe with all our heart and be wrong about our beliefs. I thought sickness and disease were in our past. It was a fair thought pattern after all I had endured personally, and the kids had each suffered, too. But, we all know life is not fair.

I do completely understand why God instructs us to "fear not." Fear only brings on stress and anxiety. It is destructive to our lives. I cannot control the fact Kevin has Multiple Sclerosis, but I can control my thought patterns. The Bible is clear to think about things that are good, pure, and noble. So, as waves of fear crash in my brain, I let them hit the sand and sink. I refuse to play with the thoughts which bring torment. I choose peace by literally capturing my thoughts and replacing them with God's word. God promised me He would never leave me or forsake me. My hope is in Him regardless of the storms. I trust God to calm my heart and carry me through.

Kevin sat down on the couch and expressed his heartache. He said he did not want to miss the good things in our future. He wanted to see Micah and Miranda graduate from college, fall in love, walk Miranda down the aisle when she married, and be there when we had a grandchild. I just sat on the couch and listened. I knew Kevin's health was critical, and it would take God to sustain Kevin's body.

CHAPTER 25

I SURRENDER

Now, the reality of Kevin's life altering illness has set in, and I have had time to think about how unbelievable it is he would have a disease with brain and spinal cord issues. I mean really, what are the odds of two people falling in love and both have terrible brain and spinal cord diseases? And, let's not forget both of our children also have them! Truly, it is unbelievable, but it is our life. This is the only life we will get, and I have settled in my heart no matter what I endure this side of Heaven, I am a disciple of Jesus Christ. My mind is made up. So, I no longer ask, "Where are you God?" Instead, I surrender and say, "Here am I God, have your way in my life."

Life will always present situations we as humans will never understand. But, if we let go of the desire to know 'why' and embrace God regardless, we can live a good life even through heartbreak. There have been multiple times I have asked, "Where are you God?" When life throws hard punches and the wind is knocked out of me, I can wonder where the God I love is hiding. As I have been given the opportunity to endure multiple situations which bring pain, I have learned when I feel God is not near me or has forsaken me, it is not God who has moved. At times, when painful situations arise, I tend to pull away from God. Sure, I might pray for someone, but not engage in a relationship with God. During the year 2000, this behavior caused me to grow bitter. After several months of bitterness, I decided I wanted my life back. Therefore, I repented for my anger towards God for allowing Miranda to be sick and turned to Him with all my heart. I recommitted my entire life to Him regardless of what the future may hold. With that decision, peace was restored, which gave me back my life.

A broken heart, due to whatever circumstance has crushed it, can make a person pull away from people or God. The hurting person can build walls to hide their emotions. However, God does not abandon us in our time of need; He is faithfully right there. Simply, all we must do is turn to Him. When Kevin went into the hospital in February 2010, I took each blow one at a time. My personal struggles had already trained me to not allow my mind to run down any path. Instead, I had to daily keep my thoughts captive. I did not allow myself the luxury of fear or dread. If fear tried to rear its head, I would quote scripture. I chose peace in the midst of pain. I had no control over what Kevin was enduring, but I did have control over my reaction to it one moment at a time.

Around the first of November 2009, when I was in prayer, these words dropped into my heart "Hang in there till May." Obviously, my first thought pattern was concerning school. It was only November and the curriculum was challenging. Greek along with Old Testament were demanding courses, which took many hours to study. So, I simply thought the Holy Spirit was encouraging me in the challenges I could "see" in that moment. I was wrong. Well, despite so much pain, sickness, warfare, and loss, we made it to May. Thank God!

Jesus gave interesting instructions to the disciples just before a storm came. He told them, "They were going to the other side." (Luke 8:22) The disciples proceed to get into their boat, and they are clueless to the events, which are about to unfold. When the storm came – Jesus slept! Well, my personal instructions were to "Hang in there till May." In November, I did not see our future or the storm, hurricane, our family was headed into…

List of events as they unfolded…

1. Kevin began to limp in November 2009 and fell – we thought he had a tilted hip.

2. I lost control of the function of my hands and was told it was due to the spinal cord in my neck – this news devastated my heart.

3. By December, I decided to have two arm surgeries to try to salvage my hand function. The decision was a gamble. It would either help me or make my loss of function worse.

4. Kevin went to a chiropractor and appeared to improve during Christmas.

5. Last day of December 2009, I had my first arm surgery.

6. Miranda fell down marble stairs and jerked her neck. If a person has Chiari and Ehlers-Danlos Syndrome, the smallest accident can cause great damage to their body.

7. January 14, 2010, I had my second arm surgery.

8. Micah's engine in his car burned up, and he had to buy a car in January 2010.

9. Miranda met with neurologist who suggested she have brain surgery with a fusion – I was shocked!

10. Miranda's body went downhill fast, and we took her for a Neurosurgeon consult – Dr. Neuro #6. A snow blizzard hit, and it took eleven hours to get home. Kevin was driving and was physically numb from the waist down.

11. January 28, 2010, Kevin was beginning to fall down all the time. He went back to the chiropractor.

12. Seminary started classes again the first of February.

13. Miranda had four MRI's, and we returned for a neurosurgeon consult on her 16th birthday.

14. Miranda's New York Neurosurgeon added more tests.

15. Kevin began to have more difficulty with even standing up and other bodily functions.

16. February 23, Micah was accused of a hit and run car accident.

17. February 25, Kevin was put in the hospital. By midnight, we had a report of lesions in his spinal cord. He was placed in ICU, because of his respiratory issues.

18. By February 26, Kevin and I had to withdraw from the Seminary.

19. By March 1, 2010, Kevin was diagnosed with Multiple Sclerosis with confirming lesions in the brain and spinal cord. He was paralyzed from the chest down – we were given no hope. Every question we asked was answered, "We don't know; it is different for every patient."

20. March 5, 2010, we had a medical bill crisis due to a health insurance company refusing to pay for rehabilitation for Kevin. I spent hours fighting for approval. Ultimately, we were granted the aid. The very night I taught a conference titled "Joy Regardless," Kevin was being transported by ambulance from the hospital to the rehabilitation center, while I was teaching the Word of God.

21. I had to trade our vehicles to get a car with handicap equipment for me to be able to drive. Kevin had always taken care of me. Now, I had to take care of him in my disabled body with both my arms, which had just been through operations.

22. Micah began the process of meeting with the police and insurance companies – no easy task. Ultimately, by March 18, 2010, the situation was cleared up with no charges against Micah. He was innocent.

23. On March 9, 2010, Kevin and I were married 19 years. Kevin was wheelchair bound. I spent my anniversary talking with MS life lines, because his medication was going to cost over $3,000.00 a month for the rest of his life. Our entire income for 2009 was only $8,400 – Kevin was unemployed. Ultimately, after several days with lots of phone calls, we received the news we qualified for a grant. Once again, God made a way.

24. Over the next several days, my Dad, with the help of other wonderful volunteers built a handicap accessible ramp into our house. It was not an easy task, but they did a great job.

25. Kevin was released to come home. He was using a walker and wheelchair, and still had to return three times a week for outpatient physical therapy.

26. On March 23, I drove Miranda to a neurosurgeon visit without Kevin. She had a brain MRI to determine further steps to be taken. The report was not good – a phone consult was scheduled to determine surgery options.

27. By April 1, 2010, I had a sore throat. By April 19, I was diagnosed with walking pneumonia.

28. Miranda was not well; however, we had decided to postpone decisions till we could meet with the Neurosurgeon in person.

29. April 30, Kevin had completed six weeks of outpatient therapy from Rehabilitation, and he is walking without assistance.

30. Micah finished his first semester at E.T.S.U., and has made excellent grades despite our trials.

"Hang in there till May."

Well, we made it to May 2010, and I am still here with Jesus Christ as my Strength, Shield, Peace, and Comfort. I would have never dreamed of the trials we were about to face; however, you cannot have a testimony without a test! God is faithful. He never left me – not for one moment. While my family was being tossed by the waves He was my Shelter. Honestly, I have no idea what the future will hold, but I know He holds the future.

CHAPTER 26

COURAGE

2 Kings 20:05 – ". . . I have heard your prayer; I have seen your tears: behold, I am healing you." Amplified

Have you ever contemplated the question, "What is normal?" I have had multiple opportunities to think about what 'normal' may be. As I have faced heartache and disappointment with illness, disease, and becoming physically handicapped, the thought patterns I battled often were along the lines of … I just wanted to be normal.

My heart's desire from as far back as I can remember was to be an elementary teacher. Even before I entered kindergarten, I had already set up a classroom in my bedroom to play school. I loved school, and I loved children. I always knew I would be an elementary teacher. I went to college and rushed through, so I could quickly fulfill my dream. In 1990, I took my teaching job in a local county school where I taught third grade. I loved every aspect of my job. Each morning when I woke up, it was like Christmas. I could not wait to go to work. Although I was only twenty years old, I had accomplished my dream. I was living exactly what I wanted to live. My life was good. Kevin, the only love of my life, and I married on March 9, 1991, of my first-year teaching. My life plan was going exactly like I had dreamed, and God's grace as well as forgiveness of our sins was evident. Everything was falling into place. To me, my life was normal and fulfilling. Our son Micah was born the following year, which was wonderful, even though I had thought we would not have children until I had finished higher level education. I kept teaching while Micah stayed with a dear friend of the family. Then, we built our dream home. By the next year, I was expecting our daughter Miranda. Up to this point, my entire adult life had been great even though it did not go exactly like I planned. Then, God continually put it in my heart to give up my dream job of teaching elementary education. Through prayer, God continued to impress upon me to quit my job to be a stay at home mother. Although I believe mothers are the unsung heroes, I thought I would be a mother and teacher. This leading from God to just stay at home challenged my heart at a deep level. Ultimately, I chose to resign. I spent the next sixteen years raising my daughter and son as a stay at home Mom. During the crises and throughout the fun, I was home for all the memories with special moments, I was there. I did not clearly see, when I chose to deny my professional dreams for my children, they were the real dream!

I am not normal. I am a Christian who completely loves Jesus, regardless of the price. I am a wife who has loved her husband regardless of the imperfections, illness, or difficulties. I am a mother who had the immeasurable opportunity to watch her children grow successfully no matter what the doctor's reports said. I am a disabled woman who has lost her sight, ability to hear, and been completely bed ridden for years – all to regain my life as well as sight, hearing, and walking. Now, even today, I live in a world full of unknowns with our health, but I experience love daily through my family as well as friends.

Being normal is an interesting idea. As children, we try to fit in, which only escalates in our teen years. As adults, we have dreams which, when fulfilled, can make us elated; but, when crushed can destroy us. As I fought back from loss of bodily function, often in prayer, I would just say, "I want to be normal." Even though I have overcome the roadblocks my illness threw at me, I am thankful I am not normal. For whatever definition, we as humans would place on the word "normal" I would be willing to bet no one would live a lifetime within the boundaries of that word. Today, I am grateful I chose the path less taken. Even though I am not normal, I am content. Therefore, my belief system leads me to know the only way to travel throughout your life with peace is to follow the heart of God in your own individual life. Refuse to fit a form which is either created by yourself or others. Norman Rockwell pictures express beautiful sceneries of the perfect, "normal" family. My advice would be to paint your own picture. Follow your own heart! As children of God, we are not normal, but we can be exceptional. We have the ability to overcome no matter how painful or difficult the situation. We have the ability to live despite the trials we face in this life. Honestly, I am not normal, but I am unmistakably Donna, which is who I was created to be.

II Timothy 2:13

"If we are faithless (do not believe and are untrue to Him), He remains true (faithful to His Word and His righteous character), for He cannot deny Himself." Amplified

I love the Word of God! In the past, I put pressure on myself to have "enough faith" until I realized Jesus made the way at Calvary, and as children of God we can rest in His faithfulness to any promise in our life. The pressure is off us completely. God is good, and His Word endures forever. Courage is being able to control your own fear and having the ability to face pain, the unknown, danger, or anything in this life that makes your heart tremble. In the book of Joshua, we are instructed to "be strong and very courageous." Courage is not the absence of fear or the ability to do whatever is required of you fearlessly. Courage is the ability to stand up and face your fear – whatever it may be.

After my brain surgery, every obstacle I faced was loaded with fear and took courage to overcome. The obstacles were as simple as brushing my teeth, walking, learning to read again, learning to drive again, and ultimately finding out if I would function at a level of independence. My body has the ability to double me over in severe pain, which is relentless. I never know when it will strike. So, to even get out of bed every day was a courageous step for me. My bed was safe, and my body seemed less likely to attack me when I was still. However, God required me to get up again, move forward with living, and face my fears. My choice to get up daily empowered me to face the pain and learn to live despite it.

The year, 2010, took me to a new level of courage. My dependence on Kevin, who had been my human rock, was tested at a level which required complete dependence on God. I did not even realize how very much I depended on Kevin until he was in the hospital, and I was alone. Many fast decisions had to be made for me to gain independence such as selling our vehicles and getting a car with equipment to enable me to drive with my disabilities. All the financial burdens, ministry decisions, Miranda's medical decisions, Micah's school issues, our school decisions, and my health suddenly all rested on me alone. The feeling of abandonment almost drowned me throughout the weeks I watched Kevin deteriorate and ultimately end up in the hospital. How could God possibly expect me to do all this alone? After all, I am physically disabled. I needed help to just open doors, much less complete all the daily activity in a family's life.

As I prayed late at night when silence engulfed our home, I could feel the presence of God. There are places in life so painful – no human can touch the lonely pain in your heart. I was there. I knew this destination, because I had been there before. So, this time I chose courage over bitterness. I decided to willingly face my fears in silence. I refused to talk to anyone about my fears. I simply and regularly let God know my heart. This gave me the power from within to daily get up and go face the unknown of Kevin's illness. There are times to talk to people, and there are times to be silent. This season required silence on my part. Oddly enough, courage came from the silence and complete dependence on God. Ultimately, I gained strength in my inner self and confidence that had been stolen from me when I was sick. God alone was my Hope, Strength, and Shelter. But, He also showed me that even disabled physically – I am enabled to do whatever I must. I have been told by many people how strong and courageous I am. Please understand I am weak, but God in me gives me the power to stand and face fear. My heart trembled at the reality of our lives, but God's peace prevailed even through the darkest nights.

Loving God with all your heart pays big dividends. When all else fails you – He will not!

Like it or not, there are many things we are allowed to choose on our journey in life. For instance, your job, spouse, financial choices, where you live, who you spend time with daily, how you handle your emotions, or what religion you desire. However, we as humans tend to want to blame circumstances for our choices, instead of owning our decisions. These items in your life are completely within your choice to change. You can either change your thinking, get instruction on how to improve each situation, or physically leave the situation. These are just examples, and I could list hundreds more. My point is: do not waste one minute of your life in self-pity! If you do not like your life – change it.

Illness, which is thrust upon us without any warning, is another monster to tackle. Coping realistically with a diagnosis, or multiple diagnoses, which has taken part of your physical ability away for as long as you are on this planet is not easy, but it is possible. What is self-pity? Self-pity is just a feeling of regret, sorrow, or feeling sorry for either yourself or someone else. My definition of self-pity would be the whispers we hear in our mind that tell us: "No one understands." "It will never get any better." "Why try?" "Why me?" "This is not fair." "There is no way out."

"Self-pity is more debilitating than any disease." ~ Dr. Donna Renfro

In August 2010, our family had a great week after months of horrific pain and life threatening experiences. I can testify of the goodness of the glory of God in the land of the living. As a family, we went to the Dixie Stampede in Pigeon Forge. God was so faithful! While eating dinner at the Dixie Stampede with 1,000 other individuals, a worker approached Kevin and Miranda and asked them to participate in one of the events in the arena. Both agreed. So, when it was time they went down to the circle to represent the South in the horse race. Well, at first we thought they would be riding a horse, but ultimately it was a stick horse which they had to straddle between their legs while running around barrels. I had the privilege of watching my husband run around the barrels – now you must remember it was just six months ago he was in the hospital. The neurologist did not think he would ever be out of a wheelchair. It had only been two months since he was in physical rehabilitation, and Kevin had a relapse with Multiple Sclerosis in July 2010. Also, Miranda was daily declining because of her own health issues. Therefore, when I witnessed Kevin and Miranda running around barrels' tears came to my eyes. The impossible is possible with God! By the way, not only did Kevin run – he and Miranda won the race. They were decorated with medals. This year has again brought much heartache and pain to our family. Yet, through it all, God never left me. He was my only constant security regardless of the facts we faced. This week was a beautiful example of His faithfulness to His promises. This week has been a gift from God, and one I will cherish all the days of my life. When storms come, remember they will go. If you are facing difficulties continue to trust in God. He will never fail you.

Faith does not believe God will do it – faith absolutely knows! Kevin improved enough for us to go back to Seminary and work towards our master's degree; however, he would have MS relapses at times. Miranda was losing physical ground daily. She dealt with severe headaches, vomiting, vertigo, difficulty walking, slurred speech, and numbness in her hands on a daily basis. By faith, Kevin and I took one day at a time and peacefully rested in God's ability to meet every need Miranda and our family faced. We took Miranda to New York and met with Neuro #3 on November 20, 2010. We trust him completely. He saved my life in December 2005. Neuro #3 evaluated Miranda and read her records. He wanted us to stay in New York to perform multiple medical tests on her, but she was not currently covered by out of state insurance. So, we came home, and I filed an appeal with Miranda's insurance company. The tests were needed to make final decisions about Miranda's surgery.

The current medical evaluation in the office confirmed Miranda would most likely need the same surgery I endured five years ago. Until all medical tests are complete, we would not know exactly which brain surgery she would need. There are at least four possibilities for now. However, it does appear she would need to have a brain decompression with the fusion of her head to her spine, which was difficult news for all of us – especially Miranda. I received a letter in the mail from the insurance company stating they had started the appeal process and could take up to 90 days to reach a decision. She had medical orders for a neck brace and thoracic vest, which would help stabilize her deterioration until all medical tests are complete and decisions could be made. Miranda completed high school early and was already accepted into college; however, school was out of the question. Miranda spent her days in bed. Miranda's high school graduation was in May 2011. The plan was to have the surgery as soon as she graduated.

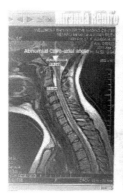 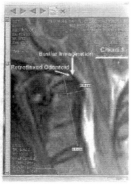 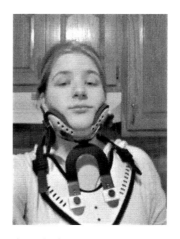

Miranda's MRI   Miranda in her thoracic vest

I spent my days fighting Miranda's insurance company, studying school work, taking care of Miranda, and watching Kevin closely. Kevin made it to February 25, 2011, without another major setback physically, and we were told that was a good sign. Micah continued in college and was extremely independent. Until we were in a health insurance battle, I had no idea how hard it could be to get out-of-state coverage. We went to court the first day on April 12, 2011, and won. In order to win, we took Miranda to another doctor who specialized in her conditions, and he confirmed the exact same medical plan as Neuro #3. Neuro #7 was located in Bethesda, Maryland. He did not know what the other neurosurgeon had medically planned, yet he dictated a letter with the same surgical solution. When I met him, he made me feel safe and there was so much peace even though we were discussing an excruciating solution. Kevin drove us to Maryland, and he slept in the car while Miranda and I met with Neuro #7. When we were leaving the office, I asked Dr. Neuro #7, if he were me, would he take his daughter to New York or come to him for Miranda's surgery. He gently placed his hand on my back and said, "I would pray about it."

Both Neurosurgeons suggested:

1. Normalization of the clivoaxial angle (whether by traction or by direction open reduction in the manner described by Kim, Rekate, Klopfenstein, Sontag, Journal of Neurosurgery, 2004) with stabilization and fusion.

2. Fuse to C2 incorporating a screw fixation at C1 level as well as C2. If C2/3 junction is extremely loose at surgery, include C3 in the fusion.

3. Perform a small suboccipital brain decompression for the Chiari at the same time.

The judge gave us the ability to use Neuro #3 as Miranda's neurosurgeon. But, we needed approval for the surgery as well. So, we had to continue to battle with the health insurance company. In the state of Tennessee, even if you win in court the insurance company had the right to overturn the decision. Therefore, the insurance company denied Miranda the right to have surgery, and we found out the day before we were leaving for New York. Miranda had already had her hair cut off and donated it to Locks of Love. Kevin received the denial through a telephone call concerning the fact Miranda would not receive medical coverage while Miranda was having her beautiful and long hair cut short to prepare for the surgery. It was unbelievable.

Certificate of Appreciation

AWARDED TO

Miranda Renfro

For selfless dedication and support of our mission to help children suffering from long-term or permanent medical hair loss.
On behalf of the Locks of Love Board of Directors, staff, volunteers, and all the children whose lives you will touch,

Thank you!

Date: June 15, 2011   *Locks of Love*

Miranda's Locks of Love Certificate

In the middle of the court battles to save Miranda's life, she graduated from high school with academic honors. Matthew 7:1, *"Do not judge, so that you may not be judged."* (NRSV) As humans, we often judge each other based on a situation or appearance. Often, Kevin and I have been told, "You look great." Well, looks can be deceiving. Both of us deal with neurological disorders, which can be difficult to "see" on the outside of our bodies. Of course, it is evident when we are unable to walk, talk, or function there is a problem; but, sometimes we are silently suffering, and it is not evident by simply looking at us.

Miranda's High School Graduation   Kevin and Donna at Miranda's Graduation

The pictures were taken at Miranda's high school graduation in May 2011. I had home-schooled her from kindergarten through graduation; so, there was no way I was going to miss being a part of the graduation. The weeks before her graduation my body began a downward spiral, which caused me to receive emergency medical treatment multiple times. I refused to be admitted into any hospital; but, I would allow treatment to aid my body in the extreme pain. The morning of her graduation, I had to have multiple shots and was heavily medicated. However, in the picture my pain is not evident. But, trust me I was suffering. The day after her graduation, I was hospitalized for over a week while an excellent neurologist diligently worked with my faithful internist to find a solution for my pain. Words simply cannot express the pain I endure when my body attacks me. I expect others who suffer with my disorders understand. However, I pray no one ever experiences the physical pain I have endured. Also, in the picture you will note I am with Kevin who is already diagnosed with Multiple Sclerosis, and Miranda looks beautiful. Personally, I think we all looked great in the pictures, and people would be shocked to know most of our day was spent resting in the bed. Fatigue and illness dominated our lives.

People assumed, because I posted a photo on Facebook or they saw us out in public, we were doing fantastic. Hopefully, when you saw us or a good picture of us – it is a representation of a great day. But, it may just be a moment in the day with laughter, happiness, and fun. In other words, there may be more to the story – just like the photos within this book. I was at Miranda's graduation; however, I had to be at the doctors before it and be hospitalized afterwards. The Bible states inn Matthew 7:1, *"Do not judge, or you too will be judged."* So, the Bible is clear in giving instructions. As believers, we need to love one another and not jump to conclusions based on appearance, race, or sin. A person may appear strong and healthy; but, maybe they are simply trusting God to carry them through the moment, because they are too weak to endure it. Another person may appear rich; but, maybe they are in extreme debt. Someone else may seem bitter; but, maybe they are hurt by past abuse. I am confident it is not our job to judge – it is our duty to love people where they are with the compassion of Christ. Letting people know "they look well" is kind, but just know, even if they look well on the outside they may be in physical, mental, spiritual, financial, or emotional pain.

The day after Miranda graduated in May 2011, I was in the hospital for over a week, due to my physical pain and headaches. Kevin and I both took a physical blow with strep throat as well. We were physically exhausted. The spiritual battle, which always seems to come with Miranda's physical situation, slammed us mentally, spiritually, financially, and emotionally. Eighteen years before in June, I became pregnant with Miranda. For her entire life, we have looked for answers, fought insurance companies, paid over the top medical bills, fought false theology, fought to find the "truth" medically, and fought to keep her alive. Now, it was time to go and receive the answer to let the healing begin. But, the insurance company kept standing in our way. People can say "the battle belongs to the Lord" which is taken from the Bible. But, I would like to point out: I made the phone calls; I held her in the night; I prayed; I fasted; I went to the doctors; I researched for answers – not to make this about me, but understand my point, which is there was much required of me for Miranda to obtain her wellness. It was not as simple as a prayer line, even though I would have loved it to be. It has been a long and painful journey. But, it is a journey I can honestly say I would do again. My love for her propelled me, and my trust in God carried me!

On June 17, 2011, we returned to court and did not win. We had already been fighting with the insurance company for eighteen months. We would have to take it to civil court to continue the battle with the health insurance company. Miranda was physically out of time. She had developed a spiraling syrinx in her spinal cord. So, Kevin and I prayed and fasted for three days. While in prayer, God reminded me He orders her steps, not the health insurance companies. So, Kevin and I took out a loan against our home. Meanwhile, Neuro #7 contacted me through email and said to bring Miranda to him. He would do the surgery.

We spoke with Neuro #3, and he was completely supportive of Miranda going to Neuro #7. Both men had great admiration of one another. The office in Bethesda, Maryland set the date for August, but Neuro #7 had them back the date up to July 21, 2011. Miranda was declining daily and needed help as soon as possible. We had no idea how it would all work out, but we packed our bags and took Miranda. In Christ alone, I placed my hope and trust!

CHAPTER 27

MIRANDA'S NEW LIFE

Kevin, Miranda, Kevin's Mom, and I left for Maryland a few days prior to the surgery. The Ronald McDonald House in Washington, D.C. gave us a home away from home during the surgery. We had to take Miranda to the hospital for pre-admitting, and tests. Also, Miranda saw Dr. Neuro #7 prior to surgery. During the office visit, Miranda found out Dr. Neuro #7 would be removing one of her ribs to place with her skull fusion. The thought of having her own rib removed to help build her fusion upset her greatly. Miranda maintained her faith. Every morning she would get up early just to read her scriptures and pray, even the morning of the surgery. On July 21, 2011, Miranda had her brain decompression and fusion surgery in Maryland by Dr. Neuro #7. We had to arrive at the hospital early in the morning, and Miranda went into surgery at 10:30 a.m. I was allowed to see her in the PICU around 5:30 p.m. Dr. Neuro #7 said she did well through the surgery, and he did fuse her from her skull to the C3 level. Peace sustained us at every turn. The only time I cried was when Miranda told the doctor all the pressure and pain in her head was gone. She had no headache, which was amazing, immediately following brain surgery. Thankfulness to a faithful God and a great surgeon was the only feeling I had.

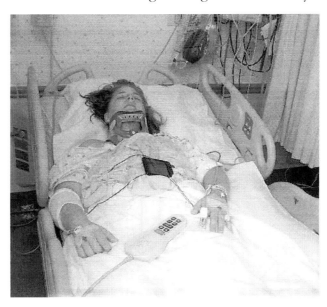

Miranda after brain decompression and fusion surgery

After her surgery, her goals were walking, changing her medications from I.V. to pill form, and washing some of the blood out of her hair. Miranda worked off the I.V. medication treatment plan. She began taking all medications by mouth. This transition was difficult, because the I.V. medications decrease pain from surgery quicker. But, Miranda did as well as can be expected. I was very proud of her. She met all her daily goals one day at a time while in the hospital. The home care nurses came by, because they would be working with us at the Ronald McDonald House for the next couple of weeks after Miranda's discharge. Dr. Neuro #7 came by to see Miranda and removed the drainage tubes. He was very encouraged by her physical improvements. His calm nature brings tremendous peace to the room. We are so thankful for him. Healing is a process, which often we do not want to endure. Many nights for Miranda were difficult. She was awake most of the night in pain. Her bladder was not functioning properly without aid. She had to leave the hospital with a catheter when she was released. The last day Miranda was in the hospital, Kevin and I were physically able to handle Miranda alone; so, Kevin's Mom flew back to Tennessee.

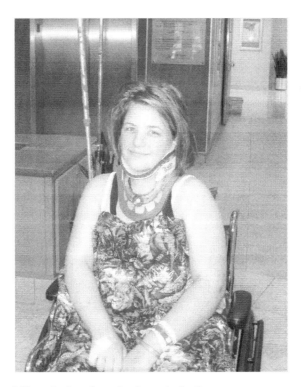

Miranda leaving the hospital after surgery

Upon release from the hospital, Miranda went to the Ronald McDonald House in Washington, D.C. She was discharged on Monday, July 25, 2011. It was a peaceful experience, and again I cannot speak highly enough of the nursing staff at the hospital. They were a constant blessing at each turn. Due to Miranda's neurogenic bladder issues, she used a catheter for a week. The home health care was scheduled to visit us and take care of Miranda for the next two weeks at the Ronald McDonald House. We received a call from the hospital stating Miranda had a urinary tract infection. Miranda was able to take a shower with my aid, which helped her feel much better. Her wound bandages were also changed. She had one small wound above her right ear, a wound on the upper left side of her back where the rib was removed, and the incision from the brain decompression and skull to C3 fusion. As far as pain, I am amazed by her experience. Dr. Neuro #7 had a wonderful pain relief plan set in place for his patients. She was doing great. Miranda continued to give thanks to God for the relief in her body from years of suffering. Kevin and I were tired, especially considering our own physical limitations. Since we have no local neurosurgeon to handle Miranda in Tennessee, we had to stay at the Ronald McDonald House until Miranda had her six-week appointment with Dr. Neuro #7.

On August 5, 2011, Miranda was two weeks out from her surgery, so we took her out to eat. It was her first outing from the Ronald McDonald house since the operation. She did well considering what her body had endured. I was concerned we were doing too much with her, but Miranda wanted to go. Once, we arrived back at the house her body gave out on her physically. She was unable to stand up. Of course, this was upsetting for her. Kevin helped her to the bed, and I held her tight while encouraging her. She had faced each obstacle with relentlessness, knowing God would carry her through. She constantly listened to worship music playing in our room to bring her the peace she needed to heal.

One night, Miranda spent several hours ministering to a young girl who had a baby in NICU. Miranda told her how she used the Message Bible to find scriptures for herself over the past several months, which she wrote over and over to memorize before the surgery. She told her each time fear would come into her mind, she would pull from the scriptures she had memorized. I just sat there in silence, listening to my daughter with joy in my heart.

Over the years, it was heartbreaking, my children who are now young adults have seen more suffering inside the four walls of their own home than anyone ever should. Miranda spoke of seeing me have seizures one night and how it scared her to the point of anger at God. Then, she went on to say ultimately it made her closer to God as she surrendered her life. Her strength of character, love of God, choices to believe despite pain, and courage was birthed during our crises. The very things I wanted to protect my children from created them to be exactly what God desired for their lives.

One day, Miranda really wanted to come home. Therefore, we went to Dr. Neuro #7, and he felt she was safe to travel home. He was as excited as we are about her results from the surgery. It was truly amazing! However, we are wise and realize healing takes time, God, and patience. Miranda was still resting most of her day. Her life was not perfect, but she had gained relief from constant physical pain through this procedure. Miranda's surgery was on July 21, and we drove home on August 19, 2011. When we left Tennessee, we had no idea how long we would be gone or what we might face. At every turn in the road, God was faithful. Although Kevin struggled daily with Multiple Sclerosis, he was physically able to do whatever Miranda needed. Also, many of you know and realize my body is not reliable as well. I had spent most of May in the hospital with my own issues from Chiari and Syringomyelia. Yet, God gave me the strength and health to be exactly what Miranda needed at every turn. I could stay with her the entire time she was in the hospital. The morning we left the Ronald McDonald House, American Idol sent two of their Idols to visit with the kids. Miranda was chosen to give one of the American Idols their honorary pin from the Ronald McDonald House when they entered the building. They were both precious and so very kind to all the children. Meeting these two young people before we left was a gift and the perfect way to end our stay.

Miranda with Ronald McDonald

Healing is a process. Miranda continued to heal from her surgery. She was doing well during the daytime; however, at night she had significant pain where her screws and rods were placed. I spoke with Dr. Neuro #7, and he said this was a normal part of the healing. With Miranda's EDS, Ehlers-Danlos Syndrome, a connective tissue disorder, healing takes longer for her body. Miranda received a big blessing while healing. This summer, Micah and Miranda's orthodontist group had a competition among all their patients. Whoever traveled the farthest away from our home town in Tennessee or went to the most unique place would win an iPad. The individual had to take a picture wearing the t-shirt provided by the orthodontist. Micah traveled to Hong Kong and China during the month of June. So, he had a picture taken with the t-shirt in front of a large Chinese landmark. Micah was excited and hoped to win. We were all pulling for him. On Monday, September 5, Micah was contacted by his orthodontist, because he won an iPad. Micah immediately picked up the iPad and as soon as he walked through the door – he gave it to Miranda. She was thrilled beyond words and hugged her brother. Miranda had so much fun with the iPad. It was perfect timing. Micah had said several times, "There should be a way for Miranda to win, because all she endured through the summer." Well, he made a way for her. I was so proud of our son, and his giving heart!

Miranda has always been a Daddy's girl! Kevin, her father, and her are like two peas in a pod. They love to pick at each other, laugh, and just have fun. There are so many pictures of Miranda with her Dad over the years, and you can see on her face how very much she loves him. Even though Kevin had Multiple Sclerosis with God, prayer, medical aid, and time, he gained back a quality of life. He had the Relapsing form of Multiple Sclerosis. Stress can bring on relapses. On Friday, September 23, 2011, Kevin let me know his feet were numb again, which is a sign of relapse for him. Kevin had been physically declining for ten days with neck pain and fatigue. However, by the time he verbally complained to me – it was evident he needed medical intervention. That night we found ourselves at the local hospital where he was immediately admitted. Honestly, we were so blessed. Kevin had an excellent team of doctors, including his internist, neurologist, and neurosurgeon. Kevin was given 3,250mg of steroids over a three-day period. Also, he had an MRI of his neck, which showed even more damage to his discs. Kevin refused to even consider neck surgery. The neurosurgeon tried less invasive treatments at our request. Kevin was discharged on Wednesday, September 28, 2011. He rested in his bed at home.

Obviously, this relapse took its toll on our entire family. Miranda was emotionally devastated at first, but I quickly reminded her God loved her Daddy more than she could imagine. Once she saw her Dad, peace came back to her heart. We were all tired, but thankful Kevin could receive medical treatment. From my heart, I thank God for all the wisdom He has given scientists and doctors for Multiple Sclerosis. We do not take it for granted. During Kevin's stay at the hospital, we found out about stem cell treatment for MS. The stem cell treatment takes the stem cell from the person with MS and after modification of the stem cells, the doctors put their own stem cells back into the same person. This process is having exceptional results for patients with Relapsing Remitting Multiple Sclerosis. Kevin was placed on a waiting list for the procedure. The stem cell transplants were in clinical trials.

Miranda continued to gain physical ground. Due to her EDS, healing takes more time for her. The good news: we have time. Miranda's scar which goes up the back of her head opened back up and tried to heal again. There are several small spots where the scar pulled apart after closing once. With a connective tissue disorder, this is not uncommon. We always watch her carefully when she is healing from anything – even simple cuts or infections. Night was still the most difficult time with pain. But, Miranda handled it with her strong spirit. She was a fighter. Over all, Miranda gained tremendous ground from the surgery. She still has not suffered from vertigo or the horrid headaches, nausea, and vomiting since the day of the operation. We were so very thankful for the outcome – it is not normal to have such an exceptional experience just out of surgery. We did not take it for granted at all.

Our family took the fall to rest, heal, and re-group. We were exhausted from all the traumas, hospitals, doctor visits, and medical bills. As we entered the holiday season, it was our desire to simply be at home with family and friends enjoying the moment without any medical crisis. Miranda, my friend, and I went to Maryland to see Dr. Neuro #5 on December 5, 2011. Miranda's scar had still not healed, and she had walking pneumonia. However, he instructed us to give it time. So, we headed home to enjoy Christmas. Miranda was still on antibiotics for the infection in her lungs, but she continued to gain ground daily. Her scar was in the process of healing, and our prayer was for it to completely heal without any intervention. Miranda had been approved to begin her college career in January 2012, at Liberty University, online to accommodate her body. She was very excited about seeking a bachelor's degree in Psychology. We gave thanks to God for all He had done on her behalf. Miranda sang in two Christmas programs even with her lung infection.

December of 2011, became an important moment in time for Miranda. She agreed to help lead praise and worship at a church for a friend we had met while in Seminary. On December 30, 2011, Miranda met Brandon Taylor at the church's New Year's Eve party. She came home and talked about him to me. Miranda was not interested in getting involved with any young man, due to the fact she had just endured major brain surgery with a fusion. It was hard for her to believe any man would love her with all her diagnoses. However, I encouraged her to give Brandon a chance. In January 2012, Miranda began attending college at Liberty University. On February 5, 2012, Miranda's friendship with Brandon turned into a relationship, and they had their first date. Miranda received a phone call on March 13, 2012, and her Make-A-Wish was granted. She was thrilled to receive the call. Her wish was to go to Honolulu, Hawaii to see where her maternal grandparents were married. Her grandfather was in the Navy when they married in Hawaii. Miranda wanted to see the church. Miranda was physically doing well in general. Her wound was still healing – slowly, but healing. Miranda loved her classes in college and was doing well academically.

Brandon and Miranda on their first date – 2/5/2012

Tuesday, March 13, 2012, Kevin flew to Chicago to meet with the neurologists. He was a possible candidate for a stem cell transplant for his Multiple Sclerosis. This particular stem cell transplant uses his own stem cells. Kevin saw the doctors on Wednesday, March 14, 2012, and then returned home on Thursday. Lifelines, a free airline for medical care, flew him and my brother-in-law, Dave Christian. From September 2011 till now, Kevin has been in the hospital multiple times, and his MS continues to progress. We were all trusting

God. Kevin was diligently eating the Multiple Sclerosis diet, as well as taking vitamins; therefore, having done all stand.

I have had a difficult season physically myself. In January 2012, I was hospitalized twice and even had the opportunity to ride in an ambulance. I met with Dr. Neuro #7, and there are many things in my brain, neck, and spine which need attention. I saw him again in April; and, it appears I need more surgery to give me quality of life. However, I was not willing to agree to any surgery at that time.

Kevin and I continued to be very focused on completing our degrees. We finished our M.A. in New Testament last year and immediately began working towards our Doctorate of Biblical Counseling. Also, I worked on a separate Master of Religious Education at the same time from Liberty University. It was my desire to complete both degrees, before any more surgery on me. Micah continued to pursue his degree and was doing well.

Thessalonians 5:24, "The one who calls you is faithful, and he will do it." (NIV)

Brandon and Miranda going to prom in 2012

CHAPTER 28

LIFE IS FRAGILE

Philippians 1:21, "For to me, to live is Christ, and to die is gain." (NKJV)

Dave and Kevin in Chicago

Kevin and Dave, my brother-in-law, went to Chicago in the middle of March 2012, with much hope they would be able to help him. It appeared Kevin met every medical criteria for the stem cell study, which only used his personal stem cells; however, when they met with the first doctor on Wednesday, it did not go very well. On Friday, Kevin met with the second doctor who had a different opinion. So, there was some confusion. By the second doctor's appointment one thing was certain, Kevin was in another MS relapse. So, my brother-in-law drove him ten hours home to meet me at the local hospital where he was admitted for 9,000mg of steroids. Yes, I said, 9,000mg! The doctors from Chicago wanted more tests run on Kevin. They seem to think he may have NMO (Neuromyelitis optica), which is a rare form of Multiple Sclerosis and much more aggressive.

After he was released from the hospital, he went to see his local doctors. Blood work was ordered, Kevin was taken off his current Multiple Sclerosis medication, and monthly infusions of steroids were set up. On Good Friday, we received a phone call which confirmed Kevin's blood work would not allow him to go on the next Multiple Sclerosis medication suggested, and I was told the doctors thought Kevin did indeed have NMO. He is off all MS medication and going for monthly infusions of solu-medrol/steroids. Our entire family felt as if we were kicked in the gut again.

2 Corinthians 4:18

"So we fix our eyes not on what is seen, but on what is unseen, since what is seen is temporary, but what is unseen is eternal." (NIV)

With God, all things are possible! Kevin and I completed our doctoral degrees in April 2012. We had the honor of walking across the stage together and receive our Doctor of Biblical Counseling in May. All our family was with us. I was in awe of a faithful God. From the moment we started down the path to fulfill the desire to complete our master's degree and a doctorate, we have faced many giants. However, the day we celebrated was incredible. We were overcomers! Together, we faced the giants and persevered to the end. The knowledge we gained while going to each Seminary was priceless. But, for me earning the degrees is secondary to all the love we had showered on us by family, friends, professors, and fellow students. We have been in a storm throughout our education, but learned a greater level of trust in God. Kevin and I were blessed – despite the odds.

Kevin and Donna Graduating with their Doctorate of Biblical Counseling

The summer was difficult for us. Kevin was not able to take the MS medication, which was suggested by the Chicago doctor. Kevin had a virus when he was a small child, which created antibodies in his blood. Due to the virus, that particular MS medication could be a dangerous for Kevin. So, he continued with having steroid infusions at the Cancer Treatment Center while we waited for insurance. Kevin was going to get insurance in August 2012, and then he could receive treatment in Chicago if he could get into their program.

So, we waited.

Around the first of September, I had a dream. In my dream, Kevin died. I woke up with my heart racing, and it took time for me to realize the dream was only a dream. It seemed so real. Two days later, on September 9, 2012, I was resting on the couch downstairs and had the thought I need to go upstairs to check on Miranda. When I approached the laundry room, Kevin said my name very quietly from his bed. I stopped at his door and said, "Did you need me?"

Kevin replied, "I have a little pain in my side."

Kevin pointed to the left side of his chest where his heart was located. I immediately called 911. I was panicked. Kevin thought I was overreacting. The paramedics finally arrived and said his heart seemed okay. They asked me if I wanted them to take him to the hospital, and I was shocked. I would not have called them if I did not want them to take him to the hospital. So, I convinced Kevin and the paramedics he needed to go. They took Kevin out of our house on a gurney. Then, the unthinkable – the ambulance driver drove the ambulance into the ditch off the right side of our driveway. I just stood there holding my head with my hands. They had to call a wrecker and another ambulance. While they were dealing with the accident in my driveway, I was trying to call every family member and friend I had. Not one person answered their phone. Micah, Miranda, and I were the only ones at home. Then, I went to my knees in the kitchen and prayed, "God help me."

Ambulance wrecked in our driveway with Kevin inside

I packed Kevin's clothes and drove behind the second ambulance to the hospital. By the time I arrived, the doctor already realized Kevin was seriously ill. She ran tests. Within thirty minutes, we were told Kevin had multiple blood clots, which had shot through his heart. It was a miracle he was alive. They admitted him immediately, and we began the process of blood thinners. We were told by multiple medical personnel how fortunate Kevin was to be alive. I had to call Chicago, and due to the blood clots, Kevin was not eligible for their stem cell protocol. Although I felt as if I had been kicked in the gut, I was so thankful Kevin was alive. The dream God gave me caused me to react and saved his life.

The fall and winter of 2012, brought a lot of heartache to our family. Kevin rapidly lost physical ground and was hospitalized multiple times – too many to talk about. Finally, we made the decision to put Kevin back on a different MS medication. It was a difficult decision, due to all the side effects of the medication. Ultimately, we were left with no other option. So, Kevin began the new MS medication. He was also going to the doctor weekly, because of the blood thinner. We had to go to the local doctor weekly for blood checks to make sure his blood was not to thick or thin.

Meanwhile, I was struggling physically. My body was in severe nerve pain and relief was difficult to obtain. Finally, the end of January 2013, I agreed to an ICP brain surgery in Maryland to determine if a shunt would bring me relief; however, the surgery proved my cerebrospinal fluid would go too high and too low. Therefore, I was not a candidate for a shunt. Our circumstances looked bleak. In February, I met with my neurologist, and he suggested I have injections to aid with my physical pain. I reluctantly agreed. By this point, I had endured several operations since the car wreck, yet was concerned about a few shots. Anyhow, I went and within two days of the shots my body was doing better. It was amazing how it helped my physical pain.

With all my degrees completed, I was applying for professorial jobs. Well, I received a phone call letting me know a man from a local radio station wanted to talk with me. I called him back, and he asked how our family was doing. I updated him and let him know I would not be coming back to radio, because I was going to work as a professor. He asked me to wait and said he wanted me to talk to the owners of the station. The next day he posted on my Facebook wall that I had two interviews. The following day, the owner of the radio station called me, and we set a time to meet on Monday, March 11, 2013. His wife, joined us at the meeting. I immediately felt a Godly connection with this couple. We talked for hours. I had turned my cell phone off for the interview. When I returned to my car, I had ten missed phone calls. My family was worried due to the fact I was gone so long. I met with them again on Wednesday and agreed to go to work at the radio station beginning April 1, 2013. When Kevin was diagnosed with Multiple Sclerosis, I literally stopped our life to take care of him. Little by little, God brought back each section of our life He desired for us to have. School came back first, completing degrees, and now a job in Christian radio with Godly people. The radio station where I agreed to work was the first radio station I went on with my program "The Word Works!" back in 2004, and now it is where God had opened a door for me to use my gifts to help others. I began work on April 1, 2013.

On June 2, I took a nap after church. My body was tired. Suddenly, I woke up, because I had a nightmare about Kevin. In my dream, Kevin was being rolled down a hospital hallway on a gurney, and I knew he was dying. I dropped to my knees and begged God to save his life. When I jerked awake, it took a few minutes to realize it was only a dream. My heart was racing, and I was deeply bothered. A few days later, I was at work when the owner of the radio station walked into my office, and told me he had a job he wanted me to do. He had just heard about the stem cell transplants in Chicago over the radio. He wanted me to call to see if Kevin could go. I sat back in my chair. This Godly man did not know we had already tried and failed at getting Kevin into the program. I explained to him Kevin had been denied. He said he wanted me to call again. I just felt hopeless.

Then, Kevin called me and was extremely ill. I was at the radio station and went outside. I literally sat down on the pavement and placed my head in my hands. I knew deep in my heart there was nowhere to go to get real help. We were without options. Kevin wanted to go to the hospital. So, I took him to the walk-in clinic, and they immediately admitted him into the local hospital. While in the emergency room, we were told Kevin was in acute renal failure. He was admitted. The doctors came by, but no one did anything to help Kevin. A dear friend came by and sat with me for hours. She was knitting and brought tremendous peace to the situation. While we were talking she said, "Donna, you need to call Chicago back."

In one week, God sent two separate people to tell me to contact Chicago. I was afraid to call them. I did not want to get my hopes up and then have them dashed. So, I decided to send them an email. Just three days after I sent the email, I received a phone call, and the doctors requested all of Kevin's medical files. Within days, they had copies. Life began to move at warp speed. The medical facility in Chicago set dates to evaluate Kevin to see if he would qualify for the stem cell transplant. Kevin's Mother and I took him to Chicago in July 2013. We spent a week going to the doctors and hospital for tests. Once we returned home, more tests were ordered. Truly, I did not think they would accept Kevin. There was a lot of confusion as to whether Kevin had Multiple Sclerosis or NMO. Another major-medical university which studied Multiple Sclerosis was asked to evaluate his case. Meanwhile, Kevin was losing physical ground. Then on August 13, 2013, I received the phone call. Kevin had been accepted for the transplant. Kevin and I were both numb by this point. The dates were rapidly set, and Kevin would need to leave Tennessee on August 25,

2013. Meanwhile, life at home continued. Micah was dating a precious young lady and entering his last year towards his bachelor degree. On August 14, 2013, Brandon proposed to Miranda. They set their wedding date for June 7, 2014. Brandon and Miranda were in college working towards their bachelor degrees. We were definitely walking in valleys and on mountain tops at the same time. Our trust in God kept our hearts stable.

Kevin's stem cell dates were set by August 16, 2013. He began treatment in Chicago on August 26, 2013. This was all extremely overwhelming. The steps of the righteous are ordered of God! I asked God for great peace, August 25, 2013, as I sent my husband and his Mother off in an airplane to Chicago, IL. I had to stay behind for medical treatment for myself.

Psalm 119:165

"Great peace have those who love thy law, nothing can make them stumble." (NIV)

On September 5, 2013, my sister had surgery in the morning. Then, I was driven to Charlotte, NC, by two dear friends, to catch a flight to Chicago, IL. I joined Kevin prior to his mobilization for the stem cell transplant. I did not want to go. Fear gripped my heart. This would be the first flight I had taken without any friends or family. Usually, when I fly my legs become paralyzed, and I end up in a wheelchair. On the plane, I met a precious Godly woman named Beulah Cure. Her name literally means "married to God" and "cure." We talked nonstop all the way to Chicago about the faithfulness of God. I never felt alone. She was a true gift and God send. My legs did fail me upon landing; but, I managed to get through the airport to the car service area. Dave, my brother-in-law, had already set up a car with a driver to take me to Kevin when I arrived in Chicago.

Kevin had completed his stem cell mobilization and harvest in Chicago on September 17, 2013. He only needed two million stem cells, and they were able to collect eight million. Due to some medication that Kevin had been taking for the Multiple Sclerosis, we had to go home and return for the transplant. Kevin had stopped taking the MS medication a couple of months prior; however, it had to be out of his body for three more months. So, we went home and planned on returning in December 2013, for the transplant. On the way home Kevin coughed once. I immediately called our internist at home. I took Kevin to him the next morning. He did not have a fever; however, our doctor put him in the local hospital. By the time Kevin was in his room, his fever was over 103 and kept rising. Infectious disease specialists evaluated Kevin. They started antibiotics and diagnosed him with pneumonia. It was a tough ride. However, many people came by and encouraged us this was just a bump in the road. The journey was dark, but our trust remained in God alone.

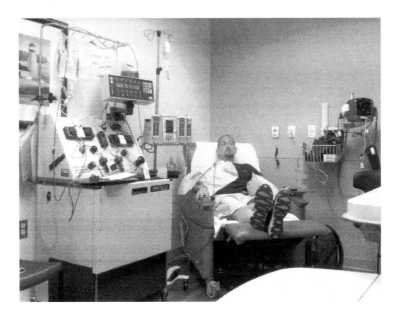

Kevin having his stem cells harvested

Dave, my brother-in-law, drove Kevin, his mother, and me to Chicago on December 2, 2013. Dave was such a blessing throughout this whirlwind. Now, Kevin began the final leg of this journey. The schedule for Kevin was physically difficult. On Tuesday, December 3, 2013, Kevin had his Triple Lumen PICC line Placement. Then, on Wednesday, December 4, 2013, Kevin was admitted into the hospital to begin the chemotherapy prior to his stem cells being put back into his body. For days Kevin endured a lethal dose of chemotherapy to prepare his body for the transplant. Finally, on December 9, 2013, Kevin received his stem cell transplant. He was extremely weak, but discharged on December 19, 2013. Dave returned to Chicago, and drove us all home. Now, we would spend the next year praying Kevin would not catch any infection. His immune system was wiped from the chemotherapy, which means he no longer had antibodies for all his vaccinations, and any prior illness, cold, or flu. We spent Christmas at home, which was a gift we did not take for granted.

CHAPTER 29

FAITH OR FEAR

Micah has been a blessing from the moment God placed him in our life. As a family, we have faced adversity – yet through it all Micah has remained stable in the moment. One of my favorite scriptures is Isaiah 40:4 which states, *"Every valley shall be raised up, every mountain and hill made low; the rough ground shall become level, the rugged places plain."* (NIV) I have prayed this over our family for years. It was my heart's desire to have the ability to be stable even if life throws us curve balls, which the Bible calls tests, trials, or tribulation. Micah was a strong example of stability in the storms of life.

In January 2011, Micah entered college at East Tennessee State University, his Dad was falling; I had two arm surgeries; and, Miranda was told she would need brain surgery with the fusion. Within a couple of weeks of his first semester, his Dad was placed in ICU at the local hospital and not given much hope. Days later, Kevin was diagnosed with Multiple Sclerosis. Our family thought we had faced all the medical nightmares we would face this side of Heaven, but we were wrong. Micah remained calm and withstood the storm. He completed his first semester with academic honors. Throughout his college career Micah was bombarded with constant medical attacks against his family and did not know if Miranda, his Dad, or Mom would be alive from day to day. His Dad had extreme health issues, including blood clots, kidney issues, and a stem cell transplant. Micah watched his sister, who he always lovingly protected, go through the same difficult brain surgery with a fusion I had endured during their childhood.

Most people would have been crushed under the constant bombardment of pain, but Micah literally stood the test. He faithfully served in church by playing the drums throughout his college years. Micah's character and strengths, which are God given, shined during extremely dark moments of our life. Even though, Micah remained focused on his academics – his precious heart wanted to run away from all the pain in our home. However, God brought a beautiful young woman into his life during his junior year in college to walk through the valley of death beside him. Sierra held his heart while they watched us suffer. She was well educated in the heartbreak of watching people you love suffer and live with the knowledge at any moment they could die. Her own mother had endured multiple heart attacks, heart surgeries, and almost died while she was a young girl. Sierra had insight very few young people could comprehend, because she had lived with it in her own home. Micah and Sierra bonded as best friends rapidly, and then their friendship turned into a relationship. God grafted Sierra into our family.

During Micah's last semester in college and just two months before Brandon would marry Miranda, on April 1, 2014, Miranda, Kevin, and I were all at home when the phone rang. Brandon called Miranda, because he was in a rear-end car wreck. Miranda and I immediately drove to the scene of the car wreck. We called Brandon's family to let them know. Brandon's car had to be towed away on a flatbed wrecker. Then, we took Brandon to the emergency room, because he was already complaining about pain in his legs and neck.

The young person who hit him totaled her car, did thousands of dollars of damage to Brandon's vehicle, and caused Brandon to hit the car in front of him as well. The person who hit Brandon never even slowed down. Brandon was at a complete stop behind several other cars prior to the impact. His car was at least one car length behind the car in front of him, when suddenly he was struck by the car which rear ended him. The rear end of his car was extremely damaged, and the front end was slightly damaged as well. The seats in his car literally broke apart, and his body was violently thrown forward and then backwards due to being hit in the back hard enough to hit the car in front of him while holding down his car brakes with his right foot. Because he was at a complete stop with his foot on the brakes, his body received the impact of the collision. Brandon's body suffered severe whip-lash as well as other physical issues. He spent the next two years going for medical treatment.

While in medical treatment, he received many medical tests, such as MRI's, scans, and x-rays, to determine how to help him. Brandon went through physical therapy, had nerves in his neck burned by pain specialist, and even met with one of the best neurosurgeon in the world. Brandon had to wear a neck brace for six months without removing it except to shower. It was used to help strengthen his neck and hopefully avoid surgery. Due to the car accident, Brandon had instability in his cervical spine. He was on medication for the pain, but through it all Brandon never stopped pursuing his college degree. Even through his own physical pain, he refused to quit.

Brandon learned a hard and painful lesson from this automobile accident. He learned what it was like to be in constant medical care, endure pain continually, and fight with car insurance companies. The claim was settled almost two years after the car accident. However, the car insurance company forced Brandon into obtaining a lawyer to sue for the car insurance policy. He had to go through depositions and mediation. Truly, until you have been an injured victim of a car wreck there is no way to understand the frustration of dealing with automobile insurance companies. Brandon and Miranda kept excellent records. In the end, the insurance was settled; however, Brandon's neck and chest continued to cause him pain. Brandon told us he had a much greater respect for the pain we live in daily, after dealing with all the physical issues he went through. Experience is often the best teacher. You can watch people endure pain, be in car wrecks, see them suffering, but when it becomes your own body it is a completely different perspective. Watching Brandon go through the pain, as well as deal with the car insurance, was emotionally difficult for me and brought back memories of my own car accident; however, my respect for Brandon grew to a whole new level. Because of Brandon's career choice of becoming a Doctor of Physical Therapy, he studied diligently to find exercises to strengthen his neck, back, and core to avoid surgical intervention. We prayed Brandon will never need a neck fusion, but only time will tell.

After four years of college, Micah graduated in May 2014, with his Bachelor of Science in Computer Science from East Tennessee State University. Many people have asked me if we were proud of Micah, and of course Kevin and I were proud. However, I must say the biggest feeling I experienced was thankfulness. I was very thankful for Micah. I was thankful he loves God. I was thankful Kevin and I were both alive to see Micah graduate. I was thankful for the peace of God in Micah and for the love Sierra has for him. I was thankful for all the friends and family who have loved us through this journey. As we celebrated a wonderful achievement, my heart was full of the reality of a faithful God, who despite pain, suffering, difficulties, and extreme circumstances, sustained Micah.

Miranda and Micah were home-schooled. I thought I would be able to help Micah transition into his first semester of college, but I was wrong. Life was going to present so many challenges, I was unable to help him in any form. I watched my determined son go after his degree with integrity and perseverance. Micah has taught me all he really needed was God all along. Micah was and continues to be a gift. It will be exciting to see what his future will hold.

Micah's College Graduation

Miranda officially became Miranda Audrey-Ruth Renfro Taylor on June 7, 2014. Kevin and I were thrilled to call Brandon Edward Taylor our son-in-law. He was a strong Christian man who loved Miranda with his heart, and their love of God and each other continues to grow even today. Brandon proposed to Miranda on August 14, 2013, which was in the middle of all the decisions being made concerning whether Kevin would receive his stem cell transplant for Multiple Sclerosis or not. Kevin was accepted into the transplant program on August 13, 2013 – the day before Brandon proposed to Miranda. Therefore, I was not available to help with much of the planning for the wedding. I spent eight weeks in Chicago from July till December of 2013. While Kevin was going through the medical treatments, and Miranda was planning her wedding, my mind would worry about a multitude of things from small insignificant issues to life and death. Peace was difficult for me to maintain. Short text messages on my phone or calls from friends and family members reminding me God loved us would encourage me to take a deep breath and keep on going. A stem cell transplant is extremely unpredictable and a wedding is a blessing; however, both brought anxiety to my heart at times.

Philippians 4:6-7

"Do not be anxious about anything, but in every situation, by prayer and petition, with thanksgiving, present your requests to God. And the peace of God, which transcends all understanding, will guard your heart and minds in Christ Jesus." (NIV)

I had to choose to trust God and not be anxious – sometimes it was moment by moment.

Miranda, with the aid of Brandon, did most of the planning for their wedding. Family and friends helped us in every aspect of the showers and wedding. Truly, it was all a gift. The Thursday prior to the wedding a team of over twenty people came to decorate the church, just because they loved Miranda and our family. Personally, I was overcome with gratitude. Kevin was still healing from the transplant and was unable to help; but, I was not alone. My disabilities or physical limitations did not matter. We had love, support, and help from multiple people. I would not want any person to ever face the pain my family has endured, but the blessings have been much greater than the pain.

James 1:2-4

"Consider it pure joy, my brothers and sisters, whenever you face trials of many kinds, because you know that the testing of your faith produces perseverance. Let perseverance finish its work so that you may be mature and complete, not lacking anything." (NIV)

Truly, throughout the stem cell transplant process and the wedding our family lacked for nothing. God made a way at every turn. Each fear I had melted away, while I watched God faithfully provide, keep us safe, and bring an army of believers by our side to walk with us through the journey. Throughout all of our trials, tests, and medical issues God faithfully provided people to love us, aid us, and enable us to keep our faith. So many people have said to me, "Donna, you are so strong." The truth is I am very weak – but I have learned with Christ I can do all things.

Brandon and Miranda's Wedding

After Micah's graduation and Miranda's wedding, we took Kevin back to Chicago for his-six month checkup. Please understand when Kevin and I agreed to the stem cell transplant it was with the knowledge there were no more medical avenues of help for him. The doctor in Chicago along with other neurologists at major universities concluded, Kevin was in secondary progressive Multiple Sclerosis. So, the offer was to allow Kevin to receive a stem cell transplant off study, because he did not meet the criteria for the research protocol. We were given no guarantees or hope the stem cell transplant would work. We were warned about all the possible things which could go wrong, yet Kevin wanted to proceed. As his wife, I supported his decision. It is his body, and I love him. Therefore, on December 9, 2013, Kevin had his stem cell transplant. The medical team warned us the first year would be the worse. They were not kidding. It was challenging in various areas. To understand our daily life, one must understand how Multiple Sclerosis had affected Kevin. Kevin had lesions in his frontal lobe. The frontal lobe is the part of the brain where we have our personality, make rational decisions, and daily living decisions. So, Kevin had difficulty with cognitive skills which caused him to make irrational decisions. Also, Kevin had lesions in his thoracic, which caused him to be numb from the waist down. Just after his diagnosis 2010, Kevin spent weeks as a patient in a Rehabilitation Center where they taught him to walk again, but the numbness is still present. Kevin still falls, passes out, and stumbles – but he is walking. Kevin was seven months out from the transplant. In my heart, I knew the best news we could receive would be Kevin's MRI's were stable with no new lesions. It was my hope and prayer. God was good. The report came back, and Kevin had no new lesions or signs of a relapse. Most of Kevin's day was spent sleeping. The doctors explained to me how Kevin's body was working hard to make new stem cells and would be tired. Also, the cognitive skills and physical issues will not rapidly improve – if they improve at all.

Although we received the best news possible, the reality of the situation was Kevin still had all his lesions. His health and cognitive skills had not improved. The doctors were clear with me, this year will continue to be difficult, and it would be another three years before we saw any improvement. And up to five years, if Kevin could gain back physical ground – absolutely no guarantee. Last year, when we agreed to the stem cell transplant, we were desperate. This past week, I was peaceful and capable of listening to the reality of the situation. We have a long walk ahead of us, years of eating healthy, exercise, doctors, prayers, and God miraculously aiding Kevin's body in healing. But, we were blessed. We still have each other and our family. We love each other and have countless people who have loved us through all the painful crises. Love is a powerful source to draw from during difficult times. God is love, and we know with Him all things are possible.

Romans 12:12

"Be joyful in hope, patient in affliction, faithful in prayer." (NIV)

Brandon and Miranda returned from their honeymoon. They went to Chicago with Kevin and me in the summer of 2014. They were only married about a month. When we arrived home from Chicago, Miranda began dealing with some serious health issues. She went by ambulance to the local hospital, which was the beginning of ongoing health issues. We had been praying for her and believing God to restore her body to health. Originally it seemed the source of her problem was her heart, but now it appears to be her gallbladder. She was scheduled to have surgery in August 2014, but the insurance company wanted more time to evaluate her case. Meanwhile, she continued to be extremely ill. Miranda was in the emergency room multiple times in the past several weeks. Her body needed intervention. The gallbladder surgery was rescheduled for August 28, 2014, and more medical tests were ordered to see if any other issue could be the root cause. We were praying for knowledge for doctors to know the exact reason Miranda was so very sick.

Matthew 10:26

"So do not be afraid of them, for there is nothing concealed that will not be disclosed, or hidden that will not be made known." (NIV)

Over and over, we have seen the goodness of God and His faithfulness in ordering Miranda's steps perfectly to restore her health. We were confident in His ability to once again move to bring her health, restoration, and wholeness. Ultimately, the insurance company would not approve the surgery; so, Miranda was left with no help and continued with pain and vomiting. God alone knew our future. We have learned through the pain of illness how to place issues we have no control over at the foot of the cross and continue living life to the best of our ability.

Philippians 4:7

"And the peace of God, which transcends all understanding, will guard your hearts and your minds in Christ Jesus." (NIV)

I was one blessed woman. Over the past twelve months I was able to witnessed my husband receive hope for his future despite Multiple Sclerosis because of a stem cell transplant, my son graduate from college, and my daughter marry a Godly man who loves her with his heart. Ten years ago, it appeared I would not live to see these precious moments in life; however, God in His faithfulness made a way through prayer, faith, and great medical professionals to give me back life. Words cannot express how fortunate I feel. I have seen the goodness of the glory of God in the land of the living. The Word of God is alive, and His promises endured regardless of the circumstances. I am living proof.

Psalm 27:13

"I remain confident of this: I will see the goodness of the Lord in the land of the living." *(NIV)*

Over the past year, my body had deteriorated. After much prayer in July of 2014, I resigned my position at the radio station, because my body was not physically able to endure the work. Once again, I had to lay down my heart's desire. Each week, I lost more physical ground. I was quietly at home praying and at times in the hospital emergency room. Once again, I had to go through medical testing. December 23, 2014, I had another ICP, intracranial pressure, brain surgery to see if there was medical aid for my deterioration. I had the procedure in Maryland. This ICP was much more difficult than the first one I endured. I was held in surgical holding for hours and then moved to an ICU unit with glass doors. It was difficult for me to keep my respirations up. I remember the nurse standing over me telling me to breathe throughout the 27 hours the monitor was in my brain. My brain pressure ruled out the need for a brain shunt once again.

When the PA went to remove my ICP, I had a serious cerebrospinal fluid, cerebrospinal fluid, leak. It was more like a spout of liquid shooting out of the hole in the front of my skull. He had to rapidly throw blue blankets over me while he held his finger in the surgical hole in my skull. The PA had just removed the ICP monitoring device and was trying to stop the cerebrospinal fluid leak. He told me to hold still. Trust me, I did not move. He proceeded to remain calm while giving me and the nurse instructions. He managed to stop the leak and sew the hole in my head up. He did warn me I may become sick with a horrific headache and listed other complications. My sister was in the room and witnessed the entire event. She had to drive me home from Maryland the same day. Each time the car stopped, I had to get out to vomit. However, she managed to get me home on December 24, 2014. Ginger told me months later, when she witnessed the cerebrospinal fluid leak she was terrified I would die right in front of her. It traumatized her, and broke her heart. By far the sick person faces the most difficulties; however, illness causes so much pain for everyone who loves the person suffering as well.

Once again, I was home for Christmas; however, I was too sick to be involved in any celebrations. I do remember Micah's girlfriend, Sierra, sitting with me on Christmas day and being so kind. She was an excellent caregiver. I could feel the love coming off her while she brought me medication and encouraged me. She was extremely peaceful and reminded me the pain would pass with time. A dear friend for over 20 years came by my house regularly while I was healing and would bring food or cook for me. She always brought love and hope with her. When I was homebound, people who took time out of their life to bring me laughter, joy, and love was a necessity which aided in my physical healing.

On Monday, January 12, 2015, Kevin, Miranda, Brandon, and I went to see Dr. Neuro #7 in Maryland. After going over recent imaging and surgical results, I agreed to two separate surgeries. Personally, I was struggling greatly with agreeing to more surgeries. I had endured the pain of brain and neck surgery before, and said I would die before I endured it again. As Christians, we all have grace, because of the gift of Jesus Christ to humanity. I was and continue to be thankful for the grace of God in my life. I needed God's grace, so I listened to a lot of praise and worship music to prepare myself mentally to go back through all the pain. I had to choose to set my face like flint, and do whatever it took to regain quality of life.

Jesus Christ is my Savior, Hope, Healer, Redeemer, and Peace in this life. Often the scriptures I am led to study are concerning fear or should I say not fearing. For instance, Isaiah 41:10, *"So do not fear, for I am with you; do not be dismayed, for I am your God. I will strengthen you and help you. I will uphold you with my righteous right hand."* (NIV) And, Isaiah 43: 2, 4, and 5: *"When you pass through the waters, I will be with you; and when you pass through the rivers, they will not sweep over you. When you walk through the fire, you will not be burned; the flames will not set you ablaze. Since you are precious and honored in my sight, and because I love you, I will give people in exchange for you, nations in exchange for your life. Do not be afraid, for I am with you; I will bring your children from the east and gather you from the west."* (NIV)

Fear may cause someone to withdraw or flee due to feeling unable to do the task in front of them. I have faced fear many times in my life as I am sure you have as well. Faith in Jesus will give you the ability to be fully persuaded and able to trust in God. Faith is not possible without an intimate relationship with God.

John 15: 5

"I am the vine; you are the branches. If you remain in me and I in you, you will bear much fruit; apart from me you can do nothing." (NIV)

My ability to walk with Jesus Christ as His disciple is due to my personal relationship with Him. God is faithful, and He has always kept His promises to me personally. However, I have faced extraordinary pain and suffering. Truly, there are no words for the physical pain I live in daily. From the moment I was in the car wreck on December 23, 2004, my entire life changed. The pain was so severe I literally agreed to let men stretch me while I was awake for 48 hours in a halo. Then in the second surgery, they did many other procedures such as a decompression of my brain and fuse my skull to C-5 with titanium rods. The car wreck literally destroyed my neck and arms. It is truly a miracle I am still able to use my hands ten years later. I have endured many major surgeries since the car wreck, but before the surgeries I literally lost all my abilities such as walking, seeing, and hearing. It took years to fight back and have a life again. But, God walked beside me in each moment of my pain.

The Bible is full of examples of great men and women of God who suffer such as David, Daniel, and Jesus our Savior, the disciples, and we must know the heart of Mary was devastated to see her son crucified. Being a Christian does not exempt us from pain; however, it empowers us to face the pain with an inner strength found in Christ Jesus alone.

The surgeries ahead of me were not a walk in the park. The surgery I had in December 2014, consisted of an incision in the front of my skull over my right eye where a probe was placed through my brain to my brain stem to monitor my brain pressure for 27 hours. The reality of the experience was painful; but, it brought more answers to help a brilliant neurosurgeon who is anointed by God to help his patients who suffer with Chiari, Syringomyelia, tethered spinal cords, Ehlers-Danlos Syndrome, bone malformations, Eagle Syndrome, and many other issues. Honestly, you are blessed if you do not know what these conditions are or what they do to people. The results were conclusive concerning my brain pressure – it was normal, which was a blessing. However, it meant my neurological decline was from other physical issues. I had to embark on two more surgeries to aid my body.

In July 2014, I knew my body had reached its limits. I was spending more time in bed than out. It was difficult to walk. I had a constant headache. By the way, when I use the word headache it is not in the "normal" context. It felt like there was a vice-grip on my head. The pressure was tolerable at times, but always present. When it was unbearable, I lost the ability to see, walk, use my hands, talk, answer simple questions, and I was at the mercy of my family to get me medical aid rapidly. I literally become desperate in pain, and would let someone drill a hole in my head to release the pressure if they offered. There are no words for the pain, no scale for it, no way to express it, and no way to explain it. However, if you saw me – you would realize the depth of it. Each time I went to the emergency room while my body deteriorated, the doctors locally were positive I was having a stroke – however, it was simply my own body attacking me.

The dates were set for my next two surgeries. On February 18, 2015, my neurosurgeon will be removing the right side of my hardware from my skull down to C-2/3 where he will saw the rod in half and leave the rest of my fusion. The right side of my fusion had failed. While removing the fusion, he will be taking four screws out of my brain and one out of my neck. My fusion was placed nine years and two months ago; therefore, it has been in my body for a long time. He will leave in the left side of my fusion, which was from my skull to C-5, because my neck is not stable enough without it. After he removes the titanium hardware, he will be taking a cadaver bone as well as removing bone marrow from my hip to rebuild my skull. He has to cut down the back of my head to do this surgery. Healing from an incision down the back of your skull and neck is excruciating. I have already walked this path, but with God I can walk down it again.

Isaiah 50:7

"Because the Sovereign Lord helps me, I will not be disgraced. Therefore have I set my face like flint, and I know I will not be put to shame." (NIV)

Seven days later on February 24, 2015, my neurosurgeon will be going into the front of my neck at the C-6/7 level to perform an Anterior Cervical Discectomy. It felt like my neck was crushing down and the pain was relentless. I was living in a neck brace. I have a syrinx, a pathological cavity in my spinal cord which is like a bubble of fluid causing constant nerve damage, at the C-5 through C-7 level as well as spinal stenosis. Basically, my spinal cord does not have the space to allow the cerebrospinal fluid to flow appropriately, and it was causing lots of physical issues as well as pain in my body. I realize I have written a lot of information and many of you may not understand the technical parts; however, knowledge is power. I desire to bring knowledge to the world to help others who may be suffering with these issues or encourage people suffering from other problems with God you can do whatever you were created to do. Be fearless and face your future.

In February 2015, I went to face my surgeries. Both surgeries were excruciating; however, I listened to praise music and endured. There were some complications. One of which was I had a bad allergic reaction to a medication given to me by the second anesthetist. Miranda was the one who figured out which medication I was allergic to and helped me by telling the neurosurgeon. Honestly, I remember well the two weeks I spent in Maryland and prefer to not dwell on them. My daughter Miranda carried me through the storm. She fought with faith at every turn and refused to let me go. Kevin, my parents, and some friends we had in Maryland were there as well. Once I was home, I thought the worst was over. But, the suffering and pain only increased. Night after night I woke up screaming for help in pain and found it very difficult to eat anything. I could swallow frozen ice drinks, but that was about it. I thought it was from the pain of the incision in the front of my neck and would simply heal with time; however, I was wrong. Micah, Brandon, and Miranda all decided to live with us while I was going through these surgeries to help me. Kevin was weak, and they all knew it. They all sacrificed in so many ways to enable me to get through these surgeries. My heart overflows with thankfulness, and they will never know how much their help meant to me. I desperately needed them twenty-four hours a day.

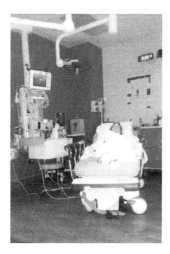
Donna in the emergency room

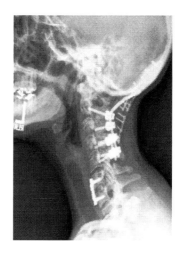
Donna's new fusion

On March 13, 2015, I went by ambulance to our local hospital. The doctors could see my body was in distress, so they did a scan to make sure I did not have complications from the surgeries. My CAT scan came back normal. Even my doctor in Maryland reviewed it. The surgeries had fixed my body, but my body was not improving. Then on March 26, my body caved. I ended up being admitted into the hospital for weeks, due to the fact I could not swallow, walk, and had lost control of my hands. I was extremely weak. After some tests, I was diagnosed with Dysphagia, which is caused by Eagle Syndrome or Ehlers-Danlos Syndrome. Therefore, I had to learn to swallow and eat again. I had a fabulous speech therapist. Also, I was put in physical therapy to aid my walking and occupational therapy for my hands as well as other issues. I was released from the hospital on April 6, 2015. Although, I was thrilled to go home the process was not over. I was placed in outpatient physical therapy. I began the outpatient therapy on April 14, 2015, and it was evident at that moment there was not an end date in sight. Walking was extremely challenging for me. I had wonderful physical therapists who were willing to reteach my body how to walk, but again last night I woke up screaming for help. The pain in my body was in every joint. I knew prior to the beginning of this journey it was going to be difficult physically, mentally, and spiritually. However, I must say it has been far more difficult than I ever dreamed was possible.

It has been a challenging road. I have been in our local hospital three times and once for a two week stay, since my last surgery on February 24, 2015. Truly, the pain from healing was excruciating, and I pray no one ever faces the struggles I have known. My heart breaks as I watch special friends of ours go through similar surgeries. Only people who have endured them will understand the level of pain. I have been the patient and the caregiver. Watching someone you love suffer is a nightmare; however, being the patient is far worse. The patient is unable to leave their body and escape the pain. Words simply cannot express the strength and courage it takes to face these surgeries. I understand why God gave me this scripture years ago.

Joshua 1:9

"Have I not commanded you? Be strong and courageous. Do not be afraid; do not be discouraged, for the Lord your God will be with you wherever you go." (NIV)

I cling to it during the dark moments. Daily, I was growing stronger, which was a true miracle. With time, I expect to be better, physically, every day. This journey tested my resolve at every level, and I can still say God is good.

CHAPTER 30

LEGACY

James 1: 2-4 Amplified

"Consider it wholly joyful, my brethren, whenever you are enveloped in or encounter trials of any sort or fall into various temptations. Be assured and understand that the trial and proving of your faith bring out endurance and steadfastness and patience. But let endurance and steadfastness and patience have full play and do a thorough work, so that you may be [people] perfectly and fully developed [with no defects], lacking in nothing."

Miranda had been extraordinarily sick, since June 2014, with her abdomen. Last year in August 2014, the doctors wanted to take out her gallbladder, but the insurance would not approve it. She had no choice, but to suffer through vomiting and other issues with her stomach. During the past twelve months, she had managed to complete her bachelor's degree with academic honors, be a wife to Brandon, and be the primary caregiver of me with excellence through my surgeries. She had faithfully served our family through much pain and continued even though she personally suffered with her own physical disabilities. As her family, we have watched her faithfully serve, love God, and continue in the difficult moments. She is a shining example of Jesus Christ daily, even in suffering. Her health insurance company approved the surgery for the spring, and she planned to have her gallbladder removed the week after she graduated. God, once again, answered our prayers by guiding the surgeon's hands, keeping her safe, and bring healing to her body. Although, our family has faced much pain, suffering, and difficulties during 2015 – we also enjoyed watching both Miranda and Brandon complete their first degrees. Miranda graduated from Liberty University with her bachelor degree in Psychology, and Brandon graduated with his associates in Pre-Physical Therapy.

2 Corinthians 12:9

"But he said to me, "My grace is sufficient for you, for my power is made perfect in weakness." Therefore, I will boast all the more gladly about my weaknesses, so that Christ's power may rest in me." (NIV)

Miranda's College Graduation   Brandon's College Graduation

Miranda had her gallbladder removed on Thursday, May 7, 2015. She dealt with the pain of healing from the surgery; however, it has brought her much relief. She could eat without pain and sickness. She had suffered almost a year before receiving help. Even though it took time, it was removed at the right time. She was able to complete her degree prior to the surgery. Therefore, she can heal without the pressure of school. We are very thankful to God for supplying all her needs.

Kevin faced another hospitalization in May 2015. It had been about eighteen months since his stem cell transplant, and his healing process had been slow. Due to severe chest pains, Kevin was hospitalized. He went through many tests. Honestly, I did not think my own body would withstand going to the emergency room much less the days he was in the hospital. His parents were a tremendous blessing and helped us at every turn. My body was weak, especially after just going and aiding Miranda with her surgery. However, I did get through the traumas, and we found answers to help Kevin's pain. God was faithful to meet all our needs once again. The week was exhausting; but, God had used it to remind me through my weakness He is strong. He had encouraged me, healed my heart, strengthened my resolve to serve Him regardless of the cost and reminded me of all the promises He has kept. Truly, we serve a faithful God.

As humans, we look for loyalty in people, and though they may try – it is inevitable they will fail. When we place expectations on people that only God can fulfill, we will be disappointed every time. As you walk through your personal journey in this world, you will find only God will have the ability to remain faithful to you regardless of the circumstances.

Luke 14:26

"If anyone comes to me and does not hate father and mother, wife and children, brothers and sisters—yes, even their own life—such a person cannot be my disciple." (NIV)

I was saved at the age of five; however, by the age of 20, I had given my life to Jesus Christ as a bondservant. Simply put, a bondservant is a person who is dedicated to their Master without wages. Due to an encounter with God, I knew my life was not my own.

1 Corinthians 6:20

"You were bought at a price. Therefore honor God with your bodies." (NIV)

I had no idea what my future held when I made my commitment to God, but I knew God held my future. As much as I have personally endured, 2015 has been one of the hardest years on me physically, spiritually, financially, and personally.

Psalm 23:4

"Even though I walk through the darkest valley, I will fear no evil, for you are with me; your rod and your staff, they comfort me." (NIV)

As my body began to fail me June 2014, I knew in my heart what I was about to face. By August, it was confirmed. In January 2015, the surgeries were ordered. I found myself facing an obstacle I had declared I would NEVER do again. Yet, there I lay without options. My husband and Miranda made decisions on my behalf, which opened the doors for me to travel back through extraordinarily painful surgeries. Honestly, I was ready to simply go on to Heaven and be finished. Suffering in daily pain is no easy task and making it look good – well that takes talent! Mentally, preparing myself to go back through the most painful surgeries I had endured was torture. Although my physical body became extremely weak the previous year and continued to go downhill, my spiritual soul increased in power as people who I thought were loyal or my friend did not stand by my side through the darkest moments. It was a gift to be abandoned, because it caused me to put all my hope in Christ alone.

I would spend time contemplating how Jesus felt as He hung on the cross. He had been lied about by His closest friends and all the people, with exception of a few woman, He served turned their back on Him. In prayer, I just kept asking why people disappoint us in our hour of pain. Then, like a revelation, it hit me, "Why do I expect people to be God in my moment of pain?" I was in a season where only God could carry me through – my hope had to be in Him alone.

Proverbs 3:5-6

"Trust in the Lord with all your heart and lean not on your own understanding; in all your ways submit to Him, and He will make your paths straight." (NIV)

Kevin and I faced a challenging year; but, we are still here. We love one another. God continues to keep all His promises to us despite the physical pain, medical reports, and disappointment. I have learned God will place the right people at the right time in your path to fulfill His destiny for your life. So, if you have people who have walked away, talk about you in a negative way, lie about you, or use you for their own gain, and then dump you. Let go of them, and cling to Jesus Christ and Him alone.

In July 2015, we broke ground on our handicapable home. Kevin and I had built a home in 1993; however, it had three levels with lots of stairs. Our new bodies had special needs. So, Kevin's parents gave us some land, which was a tremendous blessing. We found a wonderful contractor who worked diligently to meet every physical need we individually had in building our new one level home. Kevin took the lead, which was incredible and a blessing. I was only four months out of surgery when our house construction began. I was unsure of decision making; however, Kevin was extremely confident. He picked all the flooring, tile, colors, brick, stone, and layout. He knew exactly what he wanted. I was thrilled to just let him, along with the contractor, make all the decisions. Occasionally, there were a couple of issues, and I had to aid with decisions. But, most of the burden was not on my shoulders. We began building in July 2015 and moved in the last week of January 2016. Of course, we still dealt with medical issues while building.

In November 2015, Kevin became sick unto death again. Kevin and I both caught a virus, which led to a bacterial infection. Kevin became extremely ill. One Sunday night in November 2015, I was watching the television when God moved in my heart to go and check on Kevin. He had been on antibiotics for over a week. When, I touched him it was evident he had a fever. I took his temperature and it was 102.7. I immediately knew we were in a life and death situation; however, I had no idea how extremely sick Kevin was. I called my Aunt, and she instructed me to get him to the hospital as soon as possible. She said he could be septic. Brandon, Miranda, and I took Kevin to the local hospital. I prayed the entire three miles for God to grant us favor for Kevin to be quickly seen without a wait. When I arrived at the emergency room, a friend of ours from Seminary was walking down the hall. He saw me and asked if I was okay. I told him what was going on with Kevin, and he stood by me while I talked to the intake personnel. He was quietly praying the entire time. I felt panic in my heart. The hospital took Kevin back immediately. However, the nightmare was just beginning. Once in a room and hooked up to the monitor, it was evident Kevin's body was in distress. I was taken out into the hallway to be asked about his living will. Kevin has a DNR, which means the doctors cannot intervene if he dies. I knew we were in a very serious situation. Miranda and I waited for over four hours in the emergency room before anyone gave us an update. They were running tests on Kevin, but all medical personnel were being very quiet. I would leave the room and walk the hallway praying over Kevin the scripture God put in my heart.

Hebrews 11:1

"Now faith is confidence in what we hope for and assurance about what we do not see." (NIV)

I called a dear friend of mine. She and I had been friends since June 1993. She encouraged me in my faith. She reminded me I was a child of God. I needed her voice of reassurance in the middle of chaos. I went into the bathroom and looked in the mirror. I told myself, "I am a child of God, and I can do this."

When I would enter the room with Kevin, I never let him see the concern on my face. My heart was crushed and hard pressed, but I had to walk by faith. Over four hours passed and eventually, Kevin was moved to a room. A doctor came in and confirmed Kevin was septic. He said there would be multiple tests to determine exactly what the specific infection was and how to treat it. I just sat there in shock and was not educated in the infections he listed. Kevin's heart rate was out of control and his blood pressure kept going too low. Only God was going to keep him alive, and I knew it. Miranda went home to get some rest around 1:30 a.m., and I was sent home from the hospital when it was confirmed Kevin had C. diff. I had never heard of this infection before that night. C. diff. is highly contagious and extremely dangerous. It is Clostridium difficile colitis and is deadly. I researched for about a minute, and quickly realized I did not need to know the mountain we were facing. I was going to have to set my face like flint and trust God to carry us through this storm.

Kevin was released within a couple of days to come home, but our entire lives were turned upside down. Kevin had to be in a clean environment. Our entire house reeked of bleach for weeks. Kevin mainly stayed in his bedroom for six weeks. During the timeframe that Kevin had C. diff, we cleaned constantly. His food was taken to him on paper plates and thrown away inside of his bedroom. He wore blue gowns and masks to help keep from passing the infection to the rest of the family. We were locked inside of a bubble for over six weeks. However, once again God was faithful, and Kevin conquered C. diff. It was not confirmed until late December. Kevin did struggle greatly and had two more setbacks with illness in January 2016.

1 Corinthians 10:13

"No temptation [regardless of its source] has overtaken or enticed you that is not common to human experience [nor is any temptation unusual or beyond human resistance]; but God is faithful [to His word—He is compassionate and trustworthy], and He will not let you be tempted beyond your ability [to resist], but along with the temptation He [has in the past and is now and] will [always] provide the way out as well, so that you will be able to endure it [without yielding, and will overcome temptation with joy]." (AMP)

Silence is often my best weapon when we are faced with critical conditions. Once again, I hung on to the promises of God and expected a miracle. God was so very faithful to His word, but at times I have to draw back to keep my faith ablaze. I pray as you read our story, it infuses you with faith and confidence in Christ. Regardless of the outcome, I know we are loved by God, and He is in control.

Romans 8:38-39

"For I am convinced [and continue to be convinced—beyond any doubt] that neither death, nor life, nor angels, nor principalities, nor things present and threatening, nor things to come, nor powers, nor height, nor depth, nor any other created thing, will be able to separate us from the [unlimited] love of God, which is in Christ Jesus our Lord." (AMP)

Kevin and Donna Renfro

Our family has learned life continues through trials, trauma, blessings, and illness. Years ago we made purposeful decisions to keep living despite circumstances. Life will pass you by if you sit in self-pity or marvel in accomplishments. You never know what a day may hold, but you can keep goals in front of you and always show love, kindness, and hope to people around you.

By May 2016, our family was all in their own homes. Micah bought a condo. Miranda and Brandon bought the home we built in 1993. Even when Miranda was a little girl, she would say when she grew up, she was not moving out – we were. I thought it was cute coming from a two-year-old; however, it was prophetic. Kevin, Micah, and I all moved out. It took time to get all the homes set up. But, we had a lot of help from family and friends. Although Kevin and I moved into our new home at the end of January 2016, it was the middle of July before all the tools and stored items were finally in each home. Our young adult children sacrificed so much to help Kevin and me. I watched God bless them abundantly when it was time for Kevin and me to become independent. Micah's girlfriend, Sierra, was also a blessing. She is tiny in human stature; however, she is tough. She held Micah's heart through all the storms beginning with the stem cell transplant till present. She does not flinch. Brandon has a soft and gentle spirit; however, he was a solid rock for Miranda as well. It is a gift to watch God pair our adult children with their partners. Only God could bring the right people to walk beside our children through such difficult medical crises.

2 Timothy 2:15

"Do your best to present yourself to God as one approved by him, a worker who has no need to be ashamed, rightly explaining the word of truth." (NIV)

In 2003, Kevin and I began Donna Renfro Ministries. A pastor told me, if I was going to fulfill the call on my life, I needed to go back to school and earn a theological degree. Honestly, I did not think about his advice very much. I already had a bachelor's degree in teaching. We began Donna Renfro Ministries in December 2003. In December 2004, I had the car wreck and my life changed forever this side of Heaven. By 2009, I had physically healed enough to consider degree seeking. Kevin and I made the decision to embark upon the journey of obtaining one master degree at a Seminary. Over the course of the past seven years, I earned two master's degrees and on June 26, 2016, I graduated with my second doctorate degree. I have attended four separate schools for my graduate degrees. There was no way for any human to predict in 2003, what tribulations my family was going to face, but God knew. However, the pastor who advised me concerning theological degrees had given me the perfect advice for that season of our life. I earned my master of Biblical Studies, master of Religious Education, and doctorate of Biblical Counseling after many surgeries including my first brain surgery, due to the car wreck. I then graduated with my PhD in Theology after my second brain surgery. Going back to school taught me far more than Greek, Theology, or Christian History. I realized I could still learn, retain information, make goals, and achieve the goals despite facing death, an extremely ill child, and having my husband diagnosed with Multiple Sclerosis, which was later changed to NMO. The car wreck took my neck mobility away; but, it did not take my life away.

Miranda and Donna graduating together in June 2016

From left to right: Brandon, Miranda, Donna, Kevin, Micah, and Sierra

Luke 1:37

"For with God nothing [is or ever] shall be impossible." Amplified

My official name:

Rev. Dr. Donna Lynn Russell Renfro, M.S.B.S., M.R.E.D., D.B.C., PhD.

However, my identity is not in my official name or any letters. I am Donna, a child of God. My Dad named me Donna the day I was born. I will be Donna until the day I die. I am thankful God gave me the opportunity to obtain every degree I have received. Although I support higher education and believe in it completely, the higher I went in my education the more humbled I became. A person could study the scriptures constantly and never know all there is to know about God or the Bible. At the end of my life, all these degrees are simply pieces of paper. My prayer is that I rightly divide the scriptures to bring hope to the hopeless. I do not want to be remembered for having obtained degrees. I want my legacy to be: Donna obeyed God regardless of the cost, loved her family, served with integrity from her heart, and continually testified of the faithfulness of God all the days of her life. I want to hear the words, "Well done." when I meet my Savior, Jesus Christ.

Proverbs 15:33

"Wisdom's instruction is to fear the Lord, and humility comes before honor." (NIV)

Miranda had desired to go on to further education as well. She was offered scholarships to go to multiple colleges for her master's program. However, she put her education on hold to be my caregiver. Ultimately, she received her master of Biblical Counseling the same day I received my PhD in Theology. The first doctorate I received, I had the honor of walking across the stage and graduating with my husband in May 2012. The second doctorate I obtained, I had the honor of graduating with my daughter in June 2016. These are priceless moments in my heart. Truly, only God knew how hard our family had to work and the physical, emotional, spiritual, and financial cost of higher education for each one of us. So, we do not take the opportunity of higher education for granted and know God ordered our steps.

To obtain higher education it takes perseverance, hard work, sacrifice, and a determination to never give up. Words cannot express how thankful I am for having the opportunity to live to see my daughter and son grow up, graduate college, fall in love, and continue to pursue their goals. When we were diagnosed with Chiari Brain Malformation, tethered spinal cords, Ehlers-Danlos Syndrome, and a host of other health issues over 10 years ago – life looked dim on a good day. But, by faith we chose, as a family, to live in the moment and trust God regardless of circumstances.

CHAPTER 31

BE STILL

"Be still and know that He is God." Psalm 46:10

There are moments in your life when only God can carry you through. These moments tend to come when you least expect them. Life is going good, even great, then suddenly, you are thrust into a whirlwind of a storm without any warning. When you face life or death crises, you need to know God and hear His voice clearly.

On July 21, 2016, our family was elated. We had all just purchased our separate homes, moved our final items, and everyone was settled. Kevin and I were still in the process of physically healing. It takes years for a stem cell transplant to show improvement, if it even works, and after my surgeries in February 2015, healing takes time. However, July 21, 2016, was very special for our family. We were excited, because Miranda was five years out from her brain decompression and fusion surgery. She had completed her bachelor's degree and master's degree, been married to Brandon for two years, and they had bought our home. Neurologically, Miranda was doing great. We have many friends with Chiari, who have experienced our pain as well as surgeries. Miranda was an exception to the average outcome even though she was physically handicap, due to the conditions. She only had the one de-tethering and brain surgery. We were blessed beyond measure and did not take it for granted. We spent much of the day feeling so very thankful and talking about the fact, Miranda had done so well with the surgeries. Miranda and Brandon were ready to consider having a baby. Brandon was scheduled to graduate with his bachelor's degree in May 2017. So, they wanted to have a baby prior to him entering the Doctor of Physical Therapy program.

For three years prior to the car wreck, many people prayed for both Miranda and me concerning her becoming pregnant and having her own child. The promise included the fact this baby would be a little girl without Chiari Brain Malformation. Because I knew how complicated Miranda's body was physically, I struggled at the idea of her going through pregnancy. But, Miranda wanted a baby. The first year that God began speaking to us about Miranda becoming pregnant, I was angry. I would argue with God in prayer, and continually told Him I thought Miranda becoming pregnant with a child was a bad idea. Please do not misunderstand me. I wanted Brandon and Miranda to have a child, if they wanted one. It was just extremely difficult for me to line up my heart or mind to the idea of Miranda personally being pregnant, because of all the knowledge I had about her physical limitations. I had no desire to watch my daughter go through a pregnancy or have a grandchild with Chiari Brain Malformation. God moved on my heart during the three years of knowing Miranda would be pregnant. After my initial response of disagreeing with God, I finally lined up my will to His and began praying specifically over Miranda's body being prepared to carry a baby. Later, my prayer would change to asking God for the right time, right place, and right people.

Miranda and I were on the phone on July 22, 2016, when suddenly she said, "Mom, our car was just hit." I was shocked, because we were talking on cell phones. I thought she was at home; however, Brandon and Miranda were parked at a college campus in a handicap parking spot when a man rear-ended their vehicle. I rapidly asked her where they were located. Kevin and I left immediately. We were only three miles from the wreck. So, we arrived quickly. When we came to the parking lot. There were two campus police officers and a fire truck with two men who were rapid responders. Miranda had called 911. As soon as I saw her, I knew she was injured. She told me that her face was numb. One of the policemen talked with me, and I showed him a picture of the interior of her fusion. When the driver rear-ended them, Miranda was sitting still in the driver's seat and was turned towards Brandon while talking to me on the phone. When you have Ehlers-Danlos Syndrome and a fusion, it does not take much to cause great harm to your neck. Upon impact, Miranda's body took the blow and her neck was jerked. The man hit their car so hard it moved the vehicle forward and backwards in the spot it was parked. Brandon had to jump out of the car to stop the man who hit their vehicle. The other driver did not want it reported to the police; however, Miranda knew to report the accident. The numbness in Miranda's face was the first sign of a downward spiral of her health.

After talking to the police and requesting an ambulance, the police officer said he could get us to the local hospital faster. So, we followed him. He turned on his lights and ran red lights to get us there as soon as possible. Miranda's face began swelling immediately. At the hospital, she had to sit in a wheelchair to wait to be seen. When they took her back, her symptoms were increasing by the hour. She was numb in her face with her right eye drooping. Also, Miranda had extreme pain in her neck, arms, and legs. And, her hands were going numb. The doctors did a scan, gave her medicine, and her pain still increased. She began to have pain in her thoracic; so, they gave her stronger pain medication. A rapid pain went down her spine, and numbness wrapped around her abdomen, and she vomited. More medical tests were ordered such as an x-ray, and Miranda was admitted for overnight observation. The next day, they did an MRI and sent her home in pain with no medication or medical treatment.

Every day, Miranda lost physical ground. The car wreck occurred on a Friday evening. By Tuesday, Miranda went to her local internist and saw the physician's assistant. She suggested Miranda go see Dr. Neuro #7. On Wednesday, Miranda went to a local neurosurgeon and saw a physician's assistant, who basically ignored her, and only wanted to give her medication even though her body was clearly declining. Friday, July 29, 2016, Miranda ended up in another emergency room, because half of her body was numb with the other side having tremors. Also, her speech was slurred. She still had numbness in her face, extreme pain, and now leg pain had begun. The doctor at this emergency room had treated me and was aware of our diagnoses. She ran I.V. medication to help calm the symptoms, but instructed us to get Miranda to Dr. Neuro #7 as soon as possible. So, Brandon and I took Miranda to Maryland on Monday, August 1, 2016. Once again, life was spinning out of control. There was no time to think. We had to pray and react quickly to get Miranda help.

Tuesday morning, we took Miranda to the emergency room of the hospital where Dr. Neuro #7 did his surgeries. Miranda was immediately admitted. She had a new symptom of pain in her hardware located in her skull, specifically a screw from her fusion which began due to the impact from the car wreck. Dr. Neuro #7 let us know he would need to remove the hardware, because of the pain. More tests were ordered. Miranda's symptoms continued to grow. Now, her hearing was more amplified, and her vision was extremely sensitive. She was vomiting because of pain throughout the day, and it became difficult for her to even walk. Miranda had to be discharged for the sitting MRI prior to her surgery; because, the hospital did not have the machine. So, we took her to the imaging facility with the sitting MRI machine. Miranda was back in the emergency room on Monday, August 8, 2016, because her legs went numb, and Brandon had to help her. She was not able to walk anymore. Therefore, on Tuesday, August 9, 2016, Dr. Neuro #7 took her into surgery ahead of schedule. Just before she was rolled away from us, we learned he was planning on removing her entire skull and neck fusion to do an augmentation, which is a rebuild of the fusion. Miranda would be having bone marrow taken from her hip to aid with the new fusion. Brandon, Miranda, and I were all in shock. Dr. Neuro #7 prayed for Miranda. I kissed her good-bye, and Brandon hugged her. Everything happened so fast there was no time to think. As soon as I was in the waiting room, I had to run to the bathroom to vomit. We were in the middle of a nightmare.

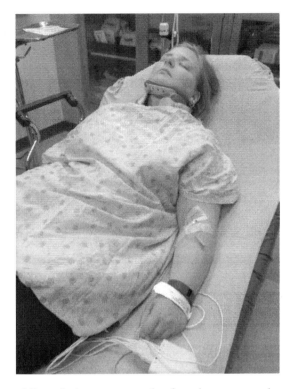

Miranda just one week after the car wreck

Brandon and I waited for hours before Dr. Neuro #7 came to give us the surgical report. He said it was extremely difficult to remove the hardware. Then, he explained he had to use human cadaver bones to rebuild her skull, and if anything hit the back of her head the bones could cave into her brain, which would kill her. I had never heard of a bone fusion prior to Dr. Neuro #7 telling us what he did to Miranda. My own fusion was rebuilt with titanium. He explained it could take up to three years for the fusion to heal, and her C3-C4 was unstable. Also, he said she can never be in another car wreck. I felt hollow on the inside. My brain could not wrap around the words I just heard. Only days prior we were celebrating, and so very thankful for how well Miranda was doing physically. Now, Miranda was tossed into the sea of pain, suffering, and her life was flipped upside down. Her dream of being a mommy was definitely on hold – maybe temporarily or maybe forever. Brandon and I handled things in a similar way. We both just sat there in silence until we could go see her in PICU. When the nurse called us back, Miranda appeared to be resting peacefully. However, the nurse explained the anesthesiologist had given her medication to help her rest better and wake up slowly. Brandon and I were not allowed to stay with her. He took me back to the hotel, and we planned to take twelve-hour shifts. We were both already exhausted from taking care of her since the day of the car wreck. So, Brandon left me and went back to the hospital.

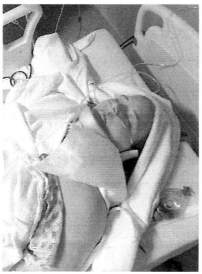

Miranda in PICU after surgery

The night was long and no one received any rest. I was awake praying in the hotel. Brandon tried to take care of Miranda. Miranda suffered in excruciating pain and was not receiving her pain medication, because the pump kept saying she did not have enough respirations. Brandon picked me up during nurse change and took me to Miranda. I did not leave her side again. Immediately, I began working on getting her pain medication issues fixed. It took me another five hours to finally get the pumps off her and have her the medications given through her I.V. Finally, Miranda received some relief. She was determined to get out of bed as soon as possible. She had been through surgery before, and knew the quicker you get up – no matter how painful – the faster you will heal. Her physical pain was unbearable, yet she continued to fight against her own body. She sat upright in a chair and wanted the catheter removed as well. Every day, she added more to her own personal goals, which were more expectations than even the doctors put on her. Miranda wanted to get out of the hospital and go home. Miranda was discharged from the hospital on August 11, 2016. Miranda and Brandon moved into our newly built handicapable home with us, because she could not walk up the stairs in their home. When we arrived home, Miranda was seen by her local internist. We were not able to fill her pain medication in Tennessee, because it was written by an out-of-state doctor. Also, when they changed her dressing from her incisions it was infected. So, Miranda had to start a high powered anti-biotic. They lived with us for six weeks. Brandon and I took care of her. During the time they were with us, Brandon began his last year in his bachelor's degree. It was difficult for him to leave Miranda, but I encouraged him I could handle it.

While Miranda was still living with us, she had a major complication. On August 29, 2016, Miranda was lethargic with slurred speech. I was unable to get her alert. When Brandon came home from school, Miranda tried to stand, but she began falling forward. I insisted we take her to the emergency room. Miranda was upset and did not want to go, but we took her anyway. The emergency room doctor was wonderful. We explained to him about the car wreck, original titanium fusion being removed, and a new bone fusion healing. He ordered a scan and admitted Miranda. The next day, the doctors ordered an MRI, which revealed a pocket of fluid at the base of her brain stem and down her neck. The fluid was from the trauma her brain, skull, and neck endured from the car wreck and surgery. After consulting with local neurosurgeons and Dr. Neuro #7, the decision was made to try to let it heal on its own. We were told it may take a year. She was released into our care after three days.

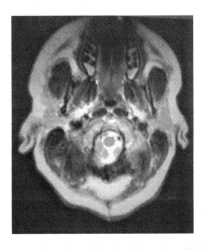
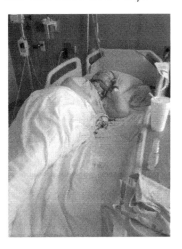

Miranda's MRI brain showing fluid   Miranda in the hospital

During the first six weeks, Miranda needed help twenty-four hours a day. She would wake up screaming, and said it felt like there were holes in her brain. I would comfort her, or Brandon would hold her. I had to help her take showers, but we were blessed to have a handicap shower in our new home. Miranda spent her days sitting upright in a recliner, taking medication, and enduring the pain of the surgery. Miranda rapidly weaned herself off all medication. We both feel strongly about not wanting medication; however, she is even more determined than I am. I watched her daily suffer and fight to gain back some sort of life. My heart ached for her and Brandon. This was Brandon's first experience witnessing this type of surgery at the hospital, and although he had watched me suffer through the rebuild of my fusion, seeing Miranda in uncontrollable pain broke his spirit.

Miranda was in so much excruciating pain, she told me one day while I was caring for her she wished she had just died in the car wreck instead of enduring the surgery and pain. I tried to comfort her with words of encouragement, but all my words were not enough. The pain was too great, and the heartbreak for Miranda was too intense. She had her normal life, even though she was handicap, ripped away from her, because of the car wreck. No one has a guarantee; however, Miranda knew pain from previous surgeries and now had experienced her life being instantly altered, due to a car wreck. Although Miranda was disabled prior to the car wreck, she had built a life within her limitations. The car wreck put her in agonizing pain and suffering.

Diane had given me a book to read about a family who endured a car wreck. I was bothered at first about the book, but read it anyhow. In the book, the mother of a daughter severely injured had to come to a place of surrendering her daughter to Jesus, whether she lived or died. In all the years of fighting for Miranda to live, in the past I had surrender her life to Jesus at the level of letting go completely– even if she died. But, this particular trauma brought me to my knees. I had watched Miranda suffer in hospitals, with illness, through surgeries, and seen her never let go of her own hope in Christ. When the car wreck from July 22, 2016, took away her hope, it was devastating to my heart. I heard my daughter, for the first time in her life, question why God would allow such relentless pain and illness in our family for twenty-three years. I did something I had never done. I went into a quiet place, with a broken heart, and prayed. While I was praying, I gave Miranda to God completely. I even said, "If Miranda is not able to live the life she dreamed of, I am willing to let her go even if it means she dies." I would rather bury my daughter and know she is not in relentless pain, then have her alive with all her dreams crushed. I let go, and trusted God at a new level with my daughter. I surrendered her life and death into His perfect plan for her, and I committed to serve Jesus Christ regardless of the outcome.

We were all in post-traumatic stress. I dealt with the post-traumatic stress by praying, cleaning, and taking care of Miranda. Also, I suffered with night terrors, which I used praise music to combat my fears. Kevin was still battling with Multiple Sclerosis in the form of NMO, Devic's Disease; and, he did not want to deal with the reality of the fact, Miranda had been injured in a life altering way due to the car wreck. So, he stayed in bed most of the time, which was not unusual for Kevin prior to the car wreck. My neck was destroyed by a low impact rear-end car wreck; therefore, we all had too many memories and concerns, because we had walked this path before. Even Brandon knew from experience what damage a car wreck can do to the human body. Brandon and Miranda began counseling with one of Miranda's professors, who was a trained counselor, to work through their post-traumatic stress.

Brandon and Miranda moved back to their home when she was six weeks out of surgery. Prior to them going home, we took Miranda back to see Dr. Neuro #7 in Maryland. He encouraged her, but the report was difficult to hear. He noted multiple disc issues below the new bone fusion; however, she would need to wait to have more surgery. First, Miranda needed to heal from her recent surgery and the pocket of fluid in her head. So, the plan was for Miranda to continue to heal and return in six months. We stayed with another family who has a daughter with Chiari. She is Miranda's age and a loving young lady. It made the trip a blessing.

The easiest part of Miranda's car wreck, should have been the car insurance companies settling. But, it was not. Miranda's medical bills were extremely high, due to the damage to her body from the car wreck. Once again, Miranda tried to simply settle with the car insurance; however, they did not settle – even though her bills justified settlement, and it was well documented she may need more neurosurgery. Brandon and Miranda obtained a lawyer, and put the car wreck settlement on a shelf. They paid all the bills they could, and communicated with all the doctors, hospitals, and places she received treatment to let everyone know they were forced by the car insurance to obtain a lawyer to receive a settlement to pay all the bills and obtain money to reimburse her health insurance. Our family had already been through this ordeal enough to realize, when you are injured in a car wreck most likely you will need a lawyer. Miranda and Brandon did what they had to do, and went on with life.

I had concerns about all Brandon had to do on his own. Taking care of Miranda was a full-time job, and he was in college, working part-time, as well as earning a lot of volunteer hours. But, Brandon did it with excellence. He took care of all the household duties, yard, Miranda, doctor appointments, and his school work. Brandon was truly amazing. At the end of November, I was praying when God moved in my heart concerning Miranda. I just had a sudden knowing she was pregnant.

By the end of December 2016, I dropped off a pregnancy test at her house, and it was positive on December 23, 2016. Miranda was pregnant. Wow! The time frame concerned me greatly. She was only a little over three months since her skull and cervical rebuild surgery, due to the car wreck, and she had the pocket of fluid in her neck. It was also a reality, Miranda may need more surgery, but all treatment for the car wreck had to come to a halt. I was concerned her body could not handle healing from the surgery and being pregnant at the same time. Miranda was immediately put with high risk OB doctors. The OB doctors set her up with a local heart doctor, endocrinologist, and neurosurgeon immediately. They did ultrasounds and genetic testing. Becoming pregnant, gave Miranda a reason to fight for her own life as well as her child. It brought her hope, while she was in a hopeless situation and enduring excruciating physical pain.

The spring of 2017 was difficult for our entire family. I went into the hospital in March with significant chest pain. I was tested for a couple of days and released. I was not able to follow up with my heart specialist until August 2017, because of all the other multiple medical crises in our life. I entered the hospital with chest pain, nausea, dizziness, left arm pain, and it was difficult to breathe. When I met with the heart doctor, he told me I did the right thing by going to the hospital, and he believed my symptoms were from POTS, Postural Orthostatic Tachycardia, which I had dealt with for years. He said the most amazing thing to me – he told me I was a very healthy woman. He said my CTA was great, and I had a very clean heart. What amazed me was that God had spoken those words to me before my car wreck. Over and over He would say, "Donna, you are a very healthy woman." After all my medical treatment, I would have never dreamed those words would come out of a doctor's mouth. But in August 2017, the very words God promised me were spoken by a heart doctor. I left the office so excited in my spirit. Even though I am disabled, due to all the titanium in my neck, I am physically heart healthy!

In April 2017, Kevin lost consciousness at the house, and I was not sure how to handle it. He had told me he did not want any more medical intervention. However, a dear friend of mine who is a missionary in the Dominican Republic private messaged me, and said she could not stop praying for Kevin. I stayed awake all night praying. Finally, I remembered when Kevin first became ill with Multiple Sclerosis, NMO, he sat on the couch in our bedroom and made a list of all things he did not want to miss. He wanted to see our children graduate from college, fall in love, walk Miranda down the aisle at her wedding, and become a grandfather. Because of the list he made verbally to me seven years prior, I made the decision to take him to a local hospital. Brandon came over and helped me get Kevin in the car. I had no idea what was wrong with him, but I knew without help, he may not live. The emergency room doctor rapidly listened to me give a medical history of Kevin, and she proceeded to order a lot of tests. Oddly enough, his blood sugar had dropped extremely low and had caused him to be unresponsive. If I had not taken him to the hospital, he may have never woken back up. Kevin had never had sugar issues in the past. Eventually, the doctors figured out his thyroid was not in the appropriate range. So, they changed his thyroid medication. Kevin, listing the desires of his heart to me, gave me the courage to continue to fight for his life. I knew he wanted to hold his grandchild.

Miranda was seeing specialist and the high-risk doctors on a regular basis. All the medical stuff was exhausting. Every time we went to the high-risk OB, we had to go over her past medical history. Each visit took hours. We never left a visit with peace. Each visit would upset Miranda, and she was tired of the process they had her endure. However, she endured. Miranda did everything in her power to ensure her pregnancy could be as healthy for the baby as possible. Even though she suffered in neck pain and constant right arm pain because of the cervical damage from the car wreck, she refused medication. Also, she watched every bite of food she consumed. Miranda researched constantly to make sure the baby would receive all she needed. Around twenty-four weeks into the pregnancy, Miranda began having pain in her hips. She said it felt like the bones were grinding when she walked. She told the doctors, but they did nothing to help her except offer medication. Miranda was not willing to take medication because of the side effects it could have on the baby.

Matthew 6:9-13 (NIV)
"This, then, is how you should pray:

"'Our Father in heaven,
hallowed be your name,
[10] your kingdom come,
your will be done,
on earth as it is in heaven.
[11] Give us today our daily bread.
[12] And forgive us our debts,
as we also have forgiven our debtors.
[13] And lead us not into temptation,
but deliver us from the evil one."

CHAPTER 32

NOT MY WILL

God is so very faithful to not let us know everything before it happens. On May 26, 2017, I was tired. Life had been throwing a lot of curve balls, and my body was worn out. However, as always, I woke up and kept on going. A dear friend of mine who is a missionary came over during the morning to spend some time with me. She and I have grown so very close. When Kevin was in the hospital in April, she was messaging me because she knew in her heart something was wrong with him. She is a powerful prayer warrior. When she arrived at my house, she could see I was exhausted at a deep level. We were talking and laughing when my phone rang. Now, you need to understand I am not the type of person who keeps their phone beside them at all times. However, my phone was sitting on the end table of my couch, and I looked down and saw it was Miranda calling. First, I asked my friend if it would bother her if I answered the phone. She encouraged me to answer it.

Miranda was extremely upset. Brandon awakened during the night and was vomiting. Instantly, I knew it was his appendix. I told Miranda I was on my way over. Just minutes prior, I was almost in tears, because I was so very tired. But, suddenly I had the endurance from God to do whatever was necessary. My friend prayed for me and asked me to keep her posted. I immediately drove to Miranda's house and picked them both up to head to the hospital. As soon as the nurse practitioner walked into the room, she ordered blood work, fluids, and a scan of his abdomen. I knew it would come back and reveal his appendix as the issue; however, Miranda as well as Brandon thought he had food poisoning. His stats were clearly showing he was in pain, and his oxygen was at 100 percent. Around the time we arrived in the room, two precious people in our life, Glen and Diane, texted looking for Miranda and Brandon. I let them know we were in the emergency room. They arrived with food for Miranda about the time Brandon returned from his scan. Life was already rapidly moving, I had not even had the time to let any family or friends know we were at the hospital. The nurse practitioner walked in and told Brandon he had an issue with his appendix. Within minutes, the surgeon appeared and asked Brandon a lot of questions about his pain. He let us know Brandon would be having surgery to remove his appendix, but it may be a while. However, a wheelchair was sent for Brandon within minutes of the surgeon leaving the room. So, we all followed Brandon to the surgical preparation area and waiting room. Miranda went back with Brandon and texted me to come back once they had him prepared. I was only in the room for about two or three minutes when Miranda looked up at me and said, "Mom, I think I am going to pass out."

I panicked, because I knew the bones in the back of her head were not healed. I was not able to physically catch Miranda, due to my own physical limitations. Brandon was in a hospital bed hooked up to multiple items and had just received the medication to help relax his body prior to surgery. I remember looking up at his monitor, and Brandon's heart rate jumped to 149. I yelled, "Help!"

Four nurses were in the doorway immediately and helped Miranda. They caught her and placed her on a gurney. I went down the hallway, opened the door, and yelled for Glen and Diane. I needed help. At this point, I am the only family member available for Brandon and Miranda. Miranda was taken to the emergency room, and Diane went with her. Glen stayed with Brandon and me, while we waited for Brandon to be taken back for surgery. Then, I received a phone call the emergency room needed me to come and sign papers on behalf of Miranda. So, I had to rapidly tell Brandon bye and go help Miranda. I had already prepared Brandon for all he would experience going into his first surgery. He was safe with Glen, and I knew it.

I called Miranda's brother Micah. I let him know what was occurring, and Miranda had asked for him. He immediately came to the hospital and brought Sierra with him to help us. There was a minor glitch. I did not tell him which hospital; so, he went to the wrong one first. But, they found us quickly and sat with Miranda. I signed all the paper work for her and gave specific instructions concerning her special needs. Then, Glen, Diane, and I returned to the waiting room where Brandon was receiving his operation. All three of us were waiting on Brandon, when a gentleman I did not recognize approached me. He asked me if my name was Donna Renfro, and I said, "Yes." He explained he was a pastor and had listened to me on the radio. When he heard me yell for help to my friends, he had a group of people stand in a circle, hold hands, and prayed for our family. A few of the other people came over to tell me they had prayed too. I was stunned, but very thankful.

Miranda was in the emergency room. Brandon was in surgery. I was with Glen and Diane, and all I could feel was shock. I did text my missionary friend. However, my brain was in overload. I had not even processed what I had just witnessed in about an hour. Once again, our life was rapidly turned upside down. Then, my phone rang and it was Brandon's family. I had not even thought to contact them or anyone else yet. So, I answered to let them know.

Then, I called Kevin. He let his parents know. I texted out to my prayer team and contacted my family. The surgeon came out and asked for me. Glen, Diane, and I went into the family room to meet with the surgeon, because no one else had arrived yet. The surgeon was wonderful. He told us everything went great and Brandon would probably be able to go home later in the day. We thanked him and went back to sit down. Then, I received a phone call. The lady on the other end identified herself and proceeded to tell me I would not be able to see Brandon. When I began to question her, she would only tell me there was a complication, and he was in critical condition. Instantly, I knew it was his oxygen; so, I asked the nurse what his oxygen level was, and once again she stated she was not allowed to disclose any information at that time. Shock went through my body like a lightning bolt. Within no time, there was a team of people at the waiting room with us. I did not reveal all the information given to me by the nurse who called me.

Miranda arrived upstairs with Micah and Sierra. The nurse came out and I asked if Brandon could see just Miranda. I explained to her I thought it would help Brandon to know Miranda was okay. She was pregnant with his child, and he knew going into surgery she had nearly passed out. He was extremely stressed by the incident just prior to him being rolled into the operating room. The nurse agreed to take Miranda back to Brandon. Brandon was on fifty percent oxygen and not doing well. Miranda left his cell phone on his chest and came back to sit with me. I reached over and hugged her tightly. I told her he would be just fine. God had not brought them this far to let go today.

Some of the people who came to visit had left when we received the report Brandon's surgery went well; however, some people stayed. We waited for about another hour, and Brandon was moved to ICU. Brandon had aspirated into his right lung and was diagnosed with aspiration pneumonia. He was extremely ill. Seeing him in the hospital with the mask on his face broke my heart; however, I did not have the luxury of allowing anyone to know how my heart ached. I knew his situation was precarious and extremely dangerous. Miranda needed me to be the voice of reassurance and confidence. We had a lot of people praying.

2 Corinthians 12:9

*"But he said to me, "My grace is sufficient for you, for my power **is** made perfect in weakness." Therefore I will boast all the more gladly about my weaknesses, so that Christ's power may rest on me."*

Brandon was admitted into the hospital on May 26, 2017, and he remained in ICU until May 30, 2017. Brandon and Miranda came home to our house, which had been built to take care of any handicap or recovery from surgery. Brandon did not improve rapidly at all. The doctors had warned us it would take three to six months for him to heal. We had never dealt with aspiration pneumonia before; however, our home was equipped with all the medical items we needed to keep a close eye on him. During the first week, his oxygen did drop into the eighties several times, and he kept a fever every night for the first three weeks. It became evident, he was not going to bounce back rapidly. Meanwhile, Miranda was continuing to grow in her pregnancy daily.

Brandon went back to see his internist and surgeon around two weeks out from surgery. Neither of them wanted him back on more antibiotics. Brandon had left the hospital with antibiotics; however, while he was in ICU they continually ran two different types of antibiotics through his veins. He had a lot of medication. Both doctors did not want him to have more antibiotics if he could heal without them. Brandon worked diligently with the incentive spirometer and oximeter to expand his lungs, cough up the stuff from the right side of his lungs, and monitor his heart rate as well as his oxygen. Brandon would have to hold a pillow over his abdomen to cough, because of the pain from the incisions from the appendix surgery, and many times he coughed up blood. He was tough and refused to quit. He fought through the pain, so he could be the husband Miranda needed. He was a shining example of a Godly husband even in the middle of his own trauma. I was impressed.

Although Brandon graduated with his bachelor's degree in May of 2017, he had to reapply to a Doctor of Physical Therapy program. He would not be healthy enough to begin as he originally planned. Although this was disappointing, Brandon had a deep confidence that God was ordering his steps. Miranda was still physically healing from the car wreck and needed him at home with her. Also, since a baby was on the way – he would be able to help Miranda physically do the things she was unable to do alone. Brandon's dream of becoming a Doctor of Physical Therapy would have to be shelved for now.

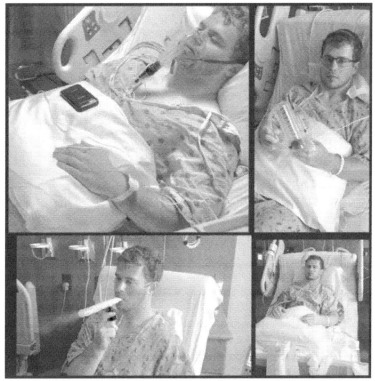

Brandon after his appendix surgery

While Brandon was healing, Miranda began a downward spiral. The first week of June her tummy dropped, and she began having contractions. As mentioned previously, Miranda was with local high risk doctors. She was immediately placed with them as soon as her primary doctor realized she was pregnant. Brandon, Miranda, and I met with these doctors for hours during the first few weeks at each visit. They set her up with three local specialists: an endocrinologist, a neurosurgeon, and an adult heart doctor. Miranda's neurosurgeon was out-of-state and would not be here when she delivered the baby. So, they wanted to make sure she had a local neurosurgeon. We were constantly going to the doctors throughout the first seven months of her pregnancy. Each time we went, we had to relive our entire medical life with each student, resident, and doctor. It was exhausting. They were the team who we thought were obtaining information to help Miranda when she went into the C-section to deliver the baby, so we endured all the questions. By twenty weeks of pregnancy, it was confirmed Miranda would be having a baby girl. Brandon and Miranda chose the name Raelynn, which means "peacemaker."

In June, we met with a surgeon for the first time, and she literally yelled at Brandon and me. She was telling us there were no notes about Miranda in the computer. We were all shocked. Then, she went on to say I needed to be in the operating room with the surgeon when the baby was delivered, because I was the only one who could save her if there was a problem. I began to stutter. I have fought hard to save Miranda's life. I have sacrificed all I have to make sure my family had the care they needed. However, I had endured an arm surgery while I was awake and the burning of my own human flesh when they cauterized me was more than I could handle. I knew I could not physically handle being in the operating room with Miranda, so I quickly pointed out Brandon was her husband. This particular surgeon continued to state Brandon could be in the C-section, but I had to be there to save Miranda. I was in shock.

We left the appointment. Brandon, Miranda and I wrote the birthing plan for Miranda, because the doctors had not created one. We had spent seven months going to these high-risk OB doctors to make a plan to save Miranda's life and her baby. We took them every medical report and gave them access to all her medical records. They did not prepare in any way for the birth or for Miranda's body to deteriorate. I was knowledgeable of all her diagnoses, surgeries, previous medications, and how she reacts to surgery. So, we wrote the birthing plan and gave it to the doctors. We went in June to do all the preadmission paper work, so the hospital would be prepared. Although, Miranda was not due until August every part of me knew she would have the baby in July. I knew her body would not be able to physically endure a full-term pregnancy.

Miranda and Brandon June 2017 – Miranda was 30 weeks pregnant

Above the door, "Grow old with me, the best is yet to be."

In July, Miranda's body began to show serious signs of decline. On July, 4, 2017, we took her to the hospital labor and delivery area, because her heart rate was over 150 beats at our house. When we arrived, the nurses were too busy having a Fourth of July party to give Miranda attention. Because we had waited so long, Brandon went out into the hallway to find a nurse to help Miranda. A nurse finally entered the room and was not very compassionate. First, she checked Miranda's blood pressure and said it was fine. I told her we were there because her heart rate was too high. Then, she checked the heart rate and realized Miranda's heart rate lying down was in the 140s, which is too high. They monitored her for several hours. While we were in the room, another nurse opened the door to ask where the cheese ball for the party was located. Miranda's nurse told her it was in the refrigerator. All the nurses were extremely unprofessional. A resident, who was training with the high-risk OB doctors, came into the triage room and was wonderful to Miranda. He felt the best plan was for Miranda to see her heart doctor. So, they discharged Miranda with a plan to go see her heart doctor. Miranda's heart doctor diagnosed her with gestational hypertension.

Daily, Miranda was losing physical ground. On July 15, 2017, we had her baby shower at the church. Brandon and Miranda were so very blessed. They had a couple of small family baby showers; however, the church shower was the last one, and it was amazing. Around twenty-five people helped throw the shower, and they received everything they could possibly need for their precious baby. It reminded me of how God talks about having so much there is not enough room to hold it. Even though the day was blessed beyond measure, Miranda was not well. Her blood pressure was extremely high, and her heart rate was running in the 150s. Miranda had been at our home resting ninety percent of the time to keep her baby safe, while her body was declining. Miranda was so careful during her pregnancy. Even though she was only three months out of her skull and neck fusion rebuild from the car wreck when she became pregnant, she refused any medication. She would only eat whole foods and drank water constantly. She endured endless nerve pain running down her neck to her right hand because of the car wreck, but refused any medication for the pain – no matter how mild the medication. She did everything humanly possible to keep Raelynn safe regardless of the physical pain she endured. Miranda wanted a healthy baby and was determined to carry her to term if her body would cooperate. During the third trimester, Miranda's body was in terrible pain from the weight of the baby pulling on her. Also, she daily would tell us about her hips feeling like they were grinding when she walked. You could see the pain in her face when she walked.

By Tuesday, July 18, Miranda was in horrible pain in her right side. She said it felt as if her tummy was being pulled away from her body. When she stood up, it was apparent her tummy had dropped further down. Also, her vision was blurry in her right eye. Her blood pressure and heart rate was high, so we called the doctors, and they sent us back to the labor and delivery side of the hospital. They monitored Miranda for several hours, and sent her home with us again. She was ordered to take a 24-hour urine. During the night, her legs went numb and walking became a problem. We called the doctor's office back, and on Wednesday, July 19, they said to return to the hospital immediately. When we returned, I had called a couple of friends to see if we could get people to listen to us, because Miranda was so sick. The doctor asked for a neurologist who knew nothing about Miranda to evaluate her. He said due to her EDS, Ehlers-Danlos Syndrome, her tummy was pressing on her nerves in both legs causing the numbness. He went on to say it would not get better, and would get worse until the baby was removed. He said she might receive the feeling in her nerves again only time would tell. I questioned him greatly, because I have experienced loss of bodily function as well as watched my husband lose his nerve function. I knew it was not easy to gain back function when nerves were involved. He was not compassionate, instead of caring about Miranda's leg numbness he was arrogant. He even said she may never walk again, but it was not life threatening. The same high-risk OB surgeon who had yelled at me and Brandon that we were the only ones who could save her life in the operating room was on call, and she discharged Miranda with the knowledge she could not walk with the numb legs. She was clear they would do nothing, but offer Physical Therapy until Miranda reached 39 weeks. Seemingly, it was irrelevant to this doctor or the neurologist if Miranda ended up permanently damaged and unable to walk.

When we left, Miranda was emotionally devastated. And, it was clear to me these were not the doctors to deliver the baby. I had already started calling every high-risk labor and delivery doctor group within a reasonable drive from our home. Also, I consulted with other medical personnel concerning our situation. We arrived home late in the afternoon. By 7:00 p.m., every person we spoke to confirmed Miranda needed immediate medical attention, and for us to take her to a hospital about thirty minutes from our house. Miranda was already 35 weeks pregnant, and the thought of changing doctors with all her complications greatly concerned me. However, it was apparent the OB high-risk group she was currently with was not going to help her. I was awake all night praying. The next morning at 6:45 a.m., Brandon, Miranda, and I arrived at the Emergency Room of the hospital every medical professional recommended. Miranda was riding in a wheelchair.

This hospital reacted with concern for Miranda, which was different from the doctors we had spent seven months trying to prepare. They took her straight to the labor and delivery floor. A dear friend of our family, who is a nurse, came to the hospital to be with us while we were meeting with all the doctors. Within two hours, Miranda was evaluated by the regular OB doctor and the high-risk OB doctor. The decision was made to admit her until delivery to keep her safe. They began pulling all her medical records from her childhood and having conferences to create a plan to save Miranda's legs, keep the baby safe, and make a plan on how to deliver via C-section without harming Miranda's skull or neck. She was not even one year out of her skull rebuild from the car wreck. Her bones were not fused, and she had several herniated discs in her neck. They could not use her back during the surgery for anesthesia, because she had previously had the de-tethering of her spinal cord. So, Miranda would have to be intubated. They quickly became knowledgeable about all her disorders including, Chiari Brain Malformation, the tethered spinal cord, Intermittent Cushing, Ehlers-Danlos Syndrome, and everything else. They planned to deliver the baby on July 31, 2017, if Miranda could physically make it to that date. They put Miranda's legs in compression hose and wrapped her legs with air compression cuffs to keep blood flow as well as prevent blood clots. Miranda was to be in the bed at all times; unless, she had to use the bathroom. If she was out of bed, she had to call a nurse. Brandon stayed with her twenty-four hours a day. I drove back and forth to take clothes, paperwork, food, or whatever they needed.

I began feeling extremely sick by Friday, July 21, and went to the doctor. They diagnosed me with a sinus infection and placed me on antibiotics. My car died while I was driving it down the interstate. I was able to get it started again and took it to a transmission shop. A dear friend of Kevin's met me there and loaned me a car to use. I was so sick on Saturday and Sunday, I could not even go see Miranda. I became sicker and by the fifth day on the medication I called my doctor, but he instructed me to stay the course. I began using essential oils to help my body, but kept going. Miranda needed me; I did not have time to stop. Kevin's family helped me with food and taking care of him. As soon as I was on the antibiotic for over twenty-four hours, I resumed driving back and forth taking Brandon and Miranda whatever they needed. Within a week, I had my car back. When we had our last oil change, the person who did it had not put oil back into the car. I was so thankful the car died causing me to rapidly get professionals to examine it. The lack of oil could have destroyed our engine. Even though it felt like life was falling apart, God still continually moved to help us.

Miranda declined daily and by Friday, July 28, she could not see out of her right eye, both legs were still numb, nerve pain was shooting down her right side, her rib cage was in tremendous pain, she had a horrible headache, neck pain, and her face was splotchy with red spots. They had given Miranda a special type of steroids the weekend before to help with the development of the baby's lungs. The high-risk OB doctor was very wise. He used a form of steroids which would suppress her cortisol instead of the type they typically give women who give birth pre-term. They planned to take Miranda to the regular operating room instead of the labor and delivery room typically used for C-sections. This upset Miranda greatly. They informed her she would have to go to PACU, and I could not be with her. Brandon would be with Raelynn. Miranda was going to be awake while they intubated her to make sure they did not harm her head or neck. Her throat was going to be numb; however, Miranda had never been awake during intubation and this information was extremely upsetting for her. I tried to remain calm and keep her focused on the bigger picture. These doctors were trying to keep Miranda safe and doing the very best by her body. However, nothing I said calmed her down.

Brandon and Miranda were also informed by the neonatal doctor, they wanted to do MRI's on the baby as soon as possible to rule out Chiari and a tethered spinal cord. Every day there was more medical information, which was extremely upsetting. Every possible scenario was discussed, even life flights if necessary. The unknown loomed over all our heads. However, I constantly reminded Miranda how God had prophesied this child for three years. He had promised her she would carry one child, it would be a girl, and she would not have Chiari Brain Malformation. I stood on the promise of God while I watched my daughter deteriorate and be emotionally stunned daily. My heart was in the hands of God.

CHAPTER 33

THE PEACEMAKER

Psalm 34:18

"The Lord is close to the brokenhearted and saves those who are crushed in spirit." (NIV)

Our pastor was continually preaching about how God uses broken vessels during the last few messages prior to Miranda being hospitalized for the birth of Raelynn. The last Sunday we were at church was the day after her baby shower and four days before she was hospitalized. Our pastor spoke about men and women of God who faced isolation, pain, and rejection. All of the great leaders were pots of clay, who needed cracks in them for the glory of God to be revealed. He even used a pregnant woman for his analogy. He talked about when a woman is about to give birth, the most painful point is transition. He strongly encouraged the entire congregation to refuse to quit when the struggles of life seem impossible.

2 Corinthians 4:6-10

"For God, who said, "Let light shine out of darkness," made his light shine in our hearts to give us the light of the knowledge of God's glory displayed in the face of Christ. But we have this treasure in jars of clay to show that this all-surpassing power is from God and not from us. We are hard pressed on every side, but not crushed; perplexed, but not in despair; persecuted, but not abandoned; struck down, but not destroyed. We always carry around in our body the death of Jesus, so that the life of Jesus may also be revealed in our body." (NIV)

Just take a few minutes and think about the reality of the men we admire in the Bible who did great things for God. Each one of them suffered to the point of becoming a broken vessel prior to their destiny. Joseph had a dream he shared with his brothers about becoming a leader over them. His brothers threw him in a pit, sold him into slavery, and he was even placed in prison unjustly. But, Joseph kept his heart right before God and eventually, he fulfilled his destiny as preordained by God (Genesis 37-42). Daniel was thrown in a pit with a lion for obeying God versus men (Daniel 6). Moses spent forty years in a desert (Acts 7: 30). David had to hide from King Saul to stay alive (I Samuel 19). Jesus remained silent when he was accused (Mark 14: 61). Each man knew pain, suffering, and humility before fulfilling their personal destiny as designed by God. The lessons we can learn from each man is: stay sweet, Joseph, keep your faith, Daniel, obedience to God is your best defense, Moses, patiently trust God when your enemy tries to kill you either with words or swords, David, and just be silent when you are falsely accused like Jesus did. As Christians, we will all face attack, but our battle is never against people.

Ephesians 6:12

"For our struggle is not against flesh and blood, but against the rulers, against the authorities, against the powers of this dark world and against the spiritual forces of evil in the heavenly realms."

My entire family was tired and hanging on by a thread. Over the past seventeen years we had faced heartache, medical diagnoses, and excruciating pain. We saw each other suffer, and endure through tragedy. Micah came to me once and was extremely upset. When I questioned him, Micah told me he felt guilty because he never had to suffer the surgeries Miranda and I endured. I was in tears. I explained to Micah how the promise God gave me over his life was the only hope I had at times of sheer desperation that God was indeed faithful to His Word and promises. Because Micah did grow up without going through the surgeries or growing tumors, I had the opportunity to see the goodness of God in our difficult journey daily. Micah was a light in the darkness and a living example of the fact God is faithful to His promises.

Now, our entire family had just been through another unbelievable year of pain and suffering. On July 22, 2016, Miranda and Brandon were in a car wreck which caused Miranda to endure the rebuild of her head and neck with cadaver bones, and she was still suffering with chronic pain in her neck as well as her right arm. I was hospitalized three times during the past twelve months, twice for complex migraines and the other time for chest pain. In April 2017, Kevin was hospitalized, because his sugar level dropped so low he lost consciousness. In May 2017, Brandon had an appendicitis attack, which led to the surgical removal of his appendix with the complication of aspiration pneumonia. In June and July, Miranda became worse physically with her car wreck complications and pregnancy. God had promised Brandon and Miranda a baby girl without Chiari Brain Malformation; however, the closer it came time for the birth of this promised child, the more difficult all our lives became. The physical toll on our bodies was almost unbearable; and, the emotional toll had caught us all as well. All of us: Kevin, Micah, Sierra, Brandon, Miranda, and I had to choose to love each other through the pain, disappointment, exhaustion of the constant bombardment of illnesses, crises, financial oppression, emotional hurts, and waves of fear. We had to trust God in the middle of circumstances, which appeared impossible. Miranda had declined to a point where I personally was not sure her physical body would be able to endure the delivery of a baby via C-section; however, she maintained a resolve in her spirit, soul, and mind to do whatever it took to keep Raelynn safe and deliver her, despite her own pain.

Miranda had been in the hospital for eleven days, and I packed my clothes to go stay with them on July 30, 2017 until the baby was born and could come home from the hospital. Kevin's family was incredible and taking great care of him. We had no idea what we may be facing during the delivery of the baby, but we all knew it would not be easy. Miranda's body began having constant contractions Sunday night on July 30, 2017. The nurse taking care of her called the doctor; however, they were not about to change the plan by taking Miranda to surgery early. The doctors were using wisdom and had an excellent plan in place to keep both Miranda and Raelynn safe. I stayed awake all night long walking the hallway, while I was praying. By 7:00 a.m. on July 31, 2017, I went to pick up Sierra so she could be with us during the delivery. Brandon contacted his family. Everything was moving at lightning speed. The nurses began prepping Miranda to go to the main OR early in the morning instead of the normal C-section operating room. There were too many physical complications in Miranda's body for her to deliver a baby unless it was in a main OR room. Brandon and Miranda were answering questions, filling out forms, and Miranda's body was in constant pain. We all knew there were no guarantees when we kissed Miranda good-bye at 11:15 a.m., and she was rolled into the pre-op area without us. In these moments, the moments when you do not know whether the people you love will live or die – you better know God.

"Be still and know that I am God." Psalm 46:10 (NIV)

The plan for Miranda's C-section was not your normal C-section. Miranda was going to a regular OR, and no one was allowed with her. The original plan was Miranda would be intubated while she was awake, but Miranda was not at peace with this decision. So, she told us as soon as she met with the anesthesiologists she was going to talk about other options. After Miranda was taken away from us, she met with the anesthesiologists to discuss the intubation.

The final plan was to put her to sleep first and then intubated her. One anesthesiologist held Miranda's neck, which was in her neck brace to keep her bone fusion safe during the intubation, while another anesthesiologist began intubation. One of the nurses who had taken excellent care of Miranda during her stay in the hospital chose to work the day of the birth just to take care of Miranda during the C-section. She even took Miranda's cell phone into the OR to take video of Raelynn when she was born. It is priceless video because no one in the family was in the OR – not even Miranda was awake for the birth of Raelynn.

Brandon, Sierra, and I waited in the OR waiting room in silence. They kept Miranda's number on the pre-op board for a long time. I could feel fear trying to rise in my heart. Brandon appeared to be solid, but we were both extremely concerned. On August 9, 2016, Brandon and I were sitting in an OR waiting room while Miranda was having her head and neck rebuilt due to a car wreck, and now – not even a year later, we were waiting in another OR waiting room for the birth of their baby girl via C-section. The risks were high and we both knew it. Sierra was a peaceful voice of encouragement, and she kept Micah informed. He had to go to work. Honestly, I was too focused in the moment to communicate with anyone. I just sat there in silence – hoping beyond all hope – God was going to do what He promised. I had arrived at the place my pastor was preaching about – I was broken. I was physically, emotionally, financially, mentally, and spiritually exhausted from years of traumas. I was completely and utterly broken, but my faith in God's ability was the highest I had ever experienced. Complete surrender to His plan, and hope in His word, scripture, was my life-line.

Suddenly, the name Taylor was called. Sierra, Brandon, and I all jumped up. Miranda's number on the surgical board had not been moved from pre-op to operation, even though it was almost 12:30 p.m. When we jumped up, I spilled my coffee on my hand. But, I quickly shook it off and followed the nurse into the hallway. Rapidly doors flung open, and a precious 37 week old baby girl was rolled from the OR room into the hallway. She was in an incubator.

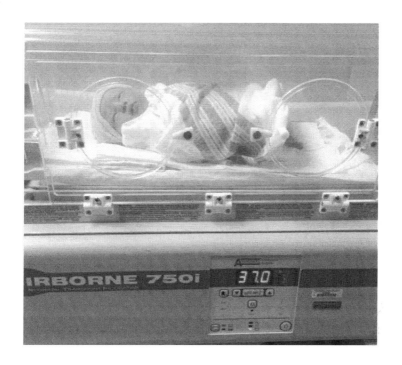

Raelynn Elizabeth Taylor was born on July 31, 2017, at 12:23 p.m.

Significance:

Name Meanings:

Raelynn (Hebrew) – Peacemaker, Defender, Informed, Divine Lamb, Beautiful Lamb, Sunshine.

Elizabeth (Hebrew) – God is my Oath, the Fullness of God, my God is abundance, God is my satisfaction.

Birthdate:

July is the seventh month. The Biblical number seven means, "perfection" or "completeness."

The Biblical number thirty-one means, "El," which is the Hebrew name of God and literally means "the strong (or primary authority)." Thirty-one is a number associated with offspring in the Bible as well.

The Biblical number 17 for 2017 means "overcoming the enemy" and "complete victory."

(www.biblestudy.org)

Therefore, God chose to bring His promise to pass on a date which literally means you are finished with complete victory, and have delivered my offspring. July 31, 2017, was a very specific date, and without doubt, God wanted Raelynn Elizabeth Taylor to enter the world. Also, Raelynn was born at exactly 12:23 p.m. My car wreck, which revealed the hidden conditions in my body, happened on 12/23/2004 – the number four means "appointed time." Raelynn being born at the exact time as the date of my car wreck was no accident. Obviously, the steps of the righteous are ordered of God – Psalm 37:23. (www.biblestudy.org)

The plan was for Brandon to go with Raelynn, and for me to wait for Miranda. Miranda was having her tubes removed, because pregnancy was too difficult on her body. One baby was all she could carry. So, I was going to wait for Miranda to come out of surgery, while Brandon went with Raelynn. Prior to Raelynn's birth, there was a lot of concern about whether her lungs would be developed or if her sugar levels would be okay. Sierra went with Brandon. She captured all the special moments with Raelynn and Brandon in pictures while Miranda was still in surgery. I paced in the hallway outside of the doors of the OR. Sierra texted me constantly, while they were checking out Raelynn. She let me know Raelynn was 20 inches long and weighed six pounds. Sierra sent me pictures of Brandon with Raelynn, and let me know her oxygen was normal. She did a wonderful job of keeping me informed, while I waited for Miranda.

After waiting another two hours, I received a phone call from the surgeon. She told me Miranda was in PACU, and I should just go to Miranda's room where Raelynn was with Brandon. It was going to be awhile before Miranda was stable. I struggled, because I promised Miranda I would be waiting on her when she came out. I always kept my promises to my children. But, the staff told me to leave and go be with Brandon. My heart was heavy for Miranda, but I headed back to the labor and delivery section of the hospital to Miranda's room. When I walked into the room, Raelynn was lying under a heat lamp and seemed perfectly content. Brandon was beaming with joy. It was obvious he was already in love with his daughter. Brandon did skin-to-skin contact with Raelynn for hours to bond to her, which was a part of their birthing plan. Typically, the mother does skin-to-skin contact; but, Miranda was in PACU. Sierra and I were both offered the opportunity to hold Raelynn; however, we both said no. We were not willing to hold Raelynn until her mother, Miranda, could have her special moments.

Miranda finally returned to the room about three hours after the birth of Raelynn. It was shocking how much physical pain Miranda was enduring. Her blood pressure and heartrate were high. As soon as Miranda entered the room, Brandon offered for her to hold Raelynn. However, Miranda was in excruciating pain and was not able to hold her daughter. It was heart-breaking. Miranda had suffered so much to bring precious Raelynn into the world, yet she could not even enjoy the first several hours of her life. Brandon continued caring for Raelynn. I went to Miranda and talked with the nurse. They had to increase her pain medication. It had not yet been a year since her skull and neck rebuild, so Miranda's body had a tolerance to the pain medications. It took time to get her pain under control. Around 6:00 p.m., Miranda was able to hold Raelynn for the first time.

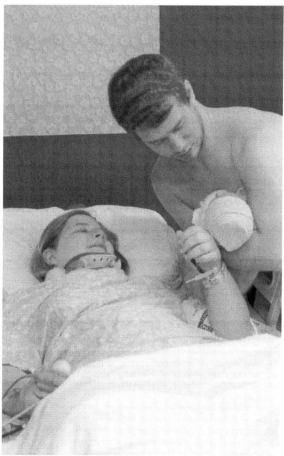

Miranda saw Raelynn for the first time

The hospital did not want visitor's due to the difficulty of the delivery. So, just immediate family were allowed to come, and they were limited on the time they could spend in Miranda's room. After Miranda held Raelynn, I held my precious granddaughter. After work, Micah came and he held Raelynn for the first time. Sierra snuggled with Raelynn, too. Kevin's mother brought him to the hospital, and they both spent time holding Raelynn. Everyone abided by the rules of the hospital to help Miranda heal. Brandon and I stayed with Miranda as well as Raelynn without leaving them. We took turns caring for whoever needed us the most.

Lots of specialists and doctors came by to see either Miranda or Raelynn. Miranda's high- risk OB was thrilled when he walked into the room and boldly said, "Well, we were successful. You are both alive!"

Then, Miranda's OB doctor who performed the actual surgery walked into the room. She asked to hold precious Raelynn. While she was standing and rocking Raelynn back and forth, she very calmly stated Raelynn had her nuchal cord wrapped around her neck three times. Kevin, his mother, his sister, Brandon, Miranda, and I were all shocked to find out about the nuchal cord. We had no idea Raelynn's life was in peril during the surgery, and we were thankful to not find out until after she was safe. Apparently, the doctors knew the entire time; however, they chose to not tell Miranda, because she was already physically struggling. They did not want to add more stress to her mind and body; but, they were monitoring Raelynn daily while Miranda was in the hospital.

Later, after we pulled the medical records from the other office and looked at the last ultrasound pictures with her original high-risk OB doctors, it was apparent on one image in the last ultrasound Miranda had with that group of doctors, Raelynn had her nuchal cord wrapped three times around her neck. The technician had printed the picture and gave it to Miranda, but we did not know how to read it. So, each time they discharged Miranda at the other hospital when she was dealing with high blood pressure, high heart rate, and numb legs – they knew about Raelynn's cord. Obviously, God ordered Miranda's and Raelynn's steps to keep them both safe.

When Raelynn was one day old, she had an MRI of her head and entire spine without any anesthesia. The doctors were checking to make sure Raelynn did not have Chiari Brain Malformation or a tethered spinal cord. Miranda and Brandon had been told they would be able to go with Raelynn to the radiology department while she was in the MRI machine; however, when the neonatal nurse came to get Raelynn, the doctors would not allow Miranda to leave the labor and delivery floor. Miranda's delivery had been so traumatic they were still concerned about her health. Miranda was emotionally devastated about being separated from Raelynn for the MRI's. Brandon immediately stepped up to the plate and comforted Miranda. With extreme compassion, he lovingly let Miranda know he would protect Raelynn. I stayed with Miranda in her room. She sat on the bed and cried. It was extremely emotional for both of us. Not only was Miranda separated from Raelynn, we both knew what these MRI's may reveal. Although, we had God's promise and clung by faith that Raelynn would not suffer from Chiari Brain Malformation or a tethered spinal cord – we were at the point where the rubber meets the road. We were in the middle of finding out if God had kept His promises. I hugged Miranda while she cried, and I prayed for her. Several nurses, as well as her OB doctor who delivered Raelynn, came in to see Miranda while Raelynn was being tested. Each one of them encouraged Miranda, and went out of their way to bring peace to Miranda's heart.

Raelynn was evaluated by the neonatal specialist as well as regular pediatricians. Her sugar levels were normal. She was able to regulate her body temperature. All physical evaluations were excellent. She did great with her Apgar scores. Each doctor who examined her gave a wonderful report. Raelynn's MRI's were read by a neuro-radiologist, and stated it appeared she did not have Chiari Brain Malformation or a tethered spinal cord. Brandon and Miranda chose to mail Raelynn's MRI's to Dr. Neuro #3 to obtain a final reading of the images by one of the world's best neurosurgeons who dealt daily with Chiari and its related disorders. The original medical video conference appointment was set up for October 2, 2017. But, it had to be moved to Friday, October 13, 2017, due to a death in Dr. Neuro #3's family.

We were extremely compassionate about his loss, but waiting was difficult. We wanted medical confirmation that Raelynn did not have Chiari or a tethered spinal cord. Waiting gave us the opportunity to continue trusting, by faith, that God had kept His promises without absolute confirmation from a medical specialist in the field of Chiari Brain Malformation. Raelynn was already two months old and appeared to be doing fantastic. She slept well at night. She loved to ride in a car seat, which was the opposite of Miranda as a baby. Miranda cried and vomited whenever she rode in a car. Raelynn was meeting all her growth milestones perfectly. However, we still wanted to hear Dr. Neuro #3 confirm Raelynn did not have Chiari or a tethered cord. We trusted his ability to accurately read the MRI's with absolute medical certainty.

Raelynn Elizabeth Taylor

Raelynn was dedicated to God by Brandon and Miranda on October 9, 2017. Miranda was dedicated to God on the exact date twenty-three years prior. Brandon and Miranda asked their pastor to dedicate Raelynn on that date, because it had special significance to them and the covenant they had with God. The dedication was a beautiful ceremony with powerful spiritual meaning. Brandon and Miranda committed to surrender Raelynn to God's will according to Matthew 6:9-13. They made a parental commitment to love God with their entire hearts as well as teach Raelynn scriptures according to Deuteronomy 6:4-7, and they entrusted Raelynn's protection to God according to Psalm 91. The pastor prayed the prayer of dedication for Raelynn. Prior to the dedication, some leadership from the church, who had been significant during the past couple of years, were asked to pray for Raelynn; and, they were each led by the Holy Spirit. Pastor Dave Christian and Dr. Ginger Christian, Raelynn's great uncle and aunt, had walked the entire journey with our family; so, they were asked to pray. Also, Dr. Karen Randolph was the first person to prophesy to Miranda she would carry a baby girl without Chiari. Although, many people had prayed and prophesied Raelynn, she was the one who knew the baby would be a girl. She was the last person to pray for Raelynn at the dedication. Kevin, Micah, Sierra, and I all stood at the altar with Brandon, Miranda, and Raelynn during the time of dedication and prayer. The tangible presence of God was with us all.

On October 13, 2017, Brandon, Miranda, and I had a medical video conference with Dr. Neuro #3 for him to give us Raelynn's results. Dr. Neuro #3 greeted all of us and then asked how Raelynn was doing physically. He specifically wanted to know how she was sleeping at night. Miranda told him that Raelynn went to bed around 11:00 p.m. and woke up around 8:00 a.m. Dr. Neuro #3 jokingly said he wished his kids slept that much. He went on to say it was wise to have a second set of eyes look at the images. My heart skipped a beat because I was concerned he had found something. However, God's promise prevailed. Dr. Neuro #3 confirmed Raelynn was perfectly healthy. She was the opposite of Chiari, and even her spinal cord was without genetic conditions. Raelynn did not have Chiari Brian Malformation or a tethered spinal cord. This particular neurosurgeon had saved my life, and diagnosed both my children. He knew our family well and completely understood why we wanted to confirm that Raelynn did not have either Chiari or a tethered spinal cord, because all our conditions are genetic. Dr. Neuro #3 congratulated Brandon for his genetics trumping Miranda's. We all laughed. Dr. Neuro #3 was the happiest our family had ever seen him, while he gave us the great news. It was peaceful, incredible, and humbling to actually – for the first time in seventeen years – receive fantastic medical news from a neurosurgeon. Originally, hearing good news from a neurosurgeon meant they found the root of our medical issues, and now good news meant Miranda did not pass it genetically to Raelynn. It made the entire journey with all its pain, loss, and disappointment worth it. Despite all odds, God kept his promise to give Brandon and Miranda a precious baby girl without Chiari Brain Malformation. God was faithful to His promise!

"When your faith and your fears collide, miracles are inevitable." – Dr. Donna Renfro

CHAPTER 34

HIS WAY IS PERFECT

Raelynn, Miranda, and Donna

"If you fully obey the Lord your God and carefully follow all his commands I give you today, the Lord your God will set you high above all the nations on. All these blessings will come on you and accompany you if you obey the Lord your God: You will be blessed in the city and blessed in the country. The fruit of your womb will be blessed, and the crops of your land and the young of your livestock—the calves of your herds and the lambs of your flocks. Your basket and your kneading trough will be blessed. You will be blessed when you come in and blessed when you go out. The Lord will grant that the enemies who rise up against you will be defeated before you. They will come at you from one direction but flee from you in seven. The Lord will send a blessing on your barns and on everything you put your hand to. The Lord your God will bless you in the land he is giving you. The Lord will establish you as his holy people, as he promised you on oath, if you keep the commands of the Lord your God and walk in obedience to him. Then all the peoples on earth will see that you are called by the name of the Lord, and they will fear you. The Lord will grant you abundant prosperity—in the fruit of your womb, the young of your livestock and the crops of your ground—in the land he swore to your ancestors to give you. The Lord will open the heavens, the storehouse of his bounty, to send rain on your land in season and to bless all the work of your hands. You will lend to many nations but will borrow from none." Deuteronomy 28:1-12 (NIV)

When I began this book by faith, I had no idea all the giants our family was going to face. I was taught through the blood of Jesus and the price He paid on the cross all the blessings of Abraham belonged to us as a part of His church. I received the promises, set stakes in the ground, and refused to quit until I saw all the promises fulfilled. I literally had a picture in my mind of a stake in the ground with a rope tied around my waist. I was going to make it to the stake no matter how hard the wind blew. I was not going to give up on the promises God gave me. When I was tired, in pain, or could not take the heartache one more day, God always sent someone to encourage me along our path. I was never alone – not only was the Holy Spirit with me, but He sent people to comfort me. We found encouragement from the Body of Christ, family, friends, strangers, and medical professionals. God placed people in our path continually to keep our focus on Him as well as His promises to our family. Two specific people who were necessary from the time Kevin and I started dating until today are my sister, Ginger and her husband, Dave. In 1996, at a Christian conference, my sister looked at me with revelation in her eyes and said, "We are sisters. I have known you since birth. We will be friends for life – we will walk through our entire lives together." There were moments so painful it appeared it would rip our extended family apart, but forgiveness, love, and grace prevailed. No one is perfect, and extremely painful circumstances with chronic health issues can cause everyone to become weary. If you have people in your life who live in chronic pain, they need your love and mercy.

Dave & Raelynn
Great Uncle Dave

October 9, 2017

Ginger & Donna:
Sisters, Friends, and
Prayer Warriors for Life
October 14, 2017

I pray as you have read our story, you see the goodness of God and realize how He took me on an adventure of faith. In the beginning, all I wanted was for Miranda to be well, and our family to be debt free. A powerful key I learned during the journey: this life is temporary. Today, all I need to be content is Jesus

– that is a true miracle. As I finish this book, I am in awe of God's faithfulness, even when I am faithless.

II Timothy 2:13

"If we are faithless, He remains faithful [true to His word and His righteous character], for He cannot deny Himself." Amplified

How many people in a family of four can have horrific neurological disorders? Well, in our family, the answer is four. I had no idea I had so many genetic malformations and conditions in my body. I would have never even believed it if tests and doctors did not confirm it. I never thought Miranda or Micah inherited their conditions from me. I was shocked and horrified to find out that I had genetically passed my children their medical conditions. I did not do it on purpose or even with knowledge, but I did pass genetic conditions to my children, which broke my heart. I had to work through the emotions of the knowledge of the fact – my genetic conditions were the root of the medical problems in my children. God always told me, "Donna, the answers lie in you." He was right. But, He went a step further and not only revealed the hidden things in my life – He brought knowledge to extend my life as well as give me a better quality of life. Even though I did not know to pray for healing in my body, God, in His grace and mercy saw the whole picture, while I only had pieces. Then, after going through so much medical heartache with my body, as well as Micah and Miranda, to find out Kevin had Multiple Sclerosis, NMO, was a kick in the gut. I did not believe I could emotionally, spiritually, or financially handle Kevin's illness. However, God graced our family and me at every turn in the road. He took the pieces of a very large puzzle and put it together to complete our family. God kept Micah safe. He made a way for Miranda to build a life despite her disabilities. He has extended Kevin's life despite many opportunities to die. And, God made me healthy beyond all hope – even though I am permanently disabled.

Faith, and the definition of its ability to make things happen has been debated in the church for years. I would like to point out the simple fact that Kevin, Micah, Miranda, and myself, all four, had major medical conditions or diseases. Each of us received extra medical issues to deal with the other one did not have. Faith in God and His promises carried us through, but our faith did not dictate the way each of us received our promise. God said, "It will not touch Micah." God led me to medical professionals and a specific diet to help Miranda, even though I went kicking and screaming. And, God used every tool available to mankind to save me, which included sheer determination, prayer, the Word of God, an army of believers, several friends, a great sister, great parents, great in-laws, great pastors, multiple churches, diet, exercise, doctors, multiple surgeries, money, and a husband who refused to let me die! Upon the diagnosis of Multiple Sclerosis, Kevin sat on our couch and asked God to lengthen his life to see our children fall in love, graduate from college, walk his daughter down the aisle at her wedding, and become a grandfather. God honored Kevin's requests even when it looked like Kevin would not be here for those special moments.

Our family had the honor of receiving instant healing through prayer. At the age of five, Miranda regained her ability to walk when our church fasted and prayed for our family for three days. Believe me; it takes far less faith to be healed in a prayer line than to put your body in the hands of mankind or a doctor. When you are thrust into a faith walk it will cost you everything. But, as Christians, we are called to pick up our cross and carry it daily. Many times you carry the cross one minute at a time. And, when you cannot possibly carry it one more step, I promise God will send someone to help you pick it up and keep walking if you keep your focus on Jesus.

Doctors are people and people can easily make mistakes. I found a lot of doctors along our journey who made serious errors. However, I also found some doctors who were obviously gifted by God to do their jobs, and their medical knowledge extended our lives! I have heard people in the church say it is lack of faith to use the medical profession. I would like to say it is foolish to not use the medical profession. For those of you who disagree, think about it. Enoch was "beamed" from one place in the Bible to another (Genesis 5); he did not use a car. Do you "beam" yourself to work or the grocery store, or do you get in a car that was built by men to drive yourself to your destination? Doctors are men who God can use to help your body heal. If you choose to ignore this precious gift from God, then you are choosing your course. I realize there are bad doctors; but, if God leads you, you will find the one you need. Do I believe you always need a doctor? No, but you better know God, and do whatever He tells you. We as Christians use money to buy things. We use glasses to improve our eyesight. We use cars to travel. We use people to pray for us. We allow God to use men and women to minister to us. Why would we not use doctors to help us?

Just as God has called and set apart some men and women to be ministers, He has also set apart some men and women to be doctors. I believe a big reason we found help in medical crises was because I was willing to do whatever it took, regardless of cost, judgment, or opinions of people. I followed God, and He led me to His promises for our lives. Please do not misunderstand me. I do not put my hope or even my trust in doctors. Simply, I recognize their gifts and use their wisdom in my life to live and be well. Honestly, I pray God continues to give the medical profession more wisdom every day. If God can give men and women the wisdom to beat some of these horrible conditions or diseases, then people do not suffer – I know that is the heart of God.

As a child, I was diagnosed with eczema, which is a skin disorder. And, I was diagnosed with Anorexia Nervosa, which I received prayer for as a teenager. God did do an extraordinary work in me that day; however, He was preparing me to live a life of faith. As an adult, all the truth came out about my genetic conditions. I did not have either eczema or Anorexia Nervosa. Ehlers-Danlos Syndrome will make your skin split open and bleed, and can appear to look like eczema. Chiari Brain Malformation can cause extreme nausea with vomiting, and certain foods make me more nauseated, so it was and still can be difficult for me to eat. I have dysphagia as well, which makes it difficult for me to swallow food. So, it was easy for the medical professionals to think I had Anorexia Nervosa, because they did not know about my physical conditions. My physical issues were medical – not psychological. God was gracious enough to reveal the truth to bring more healing to my body, while we looked for answers for Miranda. Ultimately, Miranda did have Intermittent Cushing's, which is simply a hormonal imbalance. However, it was not the root cause of her problem. The flat pituitary may be why she had the hormonal imbalances – no one really knows. As horrible as Cushing's Disease is, Miranda had much larger problems. I cried out to God to reveal the root, and He was faithful. Although, over the years, I was extremely frustrated and angry, waiting was wisdom. If a surgeon had operated on her pituitary, it would not have fixed the problem, probably only made it worse. God had warned me to be patient and allow Him to be in control. I waited, and it was worth the wait!

Our medical bills throughout this journey soared over one million dollars! I lost count when Kevin became ill with Multiple Sclerosis. Kevin and I have never had a large income and throughout the majority of the most expensive medical crises neither one of us were working. I cannot even tell you how we paid all the medical bills, but God made a way. It was as miraculous as the rest of the story. We received money from work, friends, random strangers, many churches, health insurance companies, social security disability, government support, financial assistance, and write-offs from doctors. My family did a fundraiser for us before I went to New York for my brain surgery, so my father handled the medical bills for about six months, but we had outrageous medical bills throughout the entire seventeen-year journey. Only God made the way to pay them, and I learned how to trust that He would regardless of our resources or income. Most people would have buckled under the financial pressure alone; however, I was strengthened by constantly watching God meet every need our family had regardless of our personal resources. Truly, God is the provider. Do you remember the medical technician, who told Kevin and me we had a "million dollar family?" Well, she was right. It was going to take a million dollars to make us a family!

When Miranda was around the age of twelve, she asked me: "Mommy, why were we born this way?"

I simply told her when sin entered the world, the curse of sickness, disease, or illness came with it. She continued to question me, so I told her, "Honestly I do not know why we were born with genetic conditions, but truly it does not matter, because we are overcomers due to the power of Jesus Christ, scripture, and the resolve to never quit."

I have thought often about the scripture, which states, *"For you created my inmost being; you knit me together in my mother's womb." Psalm 139:13 (NIV)*

I settled my own question of why was I created genetically flawed with the truth God created me and my personality to endure the journey of my life on this planet. God has never lied to me. At times, it appeared as if we would never find the truth or root of our medical problems, but God promised us we would. He never promised me it would be easy. God definitely created me with everything I needed to endure my life with peace.

I have been asked whether I believed it was God or Satan that caused the car wreck, which left me disabled for the time I live on this planet. Honestly, I do not believe it matters. It might have been Satan. It might have been God. And, it might have just been an accident life brought my way. It does not matter who or what caused it because again the Word of God, scripture, was stronger than the accident. Romans 8:28 states, *"And we know that in all things God works for the good of those who love him, who have been called according to his purpose." (NIV)*

If the blood of Jesus saves you, then all things in your life work for your good – even the difficult and painful things. The car wreck exposed the hidden things in my body that were destroying my health. Although I endured pain beyond words, it was the way we found the root of Miranda's problem. As her mother, I would do it all again! I love her deeply, and I honestly did not care what I had to do to help her. God was gracious enough to save Miranda's life, continue to keep Micah safe, bring health to my body, and extend Kevin's life.

Our faith walk has given me the opportunity to face questions in my heart because of the reality of the excruciatingly painful walk we were required to endure. I am permanently disabled. My disability lawyer said in thirty years of practice he had never seen a more medically disabled person than me. I suppose I can add that to my bragging list. I will live with rods in my head and extreme physical limitation for the rest of my life. My life is different forever, but the truth is: life is always changing and nobody is perfect.

I have asked myself: "What do I believe about healing?"

I believe God is the Healer.
God alone will determine how He heals.
Jesus Christ paid the price for healing at Calvary.
We are clay.
He is God.
We do not live in a perfect world, but I know with God all things are possible.
With God you can do whatever lies ahead of you.
With God you can face your worst fears and overcome.
With God you can do whatever He tells you!

I would also like to add I have had the privilege of knowing many people who "believed" for healing and ended up in Heaven instead of gaining their "healing" here on Earth. I go to scripture for clarity when I am faced with difficult questions. The Bible states in Philippians 1:21, *"For to me, to live is Christ and to die is gain." (NIV)*

In other words, as long as we are Christians on this planet, then our lives are to show Christ daily, and when we die then we are released to go live in Heaven. Although, I realize the people who love us never want to let us go. If we can gain the perspective all of us will die, unless Jesus returns first, and as Christians, we will all go to Heaven – maybe death will not be feared. With battling medical conditions or sickness, a person needs a specific word or scripture from God concerning your particular situation. God gave me: prophets, pastors, and dreams. He spoke to me personally on how to travel through absolute darkness and somehow reach light. I believe that as a Christian, I was bought with the price Jesus paid, and I am capable of receiving every promise He gives me. We received the promises God gave us. I did not dictate the passage to the answer - only God did that!

Simply, I followed God as He led me. This book clearly shows I did not like the way He sent us, but I was willing to do whatever it took to receive our promises.

I also want to say if someone you know "believed" for healing and did not get what they asked for the way they thought it should be received – probably, it was not lack of faith. Faith is easy, although it needs to be handled with care. If a person has enough faith to believe Jesus was born of a virgin, died on a cross, and rose from the dead to save them, then clearly they have enough faith! People do not receive the "healing" we expect for all kinds of reasons. Hosea 4:6 states, *"My people are destroyed for lack of knowledge." (KJV)*

Obviously, some people do not get their answer here on Earth because we do not know how to help them. The Bible is clear concerning bitterness and how it will rot your bones. So, emotions play a huge role in healing. Proverbs is a book in the Bible which will give you valuable instruction on how to handle daily living in victory. Also, it must be said, God created both natural laws and spiritual laws. Therefore, a person cannot ignore the laws of nature and expect God to heal them. A good example would be, if you stand in the middle of an intersection you will probably get hit by a car. It is not the will of God for you to get hit by a car. Your choices placed you in the intersection. Every bite of food you put in your mouth affects your health. I do not like that fact any more than you do, but it is the truth.

A person cannot eat junk food and expect their body to be healthy. As much as I would love to live on brownies, it is not beneficial and actually very harmful. I learned a lot about diet as we traveled. Believe me; it was not easy for God to reach me in that particular area of my life. I loved junk food, and I was addicted to it. I have now realized our bodies are just like machines. They require particular vitamins and minerals to function properly. I believe the best foods to eat are natural foods that God created for us to consume. Fruits, vegetables, nuts, and natural meats along with a good multivitamin as well as lots of water will increase your health tremendously. It is your body and clearly your choice. Jesus said to choose life, and I had to learn to change my diet to bring life to my body.

You are given one body while you travel through your life. The Bible tells us to take good care of our "temple," which is your body. I believe God is instructing us so we will have healthy days and enjoy our journey. Think of your body like a car. If you own a car, you put gas in it to make it go places. If you put water in it instead of gas, the car would not work. Your body is no different. It was designed to eat particular foods, and if you put the wrong foods in your body, you will pay a price for it one day. Choose life and eat right. Again, I want to tell you I believe we are individuals, even in the area of diet. What is right for one person in the area of diet may not work for another person. Therefore, once again, it is your responsibility to have a personal relationship with Jesus Christ, spend time with God, search the scriptures for yourself, and find out what God is saying to you for your personal health. We are very unique and there is not a formula that will work across all barriers for all to follow.

God created us to have an intimate relationship with Him. He desires to spend time with you; therefore, He created a system, which would require each of us to go to Him individually for our own personal answers concerning whatever circumstances you may be facing. The Bible is clear concerning the fact everyone will face tests, trials, and even tribulation. Your area may be medical, financial, physical, emotional, mental, a disabled child, habitual sin, family issues, addiction, or other issues. The issue is not the point. God giving you the answers to live a peaceful life is the desired outcome – regardless of circumstances, tests, trials, or tribulation. We are overcomers because of Jesus Christ. Revelation 12:11, *"They triumphed over him by the blood of the Lamb and by the word of their testimony; they did not love their lives so much as to shrink from death." (NIV)*

Please understand this book is my testimony. You cannot do what I did and receive my results. You alone must seek His face and turn to Him with your pain, suffering, sickness, family, and even your blessings. You alone need to know Him, Jesus Christ. Nobody knows what a day will hold, but God will hold you in the day. To become saved, read these scriptures in the book of Romans from the Bible: Romans 3:10, Romans 3:23, Romans 5:8, Romans 5:12, Romans 6:23, Romans 10:9-11, and Romans 10:13. Then, by faith, ask Jesus to be your Lord and Savior. Remember everyone who comes to Jesus is saved by grace. Grace literally means unearned favor. No one is perfect, flawless, or without sin.

Ephesians 2:8-9

"For it is by grace you have been saved, through faith—and this is not from yourselves, it is the gift of God— not by works, so that no one can boast." (NIV)

We are all individuals with individual destinies. I believe if you choose Him, Jesus Christ, then whatever lies ahead in your life, you can do it! The Word states in John 10:4, *"and the sheep follow Him because they know His voice." (NIV)* You too can hear the voice of God. It is a still small voice which rises on the inside of you. Time and practice can help you discern God's voice from your own desires. Also, a key to knowing that God is speaking is to know scripture, His Word. In other words, read the Bible. Become knowledgeable about how God speaks and why God speaks. I was prepared to go through my journey due to years of studying the Bible prior to entering the dark tunnel of death and sickness. Knowing scripture will protect you from Satan's lies. The Holy Spirit will teach you through scripture the Word of God, how to recognize Satan's lies, and embrace God's truth.

I chose to put in the time and read the Bible. I chose to study with all my heart. I chose to spend time in praise and worship. I chose to go to church.

There are things God cannot do on your behalf. You must assume responsibility for your actions and knowledge. If you want the promises of God in your life, then you must find out what they are, and you must go after them with your whole heart. Be prepared to do whatever it takes. I found obtaining our promises cost me everything, but in losing my life I found true life, peace, and contentment. If God gives you a promise, then He will keep it. The Word states in Numbers 23:19, *"God is not a man that He would lie." (KJV)*

We as a family have walked through the valley of the shadow of death and lived to tell about it. From my heart, I hope you never take a trip like ours, but if you do, know this – YOU CAN DO IT!

Remember, quitting is not an option. *Raelynn Elizabeth Taylor* is evidence of the goodness of God in the land of the living. God promised Brandon and Miranda a baby girl without Chiari Brain Malformation. It took a miracle for Miranda to physically carry her own child through pregnancy, due to her own physical limitations, as well as not pass Chiari or a tethered spinal cord to the baby. Once Miranda was in the car wreck, we all thought it would be years if the prophesy ever came to pass, because Miranda's body was so weak from pain, surgery, and neck complications. Then, despite all the pain Miranda was enduring from a car wreck, God made the impossible – possible by allowing Miranda to become pregnant just four months after the car wreck. Suddenly, God took our whole family to a new level of unbelievable circumstances with His perfect timing of Raelynn's conception. Brandon and Miranda were tossed into a faith walk where only God could receive the glory. They remained strong mentally, spiritually, and emotionally throughout her pregnancy and did not waiver in God's promise for their daughter, Raelynn. Miranda walked by faith no matter how difficult the journey. God miraculously fulfilled His prophecy in His perfect timing. We are all in awe of His faithfulness.

If I had chosen to quit or lived in self-pity, my children would have learned to live in fear versus faith. My decision to hang on to the promises of God, even with all the pain, paid unbelievable dividends I did not even know were possible. I was so focused on our daily walk, I did not see how beautiful our future could be when we reached the other side. Brandon loves Miranda, and now they have a beautiful baby girl without Chiari Brain Malformation. Sierra loves my son Micah, and they are an unstoppable team. Kevin is still my best friend and the love of my life, even though we were told constantly our marriage would not make it through all the pain, illness, or diagnoses of our children. We are not normal, but we are most definitely a faith walking, mountain moving, full of grace family who loves one another and desires to help the world find hope in the middle of darkness. There is not enough money to buy the peace of knowing your family is safe in the arms of God, loves one another, and will stand together through the toughest storms.

Brandon, Miranda,   Micah & Sierra   Kevin & Donna
& Raelynn

I was recently asked if I would have changed anything in our faith walk. My answer was, "Yes, I would have trusted God more, and rested in the fact Jesus paid the price at Calvary."

The title of this book changed from *Miraculous Miranda* to *Tetelestai: It Is Finished – The Renfro Family Faith Walk*, because as we continued to face more giants, our entire family changed. My faith grew, and my ability to trust Jesus in the middle of the storm increased with each crisis and trauma. The book was no longer about obtaining a miracle for Miranda. Our entire family needed miracles, and our faith in God's ability had to go up to the level of complete surrender. Tetelestai was the last word Jesus said just before he died. I had to come to a place in my faith where I trusted "it was finished" no matter what circumstances we were facing. I had to choose to trust Jesus whether we lived or died. My agenda had to die, and I had to embrace God's plan for our family. I pray this testimony will give you the faith to trust God in every area of your life, whatever you are personally facing. I want to give hope to the hopeless.

I began this book in the year 2000 in sheer faith, believing God would make a way for my daughter Miranda to live. God was faithful to my request, and I am forever thankful. Upon beginning the book, I had no idea of the journey we would face. Now, I have the knowledge of the genetic conditions both my children and I have in our bodies as well as Kevin's diagnoses. We will always do whatever God instructs us to do daily, and use the medical profession to watch us closely. However, I am now choosing to publish this book in faith, trusting God with our lives daily. I am not in denial concerning our medical issues, Miranda's car wreck injuries, nor do I know what a day will hold. I am well aware of the malformations and diseases we all have. But, I believe, no matter what our future may hold – whether it be life or death, our God is faithful.

Romans 8:37-39 (NIV)

"No, in all these things we are more than conquerors through him who loved us. For I am convinced that neither death nor life, neither angels nor demons, neither the present nor the future, nor any powers, neither height nor depth, nor anything else in all creation, will be able to separate us from the love of God that is in Christ Jesus our Lord."

I trust God and His way is perfect.
Tetelestai!

ABOUT THE AUTHOR

Dr. Donna Renfro, PhD

Donna is called to promote Unity in the Body of Christ, testify to the fact "The Word Works!" and evangelize the world. She is a disciple of Jesus Christ with a desire to inspire unity and build the Body of Christ through Biblical teaching, praise and worship, prayer, and testimonies. She is the wife of Dr. Kevin Renfro and the mother of Micah Renfro and Miranda Renfro Taylor.

Donna committed her life as an intercessor and a bond servant to Jesus Christ at age 20. She was determined to, without reservation, obey whatever God asked. Donna taught elementary school, served on a church staff, supported the building of many churches, and served in Christian radio. Donna's greatest desire is to testify and teach the Word of God. She wants to bring hope to the hopeless.

Donna Renfro was ordained as a minister on January 28, 2007. Her education consists of a bachelor's degree in Elementary Education with a K-8 certification, a master of Biblical Studies, a master of Religious Education, a doctor of Biblical Counseling, and PhD in Theology. Her official name is Rev. Dr. Donna Renfro, M.S.B.S., M.R.E.D., D.B.C., and PhD, but she much prefers to be called Donna. Although Donna has obtained many higher-level degrees, she has learned the more you study, the more humble you become. Her desire is to leave a legacy of loving God, loving her family, and serving Jesus without hesitation.

If you want to contact Donna Renfro Ministries, go to www.donnarenfro.org

Made in the USA
Columbia, SC
02 March 2018